Fedora® Linux®
TOOLBOX

Fedora® Linux®
TOOLBOX

1000+ Commands for Fedora, CentOS,
and Red Hat® Power Users

Christopher Negus

François Caen

Wiley Publishing, Inc.

Fedora® Linux® Toolbox:
1000+ Commands for Fedora, CentOS, and Red Hat® Power Users

Published by
Wiley Publishing, Inc.
10475 Crosspoint Boulevard
Indianapolis, IN 46256
www.wiley.com

Copyright © 2008 by Wiley Publishing, Inc., Indianapolis, Indiana

Published simultaneously in Canada

ISBN: 978-0-470-08291-1

Manufactured in the United States of America

10 9 8 7 6 5 4 3 2 1

Library of Congress Cataloging-in-Publication Data

Negus, Chris, 1957–
    Fedora Linux toolbox : 1000+ commands for Fedora, Centos and Red Hat power users / Christopher Negus, François Caen.
      p. cm.
    Includes index.
    ISBN 978-0-470-08291-1 (pbk.)
    1. Linux. 2. Operating systems (Computers) I. Caen, François. II. Title.
    QA76.76.O63N4185 2007
    005.4'32—dc22
                    2007039391

As always, I dedicate my work on this book to my wife, Sheree.

— Christopher Negus

To my dad, for teaching me BASIC when I was little.

— François Caen

About the Authors

Christopher Negus is the author of the best-selling *Fedora and Red Hat Linux Bibles*, *Linux Toys, Linux Troubleshooting Bible*, and *Linux Bible 2007 Edition*. He is a member of the Madison Linux Users Group. Prior to becoming a full-time writer, Chris served for eight years on development teams for the Unix operating system at AT&T, where Unix was created and developed. He also worked with Novell on Unix development and Caldera Linux.

François Caen, through his company Turbosphere LLC, hosts and manages business application infrastructures, with 95 percent running on Linux systems. As an open source advocate, he has lectured on OSS network management and Internet services, and served as president of the Tacoma Linux User Group. François is a Red Hat Certified Engineer (RHCE). In his spare time, François enjoys managing enterprise Cisco networks.

Credits

Acquisitions Editor
Jenny Watson

Development Editor
Sara Shlaer

Technical Editor
Thomas Blader

Copy Editor
Michael Koch

Editorial Manager
Mary Beth Wakefield

Production Manager
Tim Tate

**Vice President and
Executive Group Publisher**
Richard Swadley

Vice President and Executive Publisher
Joseph B. Wikert

Project Coordinator, Cover
Lynsey Osborn

Compositor
Laurie Stewart,
Happenstance Type-O-Rama

Proofreader
Kathryn Duggan

Indexer
Melanie Belkin

Anniversary Logo Design
Richard Pacifico

Contents at a Glance

Contents

Contents

Contents

Acknowledgments

I would like to acknowledge the Fedora development community for their tenacity in turning out a high-quality Linux distribution about every six months. Likewise, I'd like to thank Red Hat, Inc., for their sponsorship of Fedora and excellent contributions to the free and open source software community.

Special thanks to François Caen for giving up most of his free time over the past year, while juggling his existing professional obligations, to co-author the book with me. Thomas Blader did his usual excellent job tech editing this book. At Wiley, I'd like to thank Jenny Watson for sticking with us through the development of the book. And, last but not least, thanks to Sara Shlaer for keeping us on track with schedules and supplying the never-ending to-do lists we needed to accomplish to get this book published.

— *Christopher Negus*

I would like to thank Chris Negus for giving me the opportunity to co-author this book with him. We had wanted to write together for the last couple of years, and this Toolbox series was the perfect fit for our collaboration.

I couldn't have worked on this book without the unrelenting support from my wife, Tonya. Thank you for emptying the dishwasher all these times even though we both know it's my job.

Thanks to Thomas Blader for his detailed tech editing. Having done some tech editing in the past, I know what a tough job it can be. Thanks to Sara Shlaer and Jenny Watson at Wiley for being the most patient cat-herders out there. Special thanks to Wayne Tucker and Jesse Keating for all the knowledge they've shared with me during and before this project.

Finally, I would like to express my gratitude to all the volunteers who make Fedora and CentOS possible and to Red Hat, Inc. for building the best Linux distributions and staying true to the spirit of open source.

— *François Caen*

Introduction

After you've had some experience with Linux, you don't need someone telling you to click the Help button for help or to drag a file to the trash icon to delete it. What you need is a reference that shows you powerful commands and options that let you take hold of your Linux system, as well as the processes, users, storage media, network resources, and system services associated with it.

Fedora Linux Toolbox provides you with more than 1,000 specific command lines to help you become a Linux power user. Whether you are a systems administrator or desktop user, the book will show you commands to create file systems, troubleshoot networks, lock down security, and dig out almost anything you care to know about your Linux system.

This book's focus for your Linux command line journey is Fedora, the community-based Linux distribution sponsored by Red Hat, Inc. Fedora and other Linux systems derived from Fedora, such as Red Hat Enterprise Linux and CentOS, have been installed on millions of computers around the world. Tapping into the skills needed to run those systems can help you to work with your own Linux systems and to learn what you need as a Linux professional.

Who Should Read This Book

This book is for anyone who wants to access the power of a Linux system as a systems administrator or user. You may be a Linux enthusiast, a Linux professional, or possibly a computer professional who is increasingly finding the Windows systems in your data center supplanted by Linux boxes.

The bottom line is that you want to find quick and efficient ways of getting Fedora, Red Hat Enterprise Linux, or CentOS systems working at peak performance. Those systems may be a few desktop systems at work, a file and print server at your school, or a home web server that you're doing just for fun.

In the best case, you should already have some experience with Linux. However, if you are a computer professional with skills managing other types of operating systems, such as Windows, you should be able to easily adapt your knowledge to be able to use the specific commands we cover in the book.

What This Book Covers

This is not a beginner's Linux book. Before you jump in, it would be best if you have a basic working knowledge of what Linux is, how the shell works, and what processes, file systems, and network interfaces are. The book will then supplement that knowledge with information you need to do the following activities:

❑ **Get software** — Fedora offers Package Updater (pup) and Package Management (pirut) GUI tools for getting software. With tools such as rpm and yum, you'll learn the best ways to search for, download, install, update, and otherwise manage software from the command line.

❑ **Access applications** — Find what's available from massive Fedora software repositories by searching yum repositories. Then search and download using tools from the yum-utils package.

❑ **Use the shell** — Find neat techniques and tips for using the shell.

❑ **Play with multimedia** — Play and stream multimedia content from your computer. You can also modify audio and image files, and then convert the content of those files to different formats.

❑ **Work with files** — Use, manipulate, convert, and secure a wide range of file types in Linux.

❑ **Administer file systems** — Access, format, partition, and monitor your file storage hardware (hard disks, CD/DVD drives, floppy disks, USB flash drives, and so on). Then create, format, and check the file systems that exist on those hardware devices.

❑ **Back up and restore data** — Use simple commands to gather, archive, and compress your files into efficient backup archives. Then store those archives locally or on remote computers.

❑ **Work with processes** — List running processes in a variety of ways, such as by CPU use, processor use, or process ID. Then change running processes to have them run in the background or foreground. Send signals to processes to have them re-read configuration files, stop and resume processing, or stop completely (abort).

❑ **Manage the system** — Run commands to check system resources, such as memory usage, run levels, boot loaders, and kernel modules.

❑ **Monitor networks** — Bring wired, wireless, and dial-up network connections up and down. Check routing, DNS, and host information. Keep an eye on network traffic.

❑ **Get network resources** — Connect to Linux and Windows remote file systems using FTP, NFS, and Samba facilities. Use shell-based commands to browse the Web.

❑ **Do remote administration** — Access and administer other computers using remote login (ssh, telnet, and so on), and screen. Learn about remote administration interfaces, such as Webmin, SWAT, and CUPS.

❑ **Lock down security** — Set up firewalls and system logging to secure your Linux systems.

❑ **Get reference information** — Use the appendixes at the end of this book to get more information about the shell (such as metacharacters and shell variables) and the state of the system (from `/proc`).

Hopefully, if we have done it right, it will be easier to use this book than to Google for the command lines or GUI tools you need.

After you have mastered many of the features described in this book, you'll have gained the following advantages:

❑ **Hundreds of commands** — By compressing a lot of information into a small space, you will have access to hundreds of useful commands, in over 1000 command lines, in a handy form to carry with you.

❑ **Critical Linux information** — This book lists connections to the most critical information on the Web for succeeding with Linux in general and Fedora in particular.

❑ **Transferable knowledge** — Most of the same commands and options you use in Fedora will work exactly the same way on other Linux systems. Different Linux distributions, on the other hand, offer different graphical administration tools. And even within a particular distribution, graphical tools change more often than commands do.

❑ **Quick problem solving** — By the time others have started up a desktop and launched a graphical administration tool, you will have already run a half dozen commands and solved the problem.

❑ **Enduring value** — Many of the commands described in this book were used in early Unix systems. So you are gaining tools that reflect the experience of thousands of computer experts for more than 30 years.

Because the full documentation for commands used in Linux consists of thousands of man pages, info text, and help messages, you will surely want to reach beyond the pages of this book from time to time. Luckily, Fedora and other Linux systems include helpful information installed on the system itself. Chapter 1 contains descriptions of how to access that information that is probably already installed on your Fedora system.

How This Book Is Structured

This book is neither a pure reference book (with alphabetically listed components) nor a guide (with step-by-step procedures for doing tasks). Instead, the book is organized by topics and aimed at including as many useful commands and options as we could fit.

Chapter 1 starts by giving you a basic understanding of what Fedora is and how it relates to other Linux systems, such as Red Hat Enterprise Linux and CentOS. Then it describes some of the vast resources available to support your experience with this book (such as man pages, info material, and help text). Chapter 2 provides a quick overview of installation and then describes useful commands such as rpm and yum for getting and managing your Fedora software.

Commands that a regular user may find useful in Linux are described in Chapters 3, 4, 5, and 6. Chapter 3 describes tools for using the shell, Chapter 4 covers commands for working with files, and Chapter 5 describes how to manipulate text. Chapter 6 tells how to work with music and image files.

Starting with Chapter 7, we get into topics relating to system administration. Creating and checking file systems are covered in Chapter 7, while commands for doing data backups are described in Chapter 8. Chapter 9 describes how to manipulate running processes, and Chapter 10 describes administrative tools for managing basic components, such as hardware modules, CPU use, and memory use.

Chapter 11 begins the chapters devoted to managing network resources by describing how to set up and work with wired, wireless, and dial-up network interfaces. Chapter 12 covers text-based commands for web browsing, file transfer, file sharing, chats, and e-mail. Tools for doing remote system administration are included in Chapter 13.

Chapter 14 covers how to lock down security using features such as firewalls and logging. After that there are three appendixes that provide reference information for text editing, shell features (metacharacters and variables), and system settings (from the /proc file system).

What You Need to Use This Book

Although we hope you enjoy the beauty of our prose, this is not meant to be a book you curl up with in front of a nice fire with a glass of wine. We expect you will be sitting in front of a computer screen trying to connect to a network, fix a file system, or add a user. The wine is optional.

In other words, the book is meant to be a companion as you work on a Fedora, Red Hat Enterprise Linux, or CentOS operating system. All of those systems are available for the x86 and x86_64 computer architectures. Some specific versions of those systems are also available for IBM POWER (formerly known as PowerPC), SPARC, Intel ia64 (Itanium), Alpha, and IBM mainframes. If you don't already have one of those systems installed, refer to Chapter 2 for information on getting and installing those systems.

All of the commands in this book have been tested against Fedora 7 on x86 or x86_64 architecture. However, because many of these commands have been around for a long time (some dating back over 30 years to the original Unix days), most will work exactly as described here on RHEL, CentOS, and other Fedora derivative systems, regardless of CPU architecture.

Many of the commands described in this book will work on other Linux and Unix systems as well. Because this book focuses on Fedora and other Red Hat–based distributions, descriptions will differ from other Linux systems most prominently in the areas of packaging, installation, and GUI administration tools.

Conventions

To help you get the most from the text and keep track of what's happening, we've used a number of conventions throughout the book. In particular, we have created styles for showing commands that allow us to fit as many command lines as possible in the book.

With command examples, computer output (shell prompts and messages) is shown in regular monofont text, computer input (the stuff you type) is shown in bold monofont text, and a short description (if included) appears in italics. Here is an example:

```
$ ls *jpg          List all JPEG files in the current directory
hat.jpg
dog.jpg
...
```

To save space, output is sometimes truncated (or skipped altogether). Three dots (. . .) are sometimes used to indicate that additional output was cut. If a command is particularly long, backslashes will appear at the end of each line to indicate that input is continuing to the next line. Here is an example:

```
# oggenc NewSong.wav -o NewSong.ogg \
    -a Bernstein -G Classical        \
    -d 06/15/1972 -t "Simple Song"   \
    -1 "Bernsteins Mass"             \
    -c info="From Kennedy Center"
```

In the example just shown, you can literally type the backslashes to have all that information included in the single command. Or, you can simply put all the information on a single line (excluding the backslashes). Notice that command prompts are shown in one of two ways:

```
$              Indicates a regular user prompt
#              Indicates the root prompt
```

As noted, when a dollar sign prompt ($) appears, any user can run the command. With a pound sign prompt (#), you probably need to be the root user for the command to work.

Notes and warnings appear as follows:

NOTE *Warnings, notes, and tips are offset and placed in italics like this.*

As for styles in the text:

❑ We *highlight* new terms and important words with italics when we introduce them.

❑ We show keyboard combinations like this: Ctrl+a. If the command requires you to type an uppercase letter, the combination will show this: Ctrl+Shift+a.

❑ We show file names, URLs, and code within the text like so: `persistence.properties`.

One final technique we use is to highlight text that describes what an upcoming command is meant to do. For example, we may say something like, "use the following command to **display the contents of a file**." We've highlighted descriptions in this way to provide quick visual cues to the readers, so you can easily scan the page for that command you just knew had to be there.

Fedora® Linux®
TOOLBOX

1

Starting with Fedora Linux

Whether you use Fedora Linux every day or just tweak it once in a while, a book that presents efficient ways to use, check, fix, secure, and enhance your system can be an invaluable resource.

Fedora Linux Toolbox is that resource.

Fedora Linux Toolbox is aimed primarily at Fedora and Red Hat Enterprise Linux power users and systems administrators. To give you what you need, we tell you how to quickly locate and get software, monitor the health and security of your systems, and access network resources. In short, we cut to the most efficient ways of using Fedora.

Our goal with *Fedora Linux Toolbox* is to pack a lot of useful information for using Fedora Linux into a small package that you can carry around with you. To that end, we describe:

❑ **Commands** — Tons of command line examples to use Fedora in helpful and clever ways.

❑ **GUI tools** — Quick pointers to graphical administration tools to configure your system.

❑ **Software repositories** — Short procedures to find and download thousands of applications.

❑ **Online resources** — Listings of the best locations to find Fedora forums, mailing lists, IRC channels, and other online resources.

❑ **Local documentation** — Tools for gathering more information from man pages, doc directories, help commands, and other resources on your Fedora system.

Because you're not a beginner with Linux, you won't see a lot of screenshots of windows, icons, and menus. What you will see, however, is the

IN THIS CHAPTER

Find Fedora resources

Learn quick and powerful commands

Have a handy reference to many useful utilities

Work as Linux gurus do

quickest path to getting the information you need to use your Fedora Linux system to its fullest extent.

If this sounds useful to you, please read on.

About Fedora, Red Hat, and Linux

Fedora is a Linux operating system that is sponsored by Red Hat, Inc. Its roots come from Red Hat Linux, which ended its development life under that name in 2003. At that time, Red Hat transitioned its single Red Hat Linux distribution into Fedora Core (now called simply *Fedora*) and Red Hat Enterprise Linux.

❑ **Fedora** (http://fedoraproject.org) became the community-driven, rapid-development operating system that was distributed for free (as is) every six to nine months. The goal was to stay on the cutting edge of open source technology, while also providing a development platform for enterprise-quality software that could become part of Red Hat Enterprise Linux.

❑ **Red Hat Enterprise Linux** (RHEL) became the commercial, subscription-based Linux operating system produced by Red Hat, Inc. (www.redhat.com). The goal was to release RHEL on about an 18-month schedule. Red Hat has since built its product line around RHEL, offering support, training, documentation, hardware certification, and other products to support RHEL customers. In 2006, Red Hat purchased the open source Java development vendor JBoss, so Red Hat can now offer a complete application stack composed of middleware running on top of its RHEL product line.

Because Fedora and RHEL are open source operating systems, built on the GNU public license, people can take the source code from those Linux systems and create their own Linux distributions. And that's just what they have done. For that reason, the skills you learn here with Fedora could also help you if you use any of the following operating systems:

❑ **CentOS** (www.centos.org) — Many Linux consultants who don't need Red Hat's commercial support and don't want to pay Red Hat subscription fees have migrated to CentOS. CentOS is a rebuild of RHEL source code, with a goal of 100-percent binary compatibility with RHEL.

Aside from logos and other Red Hat branding information (which CentOS removed), applications and interfaces should be exactly the same for CentOS and RHEL. Of all the RHEL rebuilds, CentOS is the one most widely adopted and the one we recommend.

❑ **Yellow Dog Linux** (www.yellowdoglinux.com) — Based originally on Red Hat Linux, Yellow Dog Linux runs on a variety of Apple hardware (PowerBook, iBook, iMac, G3, G4, G5, and so on) as well as on PlayStation 3.

❑ **Other RHEL and Fedora rebuilds** — Other rebuilds of RHEL include Lineox (www.lineox.net) from Finland and Scientific Linux (www.scientificlinux .org), which was created by Fermilab of the U.S. Department of Energy. Linux distributions such as those just mentioned were created primarily to allow an organization that once relied on Red Hat Linux to roll their own enterprise-quality distribution for their organization's needs.

There is a larger list of Linux distributions built on Fedora and RHEL at DistroWatch (http://distrowatch.com/dwres.php?resource=independence). Other Linux systems also have drawn heavily from technology developed at least in part by Red Hat. For example, distributions such as Mandriva, PCLinuxOS, and Linspire use the RPM package management system described in this book for managing software packages, so descriptions of rpm in Chapter 2 will help you with Mandriva, PCLinuxOS, and Linspire as well.

Comparing Fedora to Other Linuxes

Fedora is the rapid-development, cutting edge Linux system, as compared with the more stable, less-often-updated Red Hat Enterprise Linux. The speed at which Fedora is developed (with a new release about every six months) makes it perfect for the Linux enthusiast who wants the latest releases of software and can deal with some level of instability.

Using Fedora Linux might be the best way to learn Linux if you have an eye toward becoming a Linux professional. With its short development cycle, you can be assured that you have the newest cool features to use. Because Red Hat uses Fedora as a platform for testing its commercial software, the skills you learn will scale up nicely to the largest enterprise computing environments.

Besides Red Hat, Novell is the other major corporation that is marketing Linux in the enterprise market. Novell's operating systems follow the same basic dual-distribution model, with SUSE Linux Enterprise as the basis of its commercial products and OpenSUSE as its free, community-driven Linux system. Some open source enthusiasts, however, question Novell's long-term commitment to open source because of its 2006 "covenant not to sue" with Microsoft (see www.novell.com/linux/ microsoft/covenant.html).

Debian is considered to be a high-quality Linux distribution with a strong commitment to the ideals of open source software. Many derivative Linux distributions, such as the popular Ubuntu Linux and the KNOPPIX live CD, are based on Debian. Although Debian is good for use in small business, the project doesn't have the same enterprise infrastructure (training, support, documentation, and so on) that is built around RHEL. However, Ubuntu has begun offering paid enterprise-level support contracts (www.ubuntu.com/support/paid).

Finding Fedora Resources

The center for information about the Fedora project is the FedoraProject.org web site (`http://fedoraproject.org/wiki`). This is the official site for the Fedora project. Particularly useful pages from this site include the following:

- ❏ `fedoraproject.org/wiki/Communicate` — From the Communicating and Getting Help page, follow links to documentation, FAQs, bug reporting, mailing lists, IRC chats, forums, and community web sites.

- ❏ `fedoraproject.org/wiki/Distribution` — Links to information for downloading or purchasing Fedora installation CDs or DVDs are listed on this site. Some links also take you to details on upgrading and life cycles of each Fedora release.

- ❏ `fedoraproject.org/wiki/FAQ` — This FAQ contains excellent information on how to start with Fedora, use it, get help and support, and understand the parts that make up the Fedora project. This is also the first place to go for questions on hardware compatibility and on what software is and isn't included in Fedora.

- ❏ `fedoraproject.org/wiki/ForbiddenItems` — Software that is available for Linux, but not included in Fedora because it does not meet Fedora's requirements relating to legal restrictions or source code availability, is listed on this page. We indicate how you can legally get some of these items in appropriate sections of this book.

- ❏ `fedoraproject.org/wiki/Bugs/FC6Common` — Problems you may encounter that have not yet been fixed are described on this page. There is also information on getting update disks that include software fixes.

Fedora Community Connections

If you want to communicate with the Fedora community, Table 1-1 shows a quick list of links to the most useful Fedora and RHEL communications venues.

Table 1-1: Online Resources to Connect to the Fedora Community

Fedora Activities	Internet Sites
Mailing lists	`www.redhat.com/mailman/listinfo`
IRC chats	`fedoraproject.org/wiki/Communicate#IRC`
Forums	`FedoraForum.org` `LinuxForums.org`

Communities	`FedoraFaq.org`
	`fcp.surfsite.org`
	`FedoraUnity.org`
	`FedoraSolved.org`

Table 1-1: Online Resources to Connect to the Fedora Community (*continued*)

Fedora Activities	Internet Sites
News	`FedoraNEWS.org`

Social Networks	`groups.myspace.com/fedoraproject`
	`www.frappr.com/fedora`
	`www.flickr.com/groups/fedora`

Fedora Software

Before Fedora 7, development of Fedora software consisted of the basic operating system (Fedora Core) and contributed outside packages (Fedora Extras). With the merge of Fedora Core and Fedora Extras software into one massive repository simply named Fedora, you can now go to one location to get all the software projects that have been packaged to run on Fedora Linux (see `http://fedoraproject.org/get-fedora.html`).

Sites that offer software packages built for Fedora that are outside the Fedora project jurisdiction include `http://rpm.livna.org`, `http://atrpms.net`, `http://freshrpms.net`, and `http://dag.wieers.com/rpm`. Information on how to use these and other Fedora software repositories is contained in Chapter 2.

Focusing on Linux Commands

These days, many important tasks in Linux can be done from both graphical interfaces and from commands. However, the command line has always been, and still remains, the interface of choice for Linux power users.

Graphical user interfaces (GUIs) are meant to be intuitive. With some computer experience, you can probably figure out, for example, how to add a user, change the time and date, and configure a sound card from a GUI. For these cases, we'll mention which graphical tool you could use for the job. For the following cases, however, you will probably need to rely on the command line:

❑ **Almost any time something goes wrong** — Ask a question at an online forum to solve some Linux problem you are having and the help you get will almost always come in the form of commands to run. Also, command line tools typically offer much more feedback if there is a problem configuring a device or accessing files and directories.

❑ **Remote systems administration** — If you are administering a remote server, you may not have graphical tools available. Although remote GUI access (using X applications or VNC) and web-based administration tools may be available, they usually run more slowly than what you can do from the command line.

❑ **Features not supported by GUI** — GUI administration tools tend to present the most basic ways of performing a task. More complex operations often require options that are only available from the command line.

❑ **GUI is broken or not installed** — If no graphical interface is available, or if the installed GUI isn't working properly, you may be forced to work from the command line. Broken GUIs can happen for lots of reasons, such as when you use a third-party, binary-only driver from NVIDIA or ATI and a kernel upgrade makes the driver incompatible.

The bottom line is that to unlock the full power of your Linux system, you must be able to use shell commands. Thousands of commands are available for Linux to monitor and manage every aspect of your Linux system.

But whether you are a Linux guru or novice, one challenge looms large. How do you remember the most critical commands and options you need, when a command shell might only show you this:

```
$
```

Fedora Linux Toolbox is not just another command reference or rehash of man pages. Instead, this book presents commands in Fedora Linux by the way you use them. In other words, instead of listing commands alphabetically, we group commands for working with file systems, connecting to networks, and managing processes in their own sections, so you can access commands by what you want to do, not only by how they're named.

Likewise, we won't just give you a listing of every option available for every command. Instead, we'll show you working examples of the most important and useful options to use with each command. From there, we'll tell you quick ways to find more options, if you need them, from man pages, the info facility, and help options.

Finding Commands

Some of the commands described in this book may not be installed when you go to run them. You might type a command and see a message similar to:

```
bash: mycommand: command not found
```

This might happen for the following reasons:

❑ You mistyped the command name.

❑ The command is not in your PATH.

❑ You may need to be the root user for the command to be in your PATH.

❑ The command is not installed on your computer.

Table 1-2 shows some commands you can run to look for a command you want to use.

Table 1-2: Finding Commands

Command and Sample Output	Description
`$ type mount` `  mount is hashed (/bin/mount)`	Show the first mount command in PATH.

`$ whereis mount`
`mount: /bin/mount /sbin/mount.cifs`
`/sbin/mount.smb /sbin/mount.smbfs`
`/usr/share/man/man2/mount.2.gz`
`/usr/share/man/man8/mount.8.gz`
	Show binary, source, and man pages for mount.

`$ locate bash.ps`	Find bash.ps anywhere in the file system.
`$ which umount` `/bin/umount`	Find the umount command anywhere in your PATH or aliases.

`$ rpm -qal |grep umount`
`/usr/share/man/man2/umount.2.gz`
`/usr/share/man/man2/umount2.2.gz`
`/bin/umount`
	Find umount in any installed package.

`$ yum whatprovides bzfs`
`...`
`bzflag.i386  2.0.8-3.fc6  extras`
`Matched from:`
`/usr/bin/bzfs`
`/usr/share/man/man6/bzfs.6.gz`
	Find bzfs in the bzflag package.

If you suspect that the command you want is not installed, you can search your Fedora repositories for terms that might be in the description of the package it contains. If you find the right package (for example, bzflag) and it isn't installed, install it from the Internet as root by typing the following:

```
# yum search "capture-the-flag"
Searching Packages:
Setting up repositories
Reading repository metadata in from local files

bzflag.i386          2.0.8-4.fc7            fedora
Matched from:
BZflag is a 3D multi-player tank battle game that allows users to play...
   ...
There are two main styles of play: capture-the-flag and free-for-all.
# yum install bzflag
```

Command Reference Information in Fedora

Original Linux and UNIX documentation was all done on manual pages, generally referred to as *man pages*. A slightly more sophisticated documentation effort came a bit later with the *info* facility. Within each command itself, help messages are almost always available.

This reference information is component oriented — in other words, there are separate man pages for nearly every command, file format, system call, device, and other component of a Linux system. Documentation more closely aligned to whole software packages is typically stored in a subdirectory of the /usr/share/doc directory.

All three reference features — man pages, info documents, and help messages — are available in Fedora.

Using help Messages

The -h or --help options are often used to display help messages for a command. The following example illustrates how to display help for the ls command:

```
$ ls --help | less
Usage: ls [OPTION]... [FILE]...
List information about the FILEs (the current directory by default).
Sort entries alphabetically if none of -cftuSUX nor --sort.

Mandatory arguments to long options are mandatory for short options.
  -a, --all                  do not hide entries starting with .
  -A, --almost-all           do not list implied . and ..
     ...
```

The preceding output shows how the ls command line is used and lists available options. Piping the output to the less command lets you page through it. You can format the help messages into a reference card using the card command. For example:

```
$ card ls --output=/tmp/ls.ps
$ lpr ls.ps
```

The result shown here is a file named ls.ps that you can open in a PostScript document reader (such as evince) to view the card. (Select View ⇨ Rotate Right to view the card properly.) You can use the lpr command to print the card or, if you don't use the --output option, it is sent to your default printer automatically.

Using man Pages

Suppose you want to find man pages for commands related to a certain word. Use the apropos command to search the man page database. This shows man pages that have crontab in the man page NAME line:

```
$ apropos crontab
  ...
```

```
/etc/anacrontab [anacrontab] (5)  - configuration file for anacron
crontab            (1)   -  maintain crontab files for individual
                              users (ISC Cron V4.1)
crontab            (1p)  -  schedule periodic background work
crontab            (5)   -  tables for driving cron (ISC Cron V4.1)
crontabs           (rpm) -  Root crontab files used to schedule the
                              execution of programs.
    ...
```

The `apropos` output here shows each man page NAME line that contains `crontab`. The number shows the man page section in which the man page appears. (We discuss sections shortly.)

The `whatis` command is a way to show NAME lines alone for commands that contain the word you enter:

$ whatis cat
```
cat        (1)  - concatenate files and print on the standard output
cat        (1p) - concatenate and print files
```

The easiest way to **display the man page for a term** is with the `man` command and the command name. For example:

$ man find
```
FIND(1)                                                FIND(1)
NAME
       find - search for files in a directory hierarchy
SYNOPSIS
       find [-H] [-L] [-P] [path...] [expression]
...
```

The preceding command displays the first man page found for the `find` command. As you saw in the earlier example, some terms have multiple man pages. For example, there is a man page for the `crontab` command and one for the `crontab` files. Man pages are organized into sections, as shown in Table 1-3.

Table 1-3: man Page Sections

Section	Description
1	General user commands
2	System calls
3	Programming routines / library functions
4	Special files

Continued

9

Table 1-3: man Page Sections (*continued*)

Section	Description
5	Configuration files and file formats
6	Games
7	Miscellaneous
8	Administrative commands and daemons

The following code shows some other examples of useful options with the man command.

```
$ man mount -a          Shows all man pages related to component
$ man 5 crontab         Shows section 5 man page for component
$ man mount -P more     Use more, not less to page through
$ man --path            List locations of man directories
/usr/kerberos/man:/usr/local/share/man:/usr/share/man/en:
/usr/share/man:/usr/X11R6/man:/usr/local/man
$ man -f mount          Same as the whatis command
$ man -k mount          Same as the apropos command
```

Over the years, more ways of displaying and working with man pages have developed. For example, you can **convert a man page into a web page** (HTML) using the man2html command. For example:

```
$ whereis -m cat
cat: /usr/share/man/man1/cat.1.gz /usr/share/man/man1p/cat.1p.gz
$ cd /tmp ; cp /usr/share/man/man1/cat.1.gz .
$ gunzip cat.1.gz
$ man2html cat.1 > cat.1.html
$ links cat.1.html
```

The first command looks for the cat man page. The following commands copy that man page to the /tmp directory and unzip it. Next the man2html command converts the man page to HTML (cat.1.html file). The links command-line web browser then lets you view the webified man page from the shell. (You may need to install the elinks package to use the links or elinks text-based web browsers.)

Man pages are also available on the Internet. A nicely organized reference site is http://linuxmanpages.com.

Using info Documents

In some cases, developers have put more complete descriptions of commands, file formats, devices, or other Linux components in the info database. You can enter the info database by simply typing the info command or by opening a particular component:

```
$ info ls
```

The previous command shows information on the ls command. Use up, down, left, and right arrows and Page Up and Page Down to move around the screen. Home and End keys go to the beginning and end of a node, respectively. When you are displaying the info screen, you can get around using the keystrokes shown in Table 1-4.

Table 1-4: Moving Through the info Screen

Keystroke	Movement
?	Display the basic commands to use in info windows.
Shift+l	Go back to the previous node you were viewing.
n, p, u	Go to the node that is next, previous, or up.
Tab	Go to the next hyperlink that is in this node.
Enter	Go to the hyperlink that is under the cursor.
Shift+r	Follow a cross-reference.
Shift+q	Quit and exit from info.

Software packages that have particularly extensive text available in the info database include gimp, festival, libc, automake, zsh, sed, tar, and bash. Files used by the info database are stored in the /usr/share/info directory.

Summary

Although you certainly can read this book from cover to cover if you like, the book is designed to be a reference to hundreds of features in Fedora Linux that are most useful to power users and systems administrators. Because information is organized by topic, instead of alphabetically, you don't have to know the commands in advance to find what you need to get the job done.

Most of the features described in this book will work equally well in Fedora, Red Hat Enterprise Linux, CentOS, and other Linux systems based on technology from Red Hat, Inc. In fact, many of the commands described here are in such widespread use that you could use them exactly as described here on most Linux and UNIX systems.

The next chapter describes how to get and install Fedora Linux software.

2

Installing Fedora and Adding Software

Critical tools for initially installing Fedora, and for adding and managing software later, include the *anaconda installer* (initial install), rpm command (install/manage local packages), and the yum command (install/manage packages from online repositories). The yum-utils package also includes useful commands for creating and managing software packages associated with *yum repositories*.

This chapter highlights critical issues you need to know during the initial Fedora installation. It covers information about online yum software repositories, such as which are best to use for different circumstances. Detailed examples of rpm, yum, and related commands are given later in the chapter.

IN THIS CHAPTER

Installing Fedora

Working with software repositories

Getting software packages with yum

Managing software packages with rpm

Extracting files from RPMs

Installing Fedora

For initial installation of Fedora, most people get an official Fedora DVD or set of CDs. Media available for the different Fedora releases include:

❑ For Fedora 6, there is a single DVD or a set of five CDs that represent the entire distribution named *Fedora Core 6*. You can add more packages from the *Fedora Extras* repository (which was only available from online repositories).

❑ For Fedora 7, Fedora Core and Fedora Extras were merged into a single, online repository. Different installation package sets are available for Fedora 7, such as a GNOME live/install CD, KDE live/install CD, and an installation DVD. Choose the set of media that best suits your need. Then use online repositories to download and install other packages you need.

Fedora media are available with books on Fedora, such as *Fedora 7 and Red Hat Enterprise Linux Bible* (Wiley, 2007) or by downloading media from the Fedora Project (`http://fedoraproject.org/wiki/Distribution/Download`). Get media for CentOS from `http://centos.org` (select Downloads). Get Red Hat Enterprise Linux media from the Red Hat downloads page (`www.redhat.com/apps/download`). Subscription fees may apply for RHEL products.

Preparing to Install

To simply erase everything on your computer's hard disk to install Fedora, you don't have to prepare your hard disks in advance. If you want to keep any data from your hard disk, back up that data before proceeding. To keep existing data on your hard disk and add Fedora, you may need to resize existing disk partitions and repartition your disk. See Chapter 7 for information on disk resizing and partitioning commands.

Choosing Installation Options

All Red Hat–based Linux distributions (Fedora, RHEL, and CentOS) use the *anaconda* installer to initially install the system. New features in the current Fedora version of anaconda will most likely make their way into upcoming versions of the RHEL and CentOS installers as well.

> **NOTE** *If you have a Fedora live CD, you can bypass the anaconda installer to install Fedora to your hard disk. After booting the live CD, you can select an install icon from the desktop and copy the contents of the live CD to your hard disk. You don't have the flexibility that comes with the anaconda installer, but you get a good basic set of desktop packages installed to start with.*

Starting the Install Process

Most people start the install process from the DVD or first CD in the install set. As an alternative, use boot images contained in the images directory on the CD or DVD (refer to the README file in that directory). In Fedora, do one of the following to start anaconda:

❑ **CD or DVD** — Insert the installation DVD or CD and reboot the computer.

❑ **Minimal CD boot image** — Locate the `boot.iso` image from the `images` directory of CDs, DVDs, or online mirrors. Burn `boot.iso` to a CD and start the install from the CD, but continue from some other medium. This is useful when you're doing a quick installation and don't have the full media with you.

❑ **USB flash drive:** Locate the `diskboot.img` image from the `images` directory of CDs, DVDs, or online mirrors. Copy `diskboot.img` to a USB flash drive (also called a thumb drive or pen drive) and start the install from that drive (provided your computer's BIOS can boot from USB devices). From Linux, type the following (with your USB flash drive inserted and represented by `/dev/sda`) to copy `diskboot.img` to your flash drive:

```
# dd if=/media/cdrom/diskboot.img of=/dev/sda
```

❑ **Hard disk boot** — If your CD drive won't boot, you can start the install from hard disk. This procedure assumes you already have a version of Fedora installed on your hard disk and can modify the GRUB boot loader to start the new install. With the installed Fedora system running, copy the initrd.img and vmlinuz files from the isolinux directory on the CD/DVD to the /boot directory on your hard disk. Update the /boot/grub/grub.conf file to include an entry for the initrd.img and vmlinuz files you just installed. Reboot and select that new entry from the GRUB boot screen to start the install.

❑ **PXE boot** — With no CD or DVD drive, you can start an install using a PXE boot. To do this, your computer needs a PXE-enabled Ethernet card and the ability to set PXE in the BIOS's boot order. You also need to set up an install server to support the PXE boot. The kernel and initial RAM disk needed to start the PXE boot are in the images/pxeboot directory. Tips for setting up a PXE boot server are in the /usr/share/doc/syslinux-* directory (when the syslinux package is installed in Fedora).

NOTE *There is no floppy disk image for starting a Fedora install. Since the 2.6 kernel, there is no install image small enough to fit on a floppy disk.*

Choosing Where Fedora Software Is from the Boot Screen

Each of the methods just described should result in a Fedora installer *boot screen* appearing. With a CD or DVD install, press Enter to continue with a graphical install from that media. Type the following at the boot prompt to choose a different install type:

```
boot: linux askmethod
```

NOTE *Beginning with Fedora 7, Fedora install media use a graphical boot screen. To get to the boot prompt from that screen, press the Tab key. Then add any boot options* (askmethod, text, vnc, *and so on) after the* vmlinuz *line shown.*

When prompted, select your install method from the following:

❑ **Local CDROM** — Continue installing from the local CD or DVD.

❑ **Hard drive** — To use this method, you must copy the DVD or CD images to a local hard disk. When asked, identify the partition and directory holding the images.

❑ **NFS image** — To use this method, you must copy the DVD or CD images to a directory on a computer on your LAN and share that directory using NFS. When asked, identify the NFS resource holding the images.

❑ **FTP** — You can use this method to install from an existing Internet FTP mirror, or from your own in-house install point. When asked, identify the FTP site's URL and directory. To create your own FTP install point, you can, for example, copy the contents of the DVD or all CD images to a directory on your FTP server with a command such as cp -ar.

❑ **HTTP** — Same as FTP, but using an HTTP web server (an existing Internet mirror or your own).

Choosing How Install Proceeds from the Boot Screen

To have the install proceed in different ways, you can add boot options. Here are examples of different install types you can request from the boot prompt:

```
boot: linux text
boot: linux vnc
boot: linux vnc vncconnect=192.168.0.20 vncpassword=99pass07
boot: linux ks=floppy
boot: linux ks=hd:/dev/hda1/ks.cfg
boot: linux ks=http://example.com/ks.cfg
```

Use linux text to run the install in text mode (if your graphical screens are garbled). If you use linux vnc, you can step through the graphical section of the install remotely by connecting a VNC client to the IP of the install machine. The installer will show the IP address and display to connect to after it starts the VNC server. You can also start a VNC client on your network in listening mode and point the installer to that client using vncconnect. In the second vnc example above, vncviewer -listen is running on the machine at 192.168.0.20 with a password of 99pass07.

The three ks examples tell the installer where to find a kickstart file to guide the install process. The first looks for a ks.cfg file on the local floppy disk, the second looks for ks.cfg on the first IDE hard disk partition, and the last looks for ks.cfg in the root of the web server at example.com. A kickstart file contains information that lets the install process bypass some or all questions asked during installation. A sample kickstart file can be found in /root/anaconda-ks.cfg after a Fedora install is completed. Using that file, you can repeat the install done on that machine on another computer. For information on kickstart, refer to the following site:

```
http://fedora.redhat.com/projects/config-tools/redhat-config-kickstart.html
```

> **NOTE** *To learn more about kickstart, install the anaconda package, then refer to the* kickstart-docs.txt *file in the* /usr/share/doc/anaconda-* *directory.*

You also have the choice of going into modes other than installation mode. For example:

```
boot: linux rescue
boot: linux local
boot: linux memtest86
```

The Fedora installer CD/DVD can be used for things other than installing Fedora. The rescue option starts a mini–Linux system in rescue mode, so you can mount file systems and fix problems from the command line. The local option bypasses the CD/DVD and tries to boot from hard disk. The memtest86 option checks your computer's memory.

Choosing More Boot Options

Most boot options, besides those mentioned, are meant to help work around problems that might occur during installation. In particular, you might need to disable certain hardware components or features that aren't properly configured and enabled during installation. Type **linux**, followed by one or more of the boot options shown in Table 2-1, to deal with common problems.

Table 2-1: Boot Options When Installing Fedora

Problem	Description	Boot Options to Try
Failure to read CD/DVD drive.	Some CD/DVD drives don't properly support DMA or some power management features.	`ide=nodma nodma acpi=off all-generic-ide irqpoll`
Hardware improperly probed.	Tell the boot process to not probe hardware.	`noprobe`
System hangs trying to enable some hardware.	Disable hardware or service that is causing the system to hang.	`nousb nopcmcia nofirewire noapic nolapic`
You want to disable SELinux.	Some people prefer not to enable SELinux because of its complexity.	`selinux=0`
Your computer has a serial console, but no regular monitor.	You can run the install in text mode from the serial terminal.	`console=/dev/ttyS0`
Video is garbled or hangs.	Try to set resolution yourself or skip monitor probing.	`resolution=800x600 skipddc vga=ask`
RAM is improperly detected.	Tell the kernel how much RAM to use.	`mem=256M`
Driver needed is not available with kernel.	Add driver you need from a driver disk.	`dd`

Other information on kernel boot options is available from the `bootparam` man page and the Boot Prompt HOWTO (`www.tldp.org/HOWTO/BootPrompt-HOWTO.html`).

Answering Installation Questions

Most of the screens you see during installation are quite intuitive. Table 2-2 offers a quick review of those screens, along with tips where you might need some help.

If errors occur during the installation, press Ctrl+Alt+F1, F2, F3, F4, or F5 to see virtual terminals containing useful information. Ctrl+Alt+F1 displays the installation dialog box. Ctrl+Alt+F2 displays a shell prompt, so you can access your system during installation from the shell. Ctrl+Alt+F3 displays messages sent to the install log from the installation program. Ctrl+Alt+F4 shows system-related messages. Ctrl+Alt+F5 displays other messages. Press Ctrl+Alt+F7 to return to the X graphical installation screen.

Table 2-2: Fedora Installation Screens

Screen	Description	Tips
Test Media	Check each CD/DVD image against an md5sum implanted on that image.	On occasion, a media check will fail with good media on a drive that doesn't support DMA. If the check fails, start the installer with ide=nodma and check again. If the media passes, you can continue.
Language	Choose the install language.	If you need support for other languages, add them later.
Keyboard	Choose the keyboard by language/country.	
Install or Upgrade	Choose a fresh install or upgrade (if a Fedora version is already installed).	If multiple Fedoras are installed, choose which one to upgrade.
Disk Partitions	Either let the installer partition your disk or choose to partition it yourself.	You need at least one swap partition and one partition to hold the installation. See Chapter 7 for information on partitioning your hard disk.
Boot loader	Choose whether or not to install a boot loader on your hard disk.	GRUB is the only bootloader supported by Fedora. GRUB is configured by default in the master boot record of your first hard drive. If multiple operating systems are installed on your hard drives, you can add them to the list of bootable operating systems on your boot loader.
Network	Wired Ethernet cards are detected and configured (by default) to use dynamic addresses retrieved from a DHCP server.	You can set hostname and IP addresses manually, if you prefer. Wireless cards and modems can only be configured after Fedora is installed. (See the description of iwconfig in Chapter 11.)

Table 2-2: Fedora Installation Screens (*continued*)

Screen	Description	Tips
Timezone	Select your time zone from a map or pull-down menu.	
Root password	Set the password for the root user.	Make it difficult to guess. Don't share it.
Software packages	Package groups available from the installation medium are displayed for you to choose.	Select *Add additional software repositories* to choose online repositories that make more packages available to install. Click the *Using Software Repositories* box to see details on finding and adding repos. Click *Customize now* for details of which packages from selected groups are to be installed.
Reboot	When all packages are installed, you are asked to reboot.	

Working with Software Packages

Software delivered particularly for Fedora systems is packaged in what are called *RPM* packages. An RPM package (. rpm extension) contains not only the software you want to install, as a compressed archive, but it can also hold lots of information about the contents of the package. That information can include software descriptions, dependencies, computer architecture, vendor, size, licensing, and other information.

When a basic Fedora system is installed, you can add, remove, and otherwise manage Fedora packages to suit how you use that system. Fedora, RHEL, CentOS, and other Linux systems use *RPM Package Management* (*RPM*) tools to create and manage software for those systems. You use two primary commands to manage RPMs in Fedora:

❑ **yum** — Use yum to download and install packages from online repositories. The yum command is preferred over rpm for installing packages in most cases because yum will get dependent packages needed by those packages you request to install, and by getting packages from official repositories, you are most likely to get the latest available packages.

❑ **rpm** — Use rpm to install RPM packages available from your local system (hard disk or CD/ DVD) and otherwise manage installed packages (remove, query, and so on). Related commands and options are available for verifying software packages and repairing your local RPM database, if problems should occur.

Up until Fedora 6, Fedora was represented by an installation set (a single DVD or up to five CDs) that contained more than 2200 RPM packages. The packages in that set were referred to as *Fedora Core*. Red Hat, Inc. employees were primarily responsible for maintaining Fedora Core. Additional packages submitted by the Fedora community were tested and approved by the *Fedora Extras* committee, then added to a separate online repository.

Both Fedora Core and Extras RPM packages were held to the same standards: packages must be open source, not encumbered by patents, legal under U.S. laws such as the Digital Millennium Copyright Act (DMCA), and licensed for redistribution. That made it easier in Fedora 7 to merge Fedora Core and Extras into a single repository. So, instead of getting an installation set that included a cross-section of desktop, workstation, and server packages, separate *spins* were created for Fedora 7 desktop, server, and other package groupings. Packages outside of your spin can then be downloaded and installed from the massive, online Fedora repository.

Other software packages that work with Linux, but may not meet Red Hat requirements, are available from third-party yum software repositories. Some of those repositories build their dependencies on the main Fedora repository. The following section describes some of those repositories and how to access them.

Using yum Software Repositories

In the old days of Red Hat Linux, when people needed packages that had been left out by Red Hat, they had to hunt the packages down on the Web. If they got lucky, they located an RPM built for the exact version of Red Hat Linux they were using. If not, they had to fight against RPM dependency hell or do a dirty install from source.

The rpm command, while very powerful for installing single packages (either locally or from the Internet), did not go out and find dependent packages you needed to install your selected package. It also didn't grab the latest version of a package just by asking for it.

Debian GNU/Linux and other Linux distributions based on Debian enjoy the bliss of apt — a one-line command that allowed a user to install virtually any package out there. Dependencies are calculated and installed automagically. At first, apt4rpm emerged as a tool for letting Red Hat-based distributions get RPM packages from apt-enabled repositories. Soon, however, yum emerged as the tool for getting Fedora software.

Just as apt was borrowed from Debian, yum came from Yellow Dog Linux (a distribution based on Red Hat Linux that ran on Mac hardware). The yum utility (Yellow dog Updater, Modified) offered near-identical features to apt and has now become an integral part of Fedora; apt4rpm is no longer maintained and should no longer be used. While Fedora was adopting yum, RHEL went with its own RPM management tool: up2date. With RHEL 5, however, yum provides the underlying structure for software installation.

Enabling Repositories for yum

With the merging of Fedora Core and Fedora Extras into one massive repository, literally thousands of open source software packages are available for you to install for free. If you have an Internet connection, Fedora 7 is automatically configured to access the repository.

Repositories that are enabled are represented by .repo files in the /etc/yum.repos.d directory. Simple yum commands, described later, can be used to download and install software packages from those repositories. To have access to many more software packages that were built particularly for your version of Fedora, you can enable more software repositories for yum.

Although the Fedora Project doesn't officially bless any of the yum software repositories outside of the main Fedora repository, most Fedora users draw on one or more outside repositories to get the software they need. Keep in mind, however, that some repositories go to great lengths to be compatible with existing Fedora packages, as well as those from other outside repositories. This should reduce occurrences of packages from outside repositories not installing because of broken dependencies.

> **WARNING!** *The Fedora project doesn't officially recommend outside repositories. So, you are basically on your own when you get packages from these third-party repositories. Risks include potential conflicts with repositories that offer the same software and dangers that can come from replacing core system components. Be careful with blanket* yum upgrade. *You're sometimes better off selectively installing the specific packages you need from the third-party repository.*

To enable repositories from the following list, you need to install the .repo files needed to point to each repository and GPG keys needed to verify the authenticity of the packages you download from them. Instead of creating this information manually, most of the third-party Fedora repositories offer an RPM package you can download and install that includes that information.

Based on recommendations from Fedora users, consider using the following repositories (in the order shown):

❑ **RPMForge** (http://rpmforge.net) — Provides a wide range of packages, while striving for compatibility with the main Fedora repository. Packages are also available for RHEL/CentOS, Red Hat Linux, and other distributions across i386, x86_64, and other architectures. Several popular repositories including Dag Wieers (http://dag.wieers.com/rpm) are being merged into RPMForge.

❑ **Livna.org** (http://rpm.livna.org) — Contains packages that include codecs and drivers (such as ATI and NVIDIA video drivers) that may have restrictions that prevent them from being redistributed with Fedora. The packages may include components needed for otherwise unsupported audio and video players.

❑ **FreshRPMS** (http://freshrpms.net) — Contains packages particularly for media players and wireless network card support.

❑ **ATrpms** (http://atrpms.net) — Contains interesting packages for such things as QEMU acceleration, telephony, audio and video streaming, MythTV, and NVIDIA video card drivers. This is generally considered to have more compatibility issues than the preceding repositories.

Each of these repositories has separate locations for different distributions and versions (so be sure to choose the one that matches your installed Fedora or other Linux system). Each can be enabled manually or through a release RPM package.

> **NOTE** *Before you enable extra repositories, here are a couple of tips you should keep in mind. Each added repository can severely slow the performance of yum. So only add repositories you need and, when possible, directly identify the repository you want when you run yum. You will run into fewer compatibility issues by using fewer repositories.*

The following command lines can be used to **get and install the release packages** for the first three repositories on the list and install them for the local system. These commands need to point to different packages for different Fedora releases, so you need to modify them to work with your Fedora release:

```
# rpm -Uhv http://ftp.belnet.be/packages/dries.ulyssis.org/fedora/
fc5/i386/RPMS.dries/rpmforge-release-0.2-2.2.fc5.rf.i386.rpm
# rpm -Uhv http://rpm.livna.org/livna-release-6.rpm
# rpm -Uhv http://ftp.freshrpms.net/pub/freshrpms/fedora/linux/6/
freshrpms-release/freshrpms-release-1.1-1.fc.noarch.rpm
```

The rpm commands run in these three lines get and install release packages for RPMForge, Livna.org, and FreshRPMS repositories, respectively. The RPMForge example enables that repository for Fedora Core 5, whereas the other two repositories are enabled for Fedora Core 6. There is no release package for the ATrpms repository, so you must **add the ATrpms repository manually.** Before you do, however, you need to install the ATrpms signing key on your Fedora system by typing the following:

```
# rpm --import http://ATrpms.net/RPM-GPG-KEY.atrpms
```

Next, you need to identify the ATrpms repository to your yum facility. The first versions of yum in Fedora used a monolithic /etc/yum.conf in which users added a few state-ments to add a repository. Current Fedoras now use individual .repo files in /etc/yum.repos.d/ directory. So, for example, you could add the following lines as a sepa-rate atrpms.repo file in the /etc/yum.repos.d directory:

```
[atrpms]
name=Fedora Core $releasever - $basearch - ATrpms
baseurl=http://dl.atrpms.net/fc$releasever-$basearch/atrpms/stable
gpgkey=http://ATrpms.net/RPM-GPG-KEY.atrpms
gpgcheck=1
```

This file identifies the repository name as atrpms. The baseurl identifies the loca-tion of the ATrpms repository. The gpgkey line notes the location of the key used to verify the ATrpms packages you download. The `gpgcheck` line tells yum to verify packages against that key.

Using the yum Command

Use the `yum` command to do most of the activities for getting, installing, upgrading, checking, and searching for packages from yum repositories for Fedora. The command has many options for dealing with packages individually or in groups.

> **NOTE** *If you prefer to use a GUI tool, the Package Manager window is built on top of the yum facility in Fedora. To start it, select Applications ⇨ Add/Remove Software or run the* `pirut` *command as root. New features for Fedora 7 make it easy to search, list, and browse available packages, and then select the ones you want to add or remove.*

The following sections provide examples of some useful `yum` command lines.

Finding Packages

There are lots of options to `yum` for finding information about specific packages or searching yum repositories for specific packages or components. Use the `list` option to **list packages meeting your criteria**, as in the following examples:

```
# yum list available      List packages available to be installed
# yum list installed      List packages already installed
# yum list extras         List packages not installed from any repo
# yum list *vorbis*       List packages with "vorbis" in title
# yum list updates        List packages that have updates available
```

Use the `info` option to **see package descriptions from repos**. Here are some examples:

```
# yum info wordpress      Description for wordpress package
# yum info word*          Descriptions for packages beginning with "word"
```

To **search packages for a string** that appears in the description, packager, package name, or summary of the package, use the `search` option as follows:

```
# yum search mp3          Search for packages including the "mp3" string
```

To **search packages for a file or other feature** and list the packages found, use the `whatprovides` option. For example:

```
# yum whatprovides ogg123
...
vorbis-tools.i386                  1:1.1.1-5.fc7      installed
Matched from:
/usr/bin/ogg123
/usr/share/doc/vorbis-tools-1.1.1/ogg123rc-example
/usr/share/man/man1/ogg123.1.gz
```

Installing Packages

To **install a package from any enabled yum repository,** use the `install` option. For example:

```
# yum install wordpress
...
Dependencies Resolved
=======================================================================
 Package                Arch         Version          Repository      Size
=======================================================================
Installing:
 wordpress              noarch       2.1-0.fc7        extras          725 k
Installing for dependencies:
 php                    i386         5.2.1-3          development     1.3 M
 php-cli                i386         5.2.1-3          development     2.1 M
 php-common             i386         5.2.1-3          development     197 k
 php-mysql              i386         5.2.1-3          development      72 k
 php-pdo                i386         5.2.1-3          development      53 k

Transaction Summary
=======================================================================
Install      6 Package(s)
Update       0 Package(s)
Remove       0 Package(s)

Total download size: 4.5 M
Is this ok [y/N]: y
```

This example installs the WordPress blogging software. Package dependencies that were not yet installed were found and identified for installation. For your system, you may need other packages as well, depending on what is already installed. Typing **y** (for "yes") downloads and installs all the packages.

To use `yum` to **install a package from a directory on the local computer,** you can use the `localinstall` option. An advantage of using `yum` instead of the `rpm` command is that any dependent packages needed to install the local package can be automatically picked up from enabled repositories. Here is an example:

```
# yum localinstall heyu-2.0beta.3.1-1.i386.rpm
```

You can choose to **install all packages in an installation group.** For example, to install the entire set of XFCE desktop packages, type:

```
# yum groupinstall XFCE
```

Updating Packages

If updates are available, you can **update a single package, group of packages, or all packages.** Here are some examples:

```
# yum check-update          Lists all packages with updates ready
# yum list updates openoffice*   Find available openoffice* updates
```

```
# yum update openoffice*          Update all openoffice packages
# yum update                      Update all packages with updates ready
# yum groupupdate XFCE            Update all packages in XFCE group
```

Removing Packages

You can **remove individual packages or groups of packages**. An advantage to using yum to remove packages is that it can remove dependent packages, as well as the ones you selected. Here are some examples:

```
# yum remove beagle               Removes the beagle package
# yum remove xscreen*             Removes packages beginning with xscreen
# yum groupremove XFCE            Removes all packages in XFCE group
```

In each case with yum remove commands, you see what packages will be removed by your action and you are prompted to agree or not agree to the removal.

Cleaning Up Packages

Using the clean option to yum, you can **clean up packages, headers, metadata, cache, and dbcache** left around by the yum facility. If keepcache is set to 1 in /etc/yum.conf, as the packages and headers you request are downloaded, they are saved in packages and headers subdirectories of /var/cache/yum/repo/, respectively. Metadata are stored in repomd.xml and comps.xml files in the same directory. Here are ways of cleaning out those items:

```
# yum clean packages              Cleans out packages left over in cache
# yum clean metadata              Cleans out metadata left over in cache
# yum clean headers               Cleans out headers left over in cache
# yum clean all                   Cleans out metadata, headers, and packages
```

Useful Combinations of Options

There are some yum options that can be very useful in certain situations. For example, **enabling and disabling repositories** can be useful on certain occasions. You can use --enablerepo= and --disablerepo= with a variety of yum options shown earlier, particularly if you know which repository you are interested in at the moment. Here are some examples (they assume you have the livna repository enabled):

```
# yum --disablerepo=livna search yum-utils
# yum --enablerepo=livna install mplayer
```

In the first example, you are looking for the yum-utils package. You don't remember which repository it is in, but you know it's not in the livna repository (so you disable that). In the second example, the livna repository had been disabled (by adding an enabled 0 to the repository's .repo file), so it specifically had to be enabled to install the mplayer package.

One issue that can slow down the performance of yum is that it's constantly going out and getting fresh metadata before performing the operation you request. If you feel that what you want to do doesn't require fresh metadata, you can have yum get **metadata only from the cache on your local machine**. This will often speed up performance quite a lot, with the small risk that the package information you are looking for may have changed since your last metadata update. Using the -C option, you can tell yum to use local metadata:

```
# yum -C info yum-utils
Setting up repositories
Reading repository metadata in from local files
. . .
```

Without the -C, yum will get fresh metadata from the repository if the local cache of that information is more than 30 minutes old (by default). The expiration time of the metadata is set in seconds by the metadata_expire option in the /etc/yum.conf file (metadata_expire=1800).

Using yum Utilities

By installing the yum-utils package (yum install yum-utils), you have access to a handful of useful commands that you can use for **accessing and creating yum repositories**. The repoquery command can be used to list information about a package in a yum repository. For example:

```
# repoquery -il tomcat5
# repoquery --provides tomcat5
```

The output from the -il option (shown first) produces a listing of files the tomcat5 package contains, as well as descriptions of its contents. The second example lists the capabilities the package provides. In general, the repoquery command works much the same way that rpm -q queries information from local RPMs, but will typically run a bit slower. Type man repoquery to see more available options.

The yumdownloader is useful for **downloading packages from a yum repository to the local disk**. For example, the following command downloads the cacti package to the local directory:

```
# yumdownloader cacti
```

Managing Software with rpm

Although yum has supplanted rpm as the tool of choice for installing RPM packages from online repositories, rpm has some extraordinary options for querying RPMs and verifying installed RPMs. It is also a useful tool for installing, removing, and validating RPMs that are available on your computer.

Using the rpm Command

Using the `rpm` command, any user can query the local RPM database. To use the command to install or remove software from your system, you must have root privileges.

Installing a Package

The following command installs a new package located in the current directory. Options in this command include `i` for install, `v` for verbose, and `h` for progress hash marks.

```
# rpm -ivh rpmforge-release-0.2-2.2.fc5.rf.x86_64.rpm
Preparing...          ######################################### [100%]
  1:rpmforge-release ######################################### [100%]
```

The following example installs a new package located on the Internet. This approach works with `http` and `ftp` protocols:

```
# rpm -ivh http://ftp.belnet.be/packages/dries.ulyssis.org/fedora/fc5/x8
6_64/RPMS.dries/rpmforge-release-0.2-2.2.fc5.rf.x86_64.rpm
Retrieving http://ftp.belnet.be/packages/dries.ulyssis.org/fedora/
fc5/x86_64/RPMS.dries/rpmforge-release-0.2-2.2.fc5.rf.x86_64.rpm
Preparing...          ######################################### [100%]
   1:rpmforge-release  ######################################### [100%]
```

Upgrading a Package

If an older version of the package is already installed, an error will occur when you go to install it. Use `rpm -Uvh` to upgrade an existing package to a newer version. For example:

```
# rpm -Uhv flash-plugin-9.0.31.0-release.i386.rpm
```

Removing a Package

To remove an installed package, use the `-e` option as follows:

```
# rpm -e rpmforge-release
```

Sometimes, such as on 64-bit systems that have 32-bit packages installed for backwards compatibility, you may have two or more versions of a package installed. If you get an error when trying to remove one, you might be able to fix that using a full package name or by removing all matching packages:

```
# rpm -e  avahi-0.6.11-3.fc5
error: "avahi-0.6.11-3.fc5" specifies multiple packages
# rpm -e avahi-0.6.11-3.fc5.i386
# rpm -e --allmatches avahi-0.6.11-3.fc5
error: Failed dependencies:
  libavahi-client.so.3()(64bit) needed by (installed)
    vino-2.13.5-2.2.x86_64
```

Assuming that the avahi package was installed, the command to remove the package failed because multiple packages of the same base name were installed. The second command succeeded (although it did so silently). Notice, however, that the last command failed because of dependency issues. The best way to resolve dependency issues is to use yum or work through the dependencies by hand. However, you may reach a point where you have to force the install or removal of a package.

> **WARNING!** *Doing this is DANGEROUS and may result in an unstable system. Make sure you know precisely what you're doing.*

Here, you specify that you want to remove the i386 version of the package, and ignore dependencies:

```
# rpm -e --nodeps avahi-0.6.11-3.fc5.i386
```

Querying Information about RPM Packages

This shows how to query installed packages for a package named rsync and display version information about that package (your version numbers may be different):

```
# rpm -q rsync
rsync-2.6.9-1.FC5.1
```

Use the -qp option to get information about an RPM in the present directory:

```
# rpm -qp rpmforge-release-0.2-2.2.fc5.rf.x86_64.rpm
```

To see a list of all the packages installed on your system, type the following:

```
# rpm -qa | less
glibc-2.5.90-15
libICE-1.0.3-1.fc7
```

Check a file on your system to see what package the file belongs to, if any:

```
# rpm -qf /etc/sysctl.conf
initscripts-8.31.6-1
```

Now that you know how to select the package(s) you want to query, let's get a little more information out of them. This example lists standard details about an installed package (assuming you reinstalled the rpmforge-release package).

```
# rpm -qi rpmforge-release
Name        : rpmforge-release          Relocations: (not relocatable)
Version     : 0.2                            Vendor: Dries RPM Repository
http://dries.ulyssis.org/rpm/Release    : 2.2.fc5.rf              Build
Date: Wed 12 Apr 2006 12:57:29 AM PDT
Install Date: Wed 14 Feb 2007 01:21:54 AM PST      Build Host:
```

```
koblenz.kotnet.org
Group        : System Environment/Base        Source RPM: rpmforge-release-0.2-
2.2.fc5.rf.src.rpm
Size         : 14574                          License: GPL
Signature    : DSA/SHA1, Wed 12 Apr 2006 07:17:23 AM PDT, Key ID 9c14a19c1aa78495
Packager     : Dag Wieers <dag@wieers.com>
URL          : http://rpmforge.net/
Summary      : RPMforge release file and package configuration
Description :
RPMforge.net release file. This package contains apt, yum and smart
configuration for the RPMforge RPM Repository, as well as the public
GPG keys used to sign them.
```

This **lists the content of an RPM file** that's in the local directory:

```
# rpm -qlp rpmforge-release-0.2-2.2.fc5.rf.x86_64.rpm | less
/etc/apt
/etc/apt/sources.list.d
```

Combine various query options to check an RPM file before it's installed:

```
# rpm -qilp rpmforge-release-0.2-2.2.fc5.rf.x86_64.rpm | less
```

This example **lists preinstall and postinstall** scripts that come with an installed RPM package:

```
# rpm -q --scripts kernel | less
```

Several other query options are available. See the rpm man page for details. The most powerful rpm query option is --queryformat (or --qf). It lets you build from scratch the output string. This **queries all installed packages to see what host they were built on:**

```
# rpm -qa --queryformat 'Package %{NAME} was built on %{BUILDHOST}\n' | less
```

This **makes a sorted list of all non-Red Hat packages:**

```
# rpm -qa --queryformat '%{VENDOR} %{NAME}\n' | grep -v "Red Hat" | sort
```

Here are a few more examples:

```
# rpm -qa --qf '%{NAME} is licenced under %{LICENSE}\n'
# rpm -qa --qf 'The size of %{NAME} is %{SIZE} bytes\n'
# rpm -qa --qf 'For %{NAME} get more info here: %{URL}\n'
# rpm -qa --qf 'For %{NAME} the architecture is: %{ARCH}\n'
# rpm -qa --qf 'The %{NAME} package is: %{SUMMARY}\n'
```

As you can imagine, the combinations are endless. Here's how to **list all the variables:**

```
# rpm --querytags | less
```

Verifying Installed Packages

There are times when you will question the behavior of the software installed on a machine. For example, when a system has been compromised, the attackers will often replace system binaries such as ls or ps with corrupt versions to cover their tracks. It becomes useful to check the files on the file system against the information stored in the RPM database.

> **NOTE** *It's possible that an intruder that replaces a key binary file may also have tampered with your RPM database. So, use this tool as one way of checking the validity of your system, but not necessarily the only way.*

For each file verified, rpm runs multiple checks and displays the result in a series of characters at the beginning of the line. A dot means the check was okay. A letter or number means the check failed. Table 2-3 shows the most useful checks and the character that represents their failure.

Table 2-3: RPM Package Verification Failure Messages

Letter indicating check failure	Description
S	File size differs
M	Mode differs: includes permissions and file type
5	MD5 checksum differs
U	User ownership differs
G	Group ownership differs
T	mTime (timestamp of last modification) differs

Use the following command to **verify all installed packages** and filter for files with bin in their path:

```
# rpm -Va | grep bin
S.5....T    /usr/bin/curl
```

This shows that the curl binary on the file system has a different size, MD5 checksum, and modification time than the one that came with the curl RPM. In other words, this file has been replaced. Here are a few other examples using the verify option:

```
# rpm -Vv coreutils                       Verbose check files from coreutils
# rpm -V -f /usr/bin/pr                    Verify package containing pr
# rpm -V -g Applications/Multimedia        Verify packages from selected group
```

Rebuilding Your RPM Database

If your RPM database becomes corrupted to the point where you can no longer install packages, you can **rebuild the database** from the installed package headers. First remove the old database files, and then rebuild the new ones as follows:

```
# rm /var/lib/rpm/__db.00*
# rpm --rebuilddb
```

For further information on using the rpm command, check the rpm man page (man rpm) or display help information (rpm --help).

Building RPMs from SRPMs

By rebuilding the source code that is used to build an RPM package, you can change it to better suit the way you use the software. To begin, you need to get the source RPMs (SRPMs) you want to modify and install the rpm-build package (yum install rpm-build).

For example, you could download and install the rpmforge-release SRPM package in the current directory by typing the following command:

```
# wget http://dag.wieers.com/rpm/packages/rpmforge-release/rpmforge-release-
0.3.6-1.rf.src.rpm
# mkdir -p /usr/src/redhat/SOURCES
# rpm -ivh rpmforge-release-0.3.6-1.rf.src.rpm
```

When a source code package (src.rpm) is installed, rpm places the files it contains in the default build tree under the /usr/src/redhat directory. If you have software development tools packages and the rpm-build package installed, you can rebuild the binary RPM from this package. You can make changes to the spec file or the source code of that package, and then **rebuild the package** using the command shown in the following example:

```
# rpmbuild -bb /usr/src/redhat/SPECS/rpmforge-release.spec
```

The result of this command is an RPM file that is output to a directory that is specific to your computer architecture: /usr/src/redhat/RPMS/arch, where arch is replaced by a name indicating the computer architecture (such as i386, i586, and so on). The resulting RPM file is ready to be installed.

Extracting Files from RPMs

An RPM is basically an archive of files that you want to install to your computer and some header information that identifies the software (descriptions, checksums, build information, and so on). You can remove the archive from an RPM package and **output the archive** to a cpio archive file.

The cpio format is similar to the tar format, described in Chapter 8, and can be similarly used for backing up and transporting files. Here's an example using the rpm2cpio command to extract the cpio archive from an RPM:

```
# rpm2cpio rpmforge-release-0.3.6-1.rf.x86_64.rpm > rpmforge-release.cpio
```

In this example, the software archive contained within the rpmforge-release RPM package is extracted to a cpio archive named rpmforge-release.cpio. Instead of sending the output of the rpm2cpio command to a cpio archive file, you can pipe it through the cpio -tv command to view a long listing of the contents of that archive:

```
# rpm2cpio rpmforge-release-0.3.6-1.rf.x86_64.rpm | cpio -tv
```

The results of the preceding command can also be produced by the rpm command. For example, rpm -qlvp rpmforge-release-0.3.6-1.rf.x86_64.rpm produces the identical output of the rpm2cpio command line shown.

To extract a single file from an RPM file, you can use rpm2cpio with a cpio -idv command that indicates the file you want. In the following command, the rpmforge.yum file is extracted to the usr/doc/rpmforge-release-0.3.6 directory in the current directory.

```
# rpm2cpio rpmforge-release-0.3.6-1.rf.x86_64.rpm \
    | cpio -idv ./usr/doc/rpmforge-release-0.3.6/rpmforge.yum
```

If you try this example, the package you get will have different version numbers and the specific rpm-release directory you use must match one that exists.

Summary

Software for Fedora and other Red Hat–based distributions is packaged in RPM format. The anaconda installer is used to initially install Fedora. Using boot options, you can choose different install types and adapt to different environments. To install additional software, you can use the yum command to get packages from online yum repositories. To install packages locally or query and verify installed packages, you can use the rpm command.

3

Using the Shell

The use of a shell command interpreter (usually just called a shell) dates back to the early days of the first Unix systems. Besides its obvious use of running commands, shells have many built-in features such as environment variables, aliases, and a variety of functions for programming. Although the shell used most often with Linux systems is called the Bourne Again Shell (bash), there are other shells available as well (such as sh, csh, ksh, tcsh, and others).

This chapter offers information that will help you use Linux shells, in general, and the bash shell, in particular.

IN THIS CHAPTER

Accessing the shell

Using command history and completion

Assigning aliases

Gaining super user access

Writing simple shell scripts

Terminal Windows and Shell Access

The most common way to access a shell from a Linux graphical interface is using a Terminal window. From a graphical interface, you can often access virtual terminals to get to a shell. With no graphical interface, with a text-based login you are typically dropped directly to a shell after login.

Using Terminal Windows

To open a Terminal window from GNOME (the default Fedora desktop), select Applications ⇨ System ⇨ Terminal. This opens a gnome-terminal window, displaying a bash shell prompt. Figure 3-1 shows an example of a gnome-terminal window.

Commands shown in Figure 3-1 illustrate that the *current shell* is the bash shell (/bin/bash), the *current user* is the desktop user who launched the window (chris), and the *current directory* is that user's home directory (/home/chris). The user name (chris) and hostname (localhost) appear in the title bar.

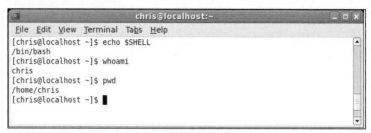

Figure 3-1: Type shell commands into a gnome-terminal window.

The gnome-terminal window not only lets you access a shell, it also has controls for managing your shells. For example, click File ➪ Open Tab to **open another shell on a different tab**, click File ➪ Open Terminal to **open a new Terminal window**, or select Terminal ➪ Set Title to **set a new title in the title bar**.

You can also use control key sequences to work with a Terminal window. Open a **shell on a new tab** by typing Shift+Ctrl+t, **open a new Terminal window** with Shift+Ctrl+n, **close a tab** with Shift+Ctrl+w, and **close a Terminal window** with Shift+Ctrl+q. Highlight text and copy it with Shift+Ctrl+c, then **paste it in the same or different window** with Shift+Ctrl+v or by clicking the center button on your mouse.

Other key sequences for controlling Terminal windows includes pressing F11 to show the window in *full screen mode*. Type Ctrl+Shift++ to **zoom in** (make text larger) or Ctrl+- (that's Ctrl and a minus sign) to **zoom out** (make text smaller). **Switch among tabs** using Ctrl+PageUp and Ctrl+PageDown (previous and next tab), or use Alt+1, Alt+2, Alt+3, and so on to go to tab one, two, or three (and so on). Type Ctrl+d to exit the shell, which closes the current tab or entire Terminal window (if it's the last tab).

The gnome-terminal window also supports profiles (select Edit ➪ Current Profile). Some profile settings are cosmetic (*allow bold text, cursor blinks, terminal bell, colors, images,* and *transparency*). Other settings are functional. For example, by default, the terminal saves 500 scrollback lines (318 kilobytes). Some people like to be able to scroll back further and are willing to give up more memory to allow that.

If you launch gnome-terminal manually, you can add options. Here are some examples:

```
# gnome-terminal -x alsamixer          Start terminal with alsamixer displayed
# gnome-terminal —tab —tab —tab        Start a terminal with three open tabs
# gnome-terminal —geometry 80x20       Start terminal 80 characters by 20 lines
# gnome-terminal —zoom=2               Start terminal with larger font
```

Besides gnome-terminal, you can use many other terminal windows. Here are some examples: xterm (basic terminal emulator that comes with the X Window System), aterm (terminal emulator modeled after the Afterstep XVT VT102 emulator), and konsole (terminal emulator delivered with the KDE desktop). The Enlightenment desktop project offers the eterm terminal (which includes features such as message logs on the screen background).

Using Virtual Terminals

When Fedora boots in multi-user mode (runlevel 2, 3, or 5), six virtual consoles (known as tty1 through tty6) are created with text-based logins. If an X Window System desktop is running, X is probably running in virtual console 7. If X isn't running, chances are you're looking at virtual console 1.

From X, you can **switch to another virtual console** with Ctrl+Alt+F1, Ctrl+Alt+F2, and so on up to F6. From a text virtual console, you can switch using Alt+F1, Alt+F2, and so on. Press Alt+F7 to return to the X GUI. Each console allows you to log in using different user accounts. Switching to look at another console doesn't affect running processes in any of them. When you switch to virtual terminal one through six, you see a login prompt similar to the following:

```
Fedora release 7
Kernel 2.6.20-1.29.22.fc7 on an i686

localhost login:
```

Separate `mingetty` processes manage each virtual terminal. Type this command to see what `mingetty` processes look like before you log in to any virtual terminals:

```
# ps awx | grep -v grep | grep mingetty
 2299 tty1     Ss+    0:00 /sbin/mingetty tty1
 2300 tty2     Ss+    0:00 /sbin/mingetty tty2
 2301 tty3     Ss+    0:00 /sbin/mingetty tty3
 2302 tty4     Ss+    0:00 /sbin/mingetty tty4
 2303 tty5     Ss+    0:00 /sbin/mingetty tty5
 2304 tty6     Ss+    0:00 /sbin/mingetty tty6
```

After I log in on the first console, `mingetty` handles my login, and then fires up a bash shell:

```
# ps awx | grep -v grep | grep tty
 1498 tty1     Ss+    0:00 -bash
 2300 tty2     Ss+    0:00 /sbin/mingetty tty2
 2301 tty3     Ss+    0:00 /sbin/mingetty tty3
 2302 tty4     Ss+    0:00 /sbin/mingetty tty4
 2303 tty5     Ss+    0:00 /sbin/mingetty tty5
 2304 tty6     Ss+    0:00 /sbin/mingetty tty6
```

Virtual consoles are configured in the `/etc/inittab` file. You can have fewer or more virtual terminals by adding or deleting `mingetty` lines from that file.

Using the Shell

After you open a shell (whether from a text-based login or Terminal window), the shell environment is set up based on the user who started the shell. Bash shell settings for all users' shells are located in /etc/bashrc, /etc/profile, and /etc/profile.d/. User-specific shell settings are determined by commands executed from several dot files in the user's home directory (if they exist): .bash_profile, .bash_login, and .profile. When a shell is closed, any commands in the user's ~/.bash_logout file are executed. Changing settings in these files permanently changes the user's shell settings but does not affect shells that are already running. (Other shells use different configuration files.)

There are a variety of ways in which you can list and change your shell environment. One of the biggest ways is to change which user you are; in particular, to become the super user (see the section "Acquiring Super User Power" later in this chapter).

Using Bash History

The Bourne Again Shell (bash) is the shell used by default by most modern Linux systems. Built into bash, as with other shells, is a history feature that lets you review, change, and reuse commands that you have run in the past.

When bash starts, it reads the ~/.bash_history file and loads it into memory. This file is set by the value of $HISTFILE. During a bash session, commands are added to history in memory. When bash exits, history in memory is written back to the .bash_history file. The **number of commands held in history during a bash session** is set by $HISTSIZE, while the **number of commands actually stored in the history file** is set by $HISTFILESIZE:

```
$ echo $HISTFILE $HISTSIZE $HISTFILESIZE
/home/fcaen/.bash_history 1000 500
```

To **list the entire history,** type **history.** To **list a previous number of history commands,** follow history with a number. This lists the previous five commands in your history:

```
$ history 5
975  mkdir extras
976  mv *doc extras/
977  ls -CF
978  vi house.txt
979  history
```

To **move among the commands** in your history, use the up arrow and down arrow. When a command is displayed, you can use the keyboard to **edit the current command** like any other command: left arrow, right arrow, Delete, Backspace, and so on. Here are some other ways to recall and run commands from your bash history:

```
$ !!                Run the previous command
$ !997              Run command number 997 from history
ls -CF
$ !997 *doc         Append *doc to command 997 from history
ls -CF *doc
$ !?CF?             Run previous command line containing the CF string
ls -CF *doc
$ !ls               Run the previous ls command
```

```
ls -CF *doc
$ !ls:s/CF/l          Run previous ls command, replacing CF with l
ls -l *doc
```

Another way to **edit the command history** is using the `fc` command. With `fc`, you open the chosen command from history using the vi editor. The edited command runs when you exit the editor. Change to a different editor by setting the FCEDIT variable (for example, `FCEDIT=gedit`) or on the `fc` command line. For example:

```
$ fc 978                  Edit command number 978, then run it
$ fc                      Edit the previous command, then run it
$ fc -e /usr/bin/nano 989  Use nano to edit command 989
```

Use Ctrl+r to **search for a string in history**. For example, typing Ctrl+r followed by the string ss resulted in the following:

```
# <Ctrl+r>
(reverse-i-search)`ss': sudo /usr/bin/less /var/log/messages
```

Press Ctrl+r repeatedly to **search backwards through your history list** for other occurrences of the ss string.

> **NOTE**   *By default, bash command history editing uses emacs-style commands. If you prefer the vi editor, you can use vi-style editing of your history by using the* set *command to set your editor to vi. To do that, type the following:* set -o vi

Using Command Line Completion

You can use the Tab key to complete different types of information on the command line. Here are some examples where you type a partial name, followed by the Tab key, to **have bash try to complete the information you want** on your command line:

```
$ tracer<Tab>         Command completion: Completes to traceroute command
$ cd /home/ch<Tab>    File completion: Completes to /home/chris directory
$ cd ~jo<Tab>         User homedir completion: Completes to /home/john
$ echo $PA<Tab>       Env variable completion: Completes to $PATH
$ ping <Alt+@><Tab>   Host completion: Show hosts from /etc/hosts
@davinci.example.com  @ritchie.example.com  @thompson.example.com
@localhost            @zooey
```

Redirecting stdin and stdout

Typing a command in a shell makes it run interactively. The resulting process has two output streams: stdout for normal command output and stderr for error output. In the following example, when /tmpp isn't found, an error message goes to stderr but output from listing /tmp (which is found) goes to stdout:

```
$ ls /tmp /tmpp
ls: /tmpp: No such file or directory
```

```
/tmp/:
gconfd-fcaen  keyring-b41WuB  keyring-ItEWbz  mapping-fcaen  orbit-fcaen
```

By default, all output is directed to the screen. Use the greater-than sign (>) to **direct output to a file**. More specifically, you can direct the standard output stream (using >) or standard error stream (using 2>) to a file. Here are examples:

```
$ ls /tmp /tmmp > output.txt
ls: /tmpp: No such file or directory
```

```
$ ls /tmp /tmmp 2> errors.txt
/tmp/:
gconfd-fcaen  keyring-b41WuB  keyring-ItEWbz  mapping-fcaen  orbit-fcaen
```

```
$ ls /tmp /tmmp 2> errors.txt > output.txt
```

```
$ ls /tmp /tmmp > everything.txt 2>&1
```

In the first example, stdout is redirected to the file output.txt, while stderr is still directed to the screen. In the second example, stderr (stream 2) is directed to errors .txt while stdout goes to the screen. In the third example, the first two examples are combined. The last example directs both streams to the everything.txt file. **To append to a file** instead of overwriting it, use two greater-than signs:

```
$ ls /tmp >> output.txt
```

If you don't ever want to see an output stream, you can simply **direct the output stream to a special bit bucket file** (/dev/null):

```
$ ls /tmp 2> /dev/null
```

> **TIP** *Another time you may want to redirect stderr is when you run jobs with crontab. You could redirect stderr to a mail message that goes to the crontab's owner. That way any error messages can be sent to the person running the job.*

Just as you can direct standard output from a command, you can also **direct standard input to a command**. For example, the following command e-mails the /etc/hosts file to the user named chris on the local system:

```
$ mail chris < /etc/hosts
```

Using pipes, you can **redirect output from one process to another process** rather than just files. Here is an example where the output of the ls command is piped to the sort command to have the output sorted:

```
$ ls /tmp | sort
```

In the next example, a **pipe and redirection are combined** (the stdout of the ls command is sorted and stderr is dumped to the bit bucket):

```
$ ls /tmp/ /tmmp 2> /dev/null | sort
```

Pipes can be used for tons of things:

```
$ rpm -qa | grep -i sql | wc -l
$ ps auwx | grep firefox
$ ps auwx | less
$ whereis -m yum | awk '{print $2}'
```

The first command line in the preceding code lists all installed packages, grabs those packages that have sql in them (regardless of case), and does a count of how many lines are left (effectively counting packages with sql in the name). The second command line displays Firefox processes taken from the long process list (assuming the Firefox web browser is running). The third command line lets you page through the process list. The last line displays the word *yum:* followed by the path to the yum man page, and then displays only the path to the man page (the second element on the line).

Using backticks, you can **execute one section of a command line first and feed the output of that command to the rest of the command line.** Here are examples:

```
$ rpm -qf `which ps`
$ ls -l `which traceroute`
```

The first command line in the preceding example finds the full path of the ps command and finds the package that contains that ps command. The second command line finds the full path to the traceroute command and does a long list (ls -l) of that command.

A more advanced and powerful way to **take the output of one command and pass it as parameters to** another is with the xargs command. For example:

```
$ ls /usr/bin/rpm* | xargs rpm -qf
```

To display the command xargs is going to run, use the following:

```
$ ls /usr/bin/rpm* | xargs -t rpm -qf
rpm -qf /usr/bin/rpm2cpio /usr/bin/rpmdb /usr/bin/rpmquery /usr/bin/rpmsign
/usr/bin/rpmverify
rpm-4.4.2-39.fc7
rpm-4.4.2-39.fc7
rpm-4.4.2-39.fc7
rpm-4.4.2-39.fc7
rpm-4.4.2-39.fc7
```

In this example, the entire output of `ls` is passed to a single `rpm -qf` command. Using the `-t` option to `xargs`, a verbose output of the command line appears before the command is executed. Now let's have `xargs` pass each output string from `ls` as input to individual `rpm` commands. We define {} as the placeholder for the string:

```
$ ls /usr/bin/rpm* | xargs -t -I{} rpm -qf {}
rpm -qf /usr/bin/rpm2cpio
rpm-4.4.2-39.fc7
rpm -qf /usr/bin/rpmdb
rpm-4.4.2-39.fc7
rpm -qf /usr/bin/rpmquery
rpm-4.4.2-39.fc7
rpm -qf /usr/bin/rpmsign
rpm-4.4.2-39.fc7
rpm -qf /usr/bin/rpmverify
rpm-4.4.2-39.fc7
```

As you can see from the output, separate `rpm -qf` commands are run for each option passed by `ls`.

Using alias

Use the `alias` command to **set and list aliases**. Some aliases are already set in your system's `/etc/bashrc` or `/etc/profile.d/*` files or the user's `~/.bashrc` file. Here's how to **list the aliases that are currently set**:

```
$ alias
alias cp='cp -i'
alias l.='ls -d .* --color=tty'
alias ll='ls -l --color=tty'
alias ls='ls --color=tty'
alias mv='mv -i'
alias rm='rm -i'
alias which='alias | /usr/bin/which --tty-only --read-alias
        --show-dot --show-tilde'
```

Notice that some aliases are set simply as a way of adding options to the default behavior of a command (such as `mv -i`, so that the user is always prompted before moving a file). You can **define your own aliases for the current bash session** as follows:

```
$ alias la='ls -la'
```

Add that line to your `~/.bashrc` file for the definition to occur for each new bash session. **Remove an alias from the current bash session** using the `unalias` command, as follows:

```
$ unalias la          Unalias the previously aliased la command
$ unalias -a          Unalias all aliased commands
```

Watching Commands

If you need to keep an eye on a command whose output is changing, use the `watch` command. For example, to keep an eye on your load average:

```
$ watch 'cat /proc/loadavg'
```

Every two seconds, `watch` runs the `cat` command again. Use Ctrl+c to quit. To change the refresh rate to 10 seconds, type the following:

```
$ watch -n 10 'ls -l'
```

To highlight the difference between screen updates, type:

```
$ watch -d 'ls -l'
```

Type Ctrl+c to exit the `watch` command.

Watching Files

You can use the `watch` command to watch the size of a file. For example, to watch a large ISO file named `mydownload.iso` as it downloads, use the following command:

```
$ watch 'ls -l mydownload.iso'
```

To watch the contents of a plain text file grow over time, you can use the `tail` command. For example, you can watch as messages are added to the `/var/log/messages` file as follows:

```
# tail -f /var/log/messages
```

Pressing Ctrl+c will exit from the `tail` command.

Acquiring Super User Power

When you open a shell, you are able to run commands and access files and directories based on your user/group ID and the permissions set for those components. Many system features are restricted to the *root user*, also referred to as the *super user*.

Using the su Command

With a shell open as a regular user, you can use the `su` (super user) command to become the root user. However, simply using `su`, as in the following code, doesn't give you a login shell with root's environment:

```
$ su
Password: *****
```

41

```
# echo $PATH
/usr/kerberos/sbin:/usr/kerberos/bin:/usr/local/bin:/usr/bin:/bin:/usr/X11R6/bin
:/home/fcaen/bin
```

After running su, the user still has fcaen's PATH. To **enable the root user's environment,** use the su command with the dash option (-), as follows:

```
# exit
$ su -
Password: *****
# echo $PATH
/usr/kerberos/sbin:/usr/kerberos/bin:/usr/local/sbin:/usr/local/bin:/sbin:/bin:/
usr/sbin:/usr/bin:/root/bin
```

In most cases, use su -, unless you have a very specific reason not to. If no user is specified, su defaults to the root user. However, su can also be used **to become other users:**

```
$ su - cnegus
```

The su command can also be used to **execute a single command as a particular user:**

```
$ su -c whoami
Password: ******
root
# su -c 'less /var/log/messages'
```

Although in the second example you are logged in as a regular user, when you run whoami with su -c, it shows that you are the root user. In the directly preceding example, the quotes are required around the less command line to identify /var/log/messages as an option to less. As seen above, whoami can be useful to **determine which user you're currently running a command as:**

```
$ whoami
fcaen
```

Delegating Power with sudo

The sudo command allows very granular delegation of power to users other than the root user. The sudo facility is a great tool when you have multiple users for granting specific escalated privileges and logging everything the users do with those privileges. Unless otherwise specified, sudo runs as root.

The sudo command is configured in /etc/sudoers.

> **WARNING!**   Never *edit this file with your normal text editor. Instead, always use the* visudo *command.*

If you look at the `sudoers` file that shipped with your distribution, you'll see different empty sections delimited by comments and one active statement:

```
root    ALL=(ALL) ALL
```

This means that the user root is allowed on any hosts to run any command as any user. Now add the following line setting the first field to a user account on your system:

```
fcaen ALL= /usr/bin/less /var/log/messages
```

Now fcaen (or whichever user you've added) can do the following:

```
$ sudo /usr/bin/less /var/log/messages
Password:
```

After fcaen types his own password, he can page through the `/var/log/messages` file. A timestamp is set at that time as well. For the next five minutes (by default), that user can type the command line above and have it work without being prompted for the password.

Every use of `sudo` gets logged in `/var/log/secure`:

```
Feb 24 21:58:57 localhost sudo: fcaen : TTY=pts/3 ; PWD=/home/fcaen ; USER=root
; COMMAND=/usr/bin/less /var/log/messages
```

Next add this line to `/etc/sudoers`:

```
fcaen        server1=(chris)      /bin/ls /home/chris
```

Now fcaen can do the following:

```
$ sudo -u chris /bin/ls /home/chris
```

The `sudo` command just shown runs as chris and will work only on the host server1. In some organizations, the `/etc/sudoers` file is centrally managed and deployed to all the hosts, so it can be useful to specify `sudo` permissions on specific hosts.

The `sudo` command also allows the definition of aliases, or predefined groups of users, commands, hosts. Check the `/etc/sudoers` file on your Linux system for examples of those features.

Using Environment Variables

Small chunks of information that are useful to your shell environment are stored in what are referred to as *environment variables*. By convention, environment variable names are all uppercase (although that convention is not enforced). If you use the bash shell, some environment variables are set for you from various bash start scripts: /etc/profile, /etc/profile.d/*.sh, /etc/bashrc, and ~/.bash_profile.

To **display all of the environment variables**, in alphabetical order, that are already set for your shell, type the following:

```
$ set | less
BASH=/bin/bash
COLORS=/etc/DIR_COLORS.xterm
COLUMNS=118
DISPLAY=:0.0
HOME=/home/fcaen
HOSTNAME=einstein
...
```

The output just shown contains only a few examples of the environment variables you will see. You can also **set, or reset, any variables yourself.** For example, to assign the value 123 to the variable ABC (then display the contents of ABC), type the following:

```
$ ABC=123
$ echo $ABC
123
```

The variable ABC exists only in the shell it was created in. If you launch a command from that shell (ls, cat, firefox, and so on), that new process will not see the variable. Start a new bash process and test this:

```
$ bash
$ echo $ABC

$
```

You can **make variables part of the environment and inheritable by children processes** by exporting them:

```
$ export ABC=123
$ bash
$ echo $ABC
123
```

Also, you can **concatenate a string to an existing variable:**

```
# export PATH=$PATH:/home/fcaen
```

To **list your bash's environment variables** use:

```
# env
```

When you go to create your own environment variables, avoid using names that are already commonly used by the system for environment variables. See Appendix B for a list of shell environment variables.

Creating Simple Shell Scripts

Shell scripts are good for automating repetitive shell tasks. Bash and other shells include the basic constructs found in various programming languages, such as loops, tests, case statements, and so on. The main difference is that there is only one type of variable: strings.

Editing and Running a Script

Shell scripts are simple text files. You can create them using your favorite text editor (such as vi). To run, the shell script file must be executable. For example, if you created a shell script with a file name of `myscript.sh`, you could **make it executable** as follows:

```
$ chmod u+x myscript.sh
```

Also, the first line of your bash scripts should always be the following:

```
#!/bin/bash
```

As with any command, besides being executable the shell script you create must also either be in your PATH or be identified by its full or relative path when you run it. In other words, if you just try to run your script, you may get the following result:

```
$ myscript.sh
bash: myscript.sh: command not found
```

In this example, the directory containing `myscript.sh` is not included in your PATH. To correct this problem, you can edit your path, copy the script to a directory in your PATH, or enter the full or relative path to your script as shown here:

```
$ mkdir ~/bin ; cp myscript.sh ~/bin/ ; PATH=$PATH:~/bin
$ cp myscript.sh /usr/local/bin
$ ./myscript.sh
$ /tmp/myscript.sh
```

Avoid putting a dot (.) into the PATH to indicate that commands can be run from the current directory. This is a technique that could result in commands with the same file name as important, well-known commands (such as `ls` or `cat`), which could be overridden if a command of the same name exists in the current directory.

Adding Content to Your Script

Although a shell script can be a simple sequence of commands, shell scripts can also be used as you would any programming language. For example, a script can produce different results based on giving it different input. This section describes how to use compound commands, such as `if`/`then` statements, `case` statements, and `for`/`while` loops in your shell scripts.

The following example code assigns the string abc to the variable MYSTRING. It then tests the input to see if it equals abc and acts based on the outcome of the test. The test is what takes place between the brackets ([ ]):

```
MYSTRING=abc
if [ $MYSTRING = abc ] ; then
echo "The variable is abc"
fi
```

To **negate the test,** use ! = instead of = as shown in the following:

```
if [ $MYSTRING != abc ] ; then
echo "$MYSTRING is not abc";
fi
```

The following are examples of **testing for numbers:**

```
MYNUMBER=1
if [ $MYNUMBER -eq 1 ] ; then echo "MYNUMBER equals 1"; fi
if [ $MYNUMBER -lt 2 ] ; then echo "MYNUMBER <2"; fi
if [ $MYNUMBER -le 1 ] ; then echo "MYNUMBER <=1"; fi
if [ $MYNUMBER -gt 0 ] ; then echo "MYNUMBER >0"; fi
if [ $MYNUMBER -ge 1 ] ; then echo "MYNUMBER >=1"; fi
```

Let's look at some **tests on file names.** In this example, you can check whether a file exists (-e), whether it's a regular file (-f), or whether it is a directory (-d). These checks are done with if/then statements. If there is no match, then the else statement is used to produce the result.

```
filename="$HOME"
if [ -e $filename ] ; then echo "$filename exists"; fi
if [ -f "$filename" ] ; then
    echo "$filename is a regular file"
elif [ -d "$filename" ] ; then
    echo "$filename is a directory"
else
    echo "I have no idea what $filename is"
fi
```

Table 3-1 shows examples of tests you can perform on files, strings, and variables.

Table 3-1: Operators for Test Expressions

Operator	Test being performed
-a *file*	Check that the file exists (same as −e).
-b *file*	Check whether the file is a special block device.
-c *file*	Check whether the file is a character special device.

Table 3-1: Operators for Test Expressions (*continued*)

Operator	Test being performed
-d *file*	Check whether the file is a directory.
-e *file*	Check whether the file exists (same as -a).
-f *file*	Check whether the file exists and is a regular file (for example, not a directory, socket, pipe, link, or device file).
-g *file*	Check whether the file has the set-group-id bit set.
-h *file*	Check whether the file is a symbolic link (same as -L).
-k *file*	Check whether the file has the sticky bit set.
-L *file*	Check whether the file is a symbolic link (same as -h).
-n *string*	Check whether the string length is greater than 0 bytes.
-O *file*	Check whether you own the file.
-p *file*	Check whether the file is a named pipe.
-r *file*	Check whether the file is readable by you.
-s *file*	Check whether the file exists and is larger than 0 bytes.
-S *file*	Check whether the file exists and is a socket.
-t *fd*	Check whether the file descriptor is connected to a terminal.
-u *file*	Check whether the file has the set-user-id bit set.
-w *file*	Check whether the file is writable by you.
-x *file*	Check whether the file is executable by you.
-z *string*	Check whether the length of the string is 0 (zero) bytes.
expr1 -a *expr2*	Check whether both the first and the second expressions are true.
expr1 -o *expr2*	Check whether either of the two expressions is true.
file1 -nt *file2*	Check whether the first file is newer than the second file (using the modification timestamp).
file1 -ot *file2*	Check whether the first file is older than the second file (using the modification timestamp).

Continued

Table 3-1: Operators for Test Expressions (*continued*)

Operator	Test being performed
file1 -ef *file2*	Check whether the two files are associated by a link (a hard link or a symbolic link).
var1 = *var2*	Check whether the first variable is equal to the second variable.
var1 -eq *var2*	Check whether the first variable is equal to the second variable.
var1 -ge *var2*	Check whether the first variable is greater than or equal to the second variable.
var1 -gt *var2*	Check whether the first variable is greater than the second variable.
var1 -le *var2*	Check whether the first variable is less than or equal to the second variable.
var1 -lt *var2*	Check whether the first variable is less than the second variable.
var1 != *var2* *var1* -ne *var2*	Check whether the first variable is not equal to the second variable.

Another frequently used construct is the case command. Using the case statement, you can test for different cases and take an action based on the result. Similar to a switch statement in programming languages, case statements can take the place of several nested if statements.

```
case "$VAR" in
   string1)
      { action1 };;
   string2)
      { action2 };;
   *)
      { default action } ;;
esac
```

You can find examples of case usage in the system start-up scripts (initscripts) found in the /etc/init.d/ directory. Each initscript takes actions based on what parameter was passed to it (start, stop, and so on) and the selection is done via a large case construct.

The bash shell also offers **standard loop constructs**, illustrated by a few examples that follow. In the first example, all the values of the NUMBER variable (0 through 9) appear on the for line:

```
for NUMBER in 0 1 2 3 4 5 6 7 8 9
do
   echo The number is $NUMBER
done
```

In the following examples, the output from the `ls` command (a list of files) provides the variables that the `for` statement acts on:

```
for FILE in `/bin/ls`; do echo $FILE; done
```

Instead of feeding the whole list of values to a `for` statement, you can increment a value and **continue through a while loop until a condition is met.** In the following example, VAR begins as 0 and the `while` loop continues to increment until the value of VAR becomes 3:

```
"VAR=0"
while [ $VAR -lt 3 ]; do
    echo $VAR
    VAR=$[$VAR+1]
done
```

Another way to get the same result as the `while` statement just shown is to use the `until` statement, as shown in the following example:

```
"VAR=0"
until [ $VAR -eq 3 ]; do echo $VAR; VAR=$[$VAR+1]; done
```

If you are just starting with shell programming, refer to the Bash Guide for Beginners (`http://tldp.org/LDP/Bash-Beginners-Guide/html/index.html`). Use that guide, along with reference material such as the bash man page, to step through many examples of good shell scripting techniques.

Summary

Despite improvements in graphical user interfaces, the shell is still the most common method for power users to work with Linux systems. The Bourne Again Shell (bash) is the most common shell used with Linux. It includes many helpful features for recalling commands (history), completing commands, assigning aliases, and redirecting output from and input to commands. You can make powerful commands of your own using simple shell scripting techniques.

4

Working with Files

Everything in a Linux file system can be viewed as a file. This includes data files, directories, devices, named pipes, links, and other types of files. Associated with each file is a set of information that determines who can access the file and how they can access it. This chapter covers many commands for exploring and working with files.

Understanding File Types

Directories and regular files are by far the file types you will use most often. However, there are several other types of files you will encounter as you use Linux. From the command line, there are many ways you can create, find, and list different types of files.

Files that provide access to the hardware components on your computer are referred to as *device files*. There are character and block devices. There are *hard links* and *soft links* you can use to make the same file accessible from different locations. Less often used directly by regular users are *named pipes* and *sockets*, which provide access points for processes to communicate with each other.

Using Regular Files

Regular files consist of data files (documents, music, images, archives, and so on) and commands (binaries and scripts). You can determine the type of a file using the `file` command. In the following example, you change to the directory containing bash shell documentation and use the file command to view some of the file types in that directory:

```
$ cd /usr/share/doc/bash*
$ file article* bash*
article.ms:   ASCII troff or preprocessor input text
article.ps:   PostScript document text conforming at level 3.0
```

```
article.txt:  ASCII English text, with escape sequences, with overstriking
bashdb:       directory
bash.html:    HTML document text
```

The `file` command that was run shows document files about the bash shell of different formats. It can look inside the files and determine that a file contains text with troff
markup (used in man pages and old Unix documentation), PostScript that can be sent
directly to a printer, plain text, or HTML (web page) markup. There is even a subdirectory shown (`bashdb`).

Creating regular files can be done by any application that can save its data. If you just
want to **create some blank files to start with**, there are many ways to do that. Here are two
examples:

```
$ touch /tmp/newfile.txt        Create a blank file
$ > /tmp/newfile2.txt           Create a blank file
```

Doing **a long list on a file is another way to determine its file type.** For example:

```
$ ls -l /tmp/newfile2.txt       List a file to see its type
-rw-rw-r--  1 chris chris 0 Sep 5 14:19 newfile2
```

A dash in the first character of the 10-character permission information (`-rw-rw-r--`)
indicates that the item is a regular file. (Permissions are explained in the "Setting File/
Directory Permissions" section later in this chapter.) Commands are also regular files,
but are saved as executables. Here are some examples:

```
$ ls -l /usr/bin/apropos
-rwxr-xr-x  1 root root 1786 Feb 13  1006 /usr/bin/apropos
$ file /usr/bin/apropos
/usr/bin/apropos: Bourne shell script text executable
$ file /bin/ls
/bin/ls: ELF 32-bit LSB executable, Intel 80386, version 1 (SYSV), for GNU/Linux
2.2.5, dynamically linked (uses shared libs), for GNU/Linux
```

You can see that the `apropos` command is executable by the x settings for owner,
group, and others. By running `file` on `apropos`, you can see that it is a shell script.
That's opposed to a binary executable, such as the `ls` command indicated above.

Using Directories

A *directory* is a container for files and subdirectories. Directories are set up in a hierarchy from the root (/) down to multiple subdirectories, each separated by a slash (/).
Directories are called *folders* when you access them from graphical file managers.

To create new directories for storing your data, you can use the `mkdir` command.
Here are examples of using `mkdir` to **create directories in different ways**:

```
$ mkdir /tmp/new             Create "new" directory in /tmp
```

```
$ mkdir -p /tmp/a/b/c/new   Create parent directories as needed for "new"
$ mkdir -m 700 /tmp/new2    Create new2 with drwx------ permissions
```

The first mkdir command simply adds the new directory to the existing /tmp directory. The second example creates directories as needed (subdirectories a, b, and c) to
create the resulting new directory. The last command adds the –m option to set directory permissions as well.

You can **identify the file as a directory** because the first character in the 10-character permission string for a directory is a d:

```
$ file /tmp/new
/tmp/new: directory
$ ls -l /tmp/new
drwxr-xr-x  2 chris chris 4096 Sep  5 14:53  /tmp/new
```

Note also that the execute bits (x) must be on, if you want people to be able to use the
directory as their current directories.

Using Symbolic and Hard Links

Instead of copying files and directories to different parts of the file system, links can
be set up to access that same file from multiple locations. Linux supports both *soft
links* (usually called *symbolic links*) and *hard links*.

When you try to open a *symbolic link* which points to a file or change to one that points
to a directory, the command you run acts on the file or directory that is the target of
that link. The target has its own set of permissions and ownership that you cannot see
from the symbolic link. The symbolic link can exist on a different disk partition than
the target. In fact, the symbolic link can exist, even if the target doesn't.

A *hard link* can only be used on files (not directories) and is basically a way of giving
multiple names to the same physical file. Every physical file has at least one hard link,
which is commonly thought of as the file itself. Any additional names (hard links) that
point to that single physical file must be on the same partition as the original target
file (in fact, one way to tell that files are hard links is that they all have the same inode
number). Changing permissions, ownership, date/time stamps, or content of any hard
link to a file results in all others being changed as well. However, deleting one link will
not remove the file; it will continue to exist until the last link to the file is deleted.

Here are some examples of using the ln command to **create hard and symbolic links**:

```
$ touch myfile
$ ln myfile myfile-hardlink
$ ln -s myfile myfile-symlink
$ ls -li myfile*
292007 -rw-rw-r--  3 francois francois 0 Mar 25 00:07 myfile
292007 -rw-rw-r--  3 francois francois 0 Mar 25 00:07 myfile-hardlink
292008 lrwxrwxrwx  2 francois francois 6 Mar 25 00:09 myfile-symlink
```

Notice that after creating the hard and symbolic link files, we used the `ls -li` command to list the results. The `-li` option shows the inodes associated with each file. You can see that `myfile` and `myfile-hardlink` both have the inode number of 292007 (signifying the exact same file on the hard disk). The `myfile-symlink` symbolic link has a different inode number. And although the hard link simply appears as a file (-), the symbolic link is identified as a link (1) with wide-open permissions. You won't know if you can access the file the symbolic link points to until you try it or list the link target.

Using Device Files

When applications need to communicate with your computer's hardware, they direct data to *device files*. By convention, device files are stored in the /dev directory. Devices are generally divided into block devices (such as storage media) and character devices (such as serial ports and terminal devices).

Each device file is associated with a major number (indicating the type of device) and minor number (indicating the instance number of the device). For example, terminal (tty) devices are represented by major character device 4, while SCSI hard disks are represented by major block device number 8. Here are **examples of device files**:

```
$ ls -l /dev/tty0 /dev/sda1    List character and block special devices
brw-r----- 1 root disk 8, 1 2007-09-05 08:34 /dev/sda1
crw-rw---- 1 root root 4, 0 2007-09-05 08:34 /dev/tty0
```

A listing of device names and numbers allocated in Linux is available in Fedora in the /usr/share/doc/MAKEDEV-*/devices.txt file. Most device files are created automatically for you at boot time, based on entries in the /etc/makedev.d directory. So most people never create device files manually. However, you can **create your own device file** using the `mknod` command. Here's an example:

```
# mknod /dev/ttyS4 c 4 68    Add device for fifth serial port
$ ls -l /dev/ttyS4           List new device file
crw-r--r-- 1 root root 4, 68 Sep  6 00:35 /dev/ttyS4
```

Using Named Pipes and Sockets

When you want to allow one process to send information to another process, you can simply pipe (|) the output from one to the input of the other. However, to provide a presence in the file system from which a process can communicate with other processes, you can create *named pipes* or *sockets*. Named pipes are typically used for interprocess communication on the local system, while sockets can be used for processes to communicate over a network.

Named pipes and sockets are often set up by applications in the /tmp directory. Here are some **examples of named pipes and sockets**:

```
$ ls -l /tmp/.TV-chris/tvtimefifo-local /tmp/.X11-unix/X0
prw------- 1 chris chris 0 Sep 26  2007 /tmp/.TV-chris/tvtimefifo-local
srwxrwxrwx 1 root  chris 0 Sep  4 01:30 /tmp/.X11-unix/X0
```

The first listing is a named pipe set up by the tvtime TV card player (note the p at the beginning indicating a named pipe). The second listing is a socket set up by the X GUI for interprocess communications.

To **create your own named pipe**, use the `mkfifo` command as follows:

```
$ mkfifo mypipe
$ ls -l mypipe
prw-rw-r--  1 chris chris 0 Sep 26 00:57 mypipe
```

To create your own socket, use the `mksock` command as follows:

```
$ /usr/sbin/mksock mysock
$ ls -l mysock
srwxrwxr-x  1 chris chris 0 Sep 26 00:57 mysock
```

Unless you are developing applications, you probably won't need to create named pipes or sockets. If you want to find where named pipes and sockets exist on your system, you can use the `-type` option to the `find` command, as described later in this chapter.

Setting File/Directory Permissions

The ability to access files, run commands, and change to a directory can be restricted with permission settings for user, group, and other users. When you do a long list (`ls -l`) of files and directories in Linux, the beginning 10 characters shown indicate what the item is (file, directory, block device, and so on) along with whether or not the item can be read, written, and/or executed. Figure 4-1 illustrates the meaning of those ten characters.

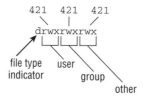

Figure 4-1: Read, write, and execute permissions are set for files and directories.

To follow along with examples in this section, create a directory called `/tmp/test` and a file called `/tmp/test/hello.txt`. Then do a long listing of those two items, as follows:

```
$ mkdir /tmp/test
$ echo "some text" > /tmp/test/hello.txt
$ ls -ld /tmp/test/ /tmp/test/hello.txt
```

```
drwxrwxr-x  2 francois sales 4096 Mar 21 13:11 /tmp/test
-rw-rw-r--  2 francois sales   10 Mar 21 13:11 /tmp/test/hello.txt
```

After creating the directory and file, the first character of the long listing shows /tmp/test as a directory (d) and hello.txt as a file (-). Other types of files available in Linux that would appear as the first character include character devices (c), block devices (b) or symbolic links (l), named pipes (p), and sockets (s).

The next nine characters represent the permissions set on the file and directory. The first rwx indicates that the owner (francois) has read, write, and execute permissions on the directory. Likewise, the group sales has the same permissions (rwx). Then all other users have only read and execute permissions (r-x); the dash indicates the missing write permission. For the hello.txt file, the user and group have read and write permissions (rw-) and others have read permission (r--).

When you set out to change permissions, each permission can be represented by an octal number (where read is 4, write is 2, and execute is 1) or a letter (rwx). Generally speaking, read permission lets you view the contents of the directory, write lets you change (add or modify) the contents of the directory, and execute lets you change to (in other words, access) the directory.

If you don't like the permissions you see on files or directories you own, you can change those permissions using the chmod command.

Changing Permissions with chmod

The chmod command lets you change the access permissions of files and directories. Table 4-1 shows several chmod command lines and how access to the directory or file changes.

Table 4-1: Changing Directory and File Access Permissions

chmod command (octal or letters)	Original Permission	New Permission	Description
chmod 0700	any	drwx------	The directory's owner can read or write files in that directory as well as change to it. All other users (except root) have no access.
chmod 0711	any	drwx--x--x	Same as for owner. All others can change to the directory, but not view or change files in the directory. This can be useful for server hardening, where you prevent someone from listing directory contents, but allow access to a file in the directory if someone already knows it's there.

Table 4-1: Changing Directory and File Access Permissions (*continued*)

chmod command (octal or letters)	Original Permission	New Permission	Description
chmod go+r	drwx------	drwxr--r--	Adding read permission to a directory may not give desired results. Without execute on, others can't view the contents of any files in that directory.
chmod 0777 chmod a=rwx	any	drwxrwxrwx	All permissions are wide open.
chmod 0000 chmod a-rwx	any	d---------	All permissions are closed. Good to protect a directory from errant changes. However, backup programs that run as non-root may fail to back up the directory's contents.
chmod 666	any	-rw-rw-rw-	Open read/write permissions completely on a file.
chmod go-rw	-rw-rw-rw-	-rw-------	Don't let anyone except owner view, change, or delete the file.
chmod 644	any	-rw-r--r--	Only the owner can change or delete the file, but all can view it.

The first 0 in the mode line can usually be dropped (so you can use 777 instead of 0777). That place holder has special meaning. It is an octal digit that can be used on commands (executables) to indicate that the command can run as a set-UID program (4), run as a set-GID program (2), or become a *sticky* program (1). With set-UID and set-GID, the command runs with the assigned user or group permissions (instead of running with permission of the user or group that launched the command).

> **WARNING!** *SUID should not be used on shell scripts. Here is a warning from the Linux Security HOWTO: "SUID shell scripts are a serious security risk, and for this reason the kernel will not honor them. Regardless of how secure you think the shell script is, it can be exploited to give the cracker a root shell."*

Having the sticky bit on for a directory keeps users from removing or renaming files from that directory that they don't own (/tmp is an example). Given the right permission settings, however, users can change the contents of files they don't own in a sticky bit directory. The final permission character is t instead of x on a sticky directory. A command with sticky bit on used to cause the command to stay in memory, even while not being used. This is an old Unix feature that is not supported in Linux.

The -R option is a handy feature of the chmod command. With -R, you can **recursively change permissions of all files and directories starting from a point in the file system**. Here are some examples:

```
# chmod -R 700 /tmp/test    Open permission only to owner below /tmp/test
# chmod -R 000 /tmp/test    Close all permissions below /tmp/test
# chmod -R a+rwx /tmp/test  Open all permissions to all below /tmp/test
```

Note that the -R option is inclusive of the directory you indicate. So the permissions above, for example, would change for the /tmp/test directory itself, and not just for the files and directories below that directory.

Setting the umask

Permissions given to a file or directory are assigned originally at the time that item is created. How those permissions are set is based on the user's current *umask* value. Using the umask command, you can **set the permissions given to files and directories** when you create them.

```
$ umask 0066   Make directories drwx--x--x and files -rw-------
$ umask 0077   Make directories drwx------ and files -rw-------
$ umask 0022   Make directories drwxr-xr-x and files -rw-r--r--
$ umask 0777   Make directories d--------- and files ----------
```

Changing Ownership

When you create a file or directory, your user account is assigned to that file or directory. So is your primary group. As root user, you can **change the ownership (user) and group assigned to a file to a different user and/or group** using the chown and chgrp commands. Here are some examples:

```
# chown chris test/          Change owner to chris
# chown chris:market test/   Change owner to chris and group to market
# chgrp market test/         Change group to market
# chown -R chris test/       Change all files below test/ to owner chris
```

The recursive option to chown (-R) just shown is useful if you need to change the ownership of an entire directory structure. As with chmod, using chown recursively changes permissions for the directory named, along with its contents. You might use chown recursively when a person leaves a company or stops using your web service. You can use chown -R to reassign their entire /home directory to a different user.

Related commands for changing group assignments and passwords include newgrp and gpasswd, as well as the /etc/gshadow file.

Traversing the File System

Basic commands for changing directories (cd), checking the current directory (pwd) and listing directory contents (ls) are well known to even casual shell users. So this section focuses on some less-common options to those commands, as well as other lesser-known features for moving around the file system. Here are some quick examples of cd for **moving around the file system**:

```
$ cd                    Change to your home directory
$ cd $HOME              Change to your home directory
$ cd ~                  Change to your home directory
$ cd ~francois          Change to francois' home directory
$ cd -                  Change to previous working directory
$ cd $OLDPWD            Change to previous working directory
$ cd ~/public_html      Change to public_html in your home directory
$ cd ..                 Change to parent of current directory
$ cd /usr/bin           Change to usr/bin from root directory
$ cd usr/bin            Change to usr/bin beneath current directory
```

If you want to **find out what your current directory is,** use pwd (print working directory):

```
$ pwd
/home/francois
```

Creating *symbolic links* is a way to access a file from other parts of the file system (see the section "Using Symbolic and Hard Links" earlier in this chapter for more information on symbolic and hard links). However, symbolic links can cause some confusion about how parent directories are viewed. The following commands **create a symbolic link** to the /tmp directory from your home directory and show how to tell where you are related to a linked directory:

```
$ cd $HOME
$ ln -s /tmp tmp-link
$ ls -l tmp-link
lrwxrwxrwx 1 francois francois 13 Mar 24 12:41 tmp-link -> /tmp
$ cd tmp-link/
$ pwd
/home/francois/tmp-link
$ pwd -P
/tmp
$ pwd -L
/home/francois/tmp-link
$ cd -L ..
$ pwd
/home/francois
$ cd tmp-link
$ cd -P ..
$ pwd
/
```

Using the -P and -L options to pwd and cd, you can **work with symbolically linked directories in their permanent or link locations,** respectively. For example, cd -L .. takes you up one level to your home directory, whereas cd -P .. takes you up one level above the permanent directory (/). Likewise, the -P and -L options to pwd show permanent and link locations.

Bash can remember a list of working directories. Such a list can be useful if you want to return to previously visited directories. That list is organized in the form of a stack. Use pushd and popd to **add and remove directories.**

```
$ pwd
/home/francois
$ pushd /usr/share/man/
/usr/share/man ~
$ pushd /var/log/
/var/log /usr/share/man ~
$ dirs
/var/log /usr/share/man ~
$ dirs -v
 0  /var/log
 1  /usr/share/man
 2  ~
$ popd
/usr/share/man ~
$ pwd
/usr/share/man
$ popd
~
$ pwd
/home/francois
```

The dirs, pushd, and popd commands can also be used to manipulate the order of directories on the stack. For example, pushd -0 pushes the last directory on the stack to the top of the stack (making it the current directory). The pushd -2 command pushes the third directory from the bottom of the stack to the top.

Copying Files

Provided you have write permission to the target directory, copying files and directories can be done with some fairly simple commands. The standard cp command will **copy a file to a new name or the same name in a new directory,** with a new time stamp associated with the new file. Other options to cp let you retain date/time stamps, copy recursively, and prompt before overwriting. Here are some examples:

```
# cd ; touch index.html
# cp -i index.html /var/www/html/
# cp -il index.html /var/www/html
```

```
# cp -a /var/www/html /mnt/sda1/var/www/
# cp -R /var/www/html /mnt/sda1/var/www/
```

Assuming you installed the Apache web server, the above examples show ways of copying files related to that server. In the first cp example above, if an index.html file exists in /var/www/html, you are prompted before overwriting it with the new file. In the next example, the index.html file is hard-linked to a file of the same name in the /var/www/html directory. In that case, because both hard links point to the same file, editing the file from either location will change the contents of the file in both locations. (The link can only be done if /var/www/html and your home directory are in the same file system.)

The cp -a command copies all files below the /var/www/html directory, retaining all ownership and permission settings. If, for example, /mnt/sda1 represented a USB flash drive, that command would be a way to copy the contents of your web server to that drive. The -R option also recursively copies a directory structure, but assigns ownership to the current user and adds current date/time stamps.

The dd command is another way to **copy data**. This command is very powerful because on Linux systems, everything is a file, including hardware peripherals. Here is an example:

```
$ dd if=/dev/zero of=/tmp/mynullfile count=1
1+0 records in
1+0 records out
512 bytes (512 B) copied, 0.000308544 s, 1.7 MB/s
```

/dev/zero is a special file that generates null characters. In the example just shown, the dd command takes /dev/zero as input file and outputs to /tmp/mynullfile. The count is the number of blocks. By default, a block is 512 bytes. The result is a 512-bytes-long file full of null characters. You could use less or vi to view the contents of the file. However, a better tool to view the file would be the od (Octal Dump) command:

```
$ od -vt x1 /tmp/mynullfile     View an octal dump of a file
```

Here's another example of the dd command:

```
$ dd if=/dev/zero of=/tmp/mynullfile count=10 bs=2
10+0 records in
10+0 records out
20 bytes (20 B) copied, 0.000595714 s, 33.6 kB/s
```

This time, we set the block size to 2 bytes and copied 10 blocks (20 bytes). The following command line **clones the first partition of the primary master IDE drive** to the second partition of the primary slave IDE drive (back up all data before trying anything like this):

```
# dd if=/dev/hda1 of=/dev/hdb2
```

The next example **makes a compressed backup** of the first partition of the primary master IDE drive. Typically the partition should be unmounted before a backup such as this.

```
# umount /dev/hda1
# dd if=/dev/hda1 | gzip > bootpart.gz
```

The following command copies a Fedora boot image (diskboot.img) from a Fedora installation DVD to your USB flash drive (assuming the drive appears as /dev/sda):

```
# dd if=diskboot.img of=/dev/sda
```

This example copies the Master Boot Record from the primary master IDE hard drive to a file named mymbrfile:

```
# dd if=/dev/hda of=mymbrfile bs=512 count=1
```

If you want to make a copy of the ISO image that was burned to a CD or DVD, insert that medium into your CD/DVD drive and (assuming /dev/cdrom is associated with your computer's CD drive) type the following command:

```
# dd if=/dev/cdrom of=whatever.iso
```

Changing File Attributes

Files and directories in Linux file systems all have read, write, and execute permissions associated with user, group, and others. However, there are also other attributes that can be attached to files and directories that are specific to certain file system types.

Files on ext2 and ext3 file systems have special attributes that you may choose to use. You can **list these attributes** with the lsattr command. Most attributes are obscure and not turned on by default. Here's an example of using lsattr to see some files' attributes:

```
# lsattr /etc/host*
------------- /etc/host.conf
------------- /etc/hosts
------------- /etc/host.allow
------------- /etc/host.deny
$ lsattr -aR /tmp/ | less      Recursively list all /tmp attributes
```

The dashes represent 13 ext2/ext3 attributes that can be set. None are on by default. Those attributes are the following: a (append only), c (compressed), d (no dump), i (immutable), j (data journaling), s (secure deletion), t (no tail-merging), u (undeletable), A (no atime updates), D (synchronous directory updates), S (synchronous updates), and T (top of directory hierarchy). You can **change these attributes** using the chattr command. Here are some examples:

```
# chattr +i /boot/grub/grub.conf
```

```
$ chattr +A -R /home/francois/images/*
$ chattr +d FC6-livecd.iso
$ lsattr /boot/grub/grub.conf /home/francois/images/* FC6-livecd.iso
----i-------- /boot/grub/grub.conf
-------A----- /home/francois/images/einstein.jpg
-------A----- /home/francois/images/goth.jpg
------d------ FC6-livecd.iso
```

As shown in the preceding example, with the +i option set, the grub.conf file becomes immutable, meaning that it can't be deleted, renamed, or changed, or have a link created to it. Here, this prevents any arbitrary changes to the grub.conf file. (Not even the root user can change the file until the i attribute is gone.)

The -R option in the example recursively sets the +A option, so all files in the images directory and below can't have access times (atime record) modified. Setting A attributes can save some disk I/O on laptops or flash drives. If you use the dump command to back up your ext2/ext3 file systems, the +d option can prevent selected files from being backed up. In this case, we chose to not have a large ISO image backed up.

To **remove an attribute** with chatter, use the minus sign (-). For example:

```
# chattr -i /boot/grub/grub.conf
```

> **NOTE** *Crackers who successfully break into a machine will often replace some system binaries (such as* ls *or* ps*) with corrupt versions and make them immutable. It's a good idea to occasionally check the attributes set for your executables (in* /bin, /usr/bin, /sbin, *and* /usr/sbin, *for example).*

Searching for Files

Fedora keeps a database of all the files in the file system (with a few exceptions defined in /etc/updatedb.conf) using features of the mlocate package. The locate command enables you to search that database. The results come back instantly, since the database is searched and not the actual file system. Before locate was available, most Linux users ran the find command to find files in the file system. Both locate and find are covered here.

Finding Files with locate

Because the database contains the name of every node in the file system, and not just commands, you can use locate to **find commands, devices, man pages, data files, or anything else identified by a name** in the file system. Here is an example:

```
$ locate e100
/lib/modules/2.6.20-1.2949.fc7/kernel/drivers/net/e100.ko
/lib/modules/2.6.20-1.2949.fc7/kernel/drivers/net/e1000/e1000.ko
```

The above example found both the e100.ko and e1000.ko kernel modules. `locate` is case sensitive unless you use the -i option. Here's an example:

```
$  locate -i itco_wdt
/lib/modules/2.6.20-1.2949.fc7/kernel/drivers/char/watchdog/iTCO_wdt.ko
```

Here are some examples using locate with regular expressions:

```
$  locate -r /ls$          Locate files ending in /ls$
/bin/ls
/usr/share/locale/l10n/ls
$  locate -r mkfs*3         Locate files with mkfs and 3 in the name
/sbin/mkfs.ext3
/usr/share/man/man8/mkfs.ext3.8.gz
$ locate -r ^/boot/grub/me  Locate files beginning with /boot/grub/me
/boot/grub/menu.1st
```

The mlocate RPM package (or slocate on some Linux distributions) includes a cron job that runs the `updatedb` command once per day to update the locate database of files. Because the file you want may have been removed since the database was last updated, you can use the `locate -e` option to check if the file found in the database still exists:

```
$ locate -e myfilename
```

To update the locate database immediately, you can run the `updatedb` command manually:

```
# updatedb
```

Locating Files with find

Before the days of `locate`, the way to find files was with the `find` command. Although `locate` will come up with a file faster, `find` has many other powerful options for finding files based on attributes other than the name.

> **NOTE**   *Searching the entire file system can take a long time to complete. Before searching the whole file system, consider searching a subset of the file system or excluding certain directories or remotely mounted file systems.*

This example searches the root file system (/) recursively for files named e100:

```
$ find / -name "e100*" -print
find: /usr/lib/audit: Permission denied
find: /usr/libexec/utempter: Permission denied
/sys/module/e100
/sys/module/mii/holders/e100
```

Running `find` as a normal user can result in long lists of `Permission denied` as `find` tries to enter a directory you do not have permissions to. You can filter out the inaccessible directories:

```
$ find / -name e100 -print 2>&1 | grep -v "Permission denied"
```

Or send all errors to the /dev/null bit bucket:

```
$ find / -name e100 -print 2> /dev/null
```

Because searches with `find` are case sensitive and must match the name exactly (e100 won't match e100.ko), you can use regular expressions to make your searches more inclusive. Here's an example:

```
$ find / -name 'e100*' -print
/lib/modules/2.6.20-1.2982.fc7/kernel/drivers/net/e1000
```

You can also find files based on timestamps. This command line finds files in /usr/bin/ that have been accessed in the past two minutes:

```
$ find /usr/bin/ -amin -2 -print
/usr/bin/
/usr/bin/find
```

This finds files that have not been accessed in /home/chris for more than 60 days:

```
$ find /home/chris/ -atime +60
```

Use the `-type d` option to find directories. The following command line finds all directories under /etc and redirects stderr to the bit bucket (/dev/null):

```
$ find /etc -type d -print 2> /dev/null
```

This command line finds files in /sbin with permissions that match 750:

```
$ find /sbin/ -perm 750 -print
```

The `exec` option to `find` is very powerful, because it lets you act on the files found with the find command. The following command finds all the files in /var owned by the user francois (must be a valid user) and executes the `ls -l` command on each one:

```
$ find /var -user francois -exec ls -l {} \;
```

An alternative to the `find` command's `exec` option is `xargs`:

```
$ find /var -user francois -print | xargs ls -l
```

There are big differences on how the two commands just shown operate, leading to very different performance. The `find -exec` spawns the command `ls` for each result it finds. The `xargs` command works more efficiently by passing many results as input to a single `ls` command.

To negate a search criterion, place an exclamation point (!) before that criterion. The next example finds all the files that are not owned by the group root and are regular files, and then does an `ls -l` on each:

```
$ find / ! -group root -type f -print 2> /dev/null | xargs ls -l
```

The next example finds the files in /sbin that are regular files and are not executable by others, then feeds them to an ls -l command:

```
$ find /sbin/ -type f ! -perm /o+x -print | xargs ls -l
-rwxr-x--- 1 root root 295884 2007-03-02 17:44 /sbin/audispd
-rwxr-x--- 1 root root  88024 2007-03-02 17:44 /sbin/auditctl
```

Finding files by size is a great way to determine what is filling up your hard disks. The following command line finds all files that are greater than 10 MB (+10M), lists those files from largest to smallest (ls -lS) and directs that list to a file (/tmp/bigfiles.txt):

```
$ find / -xdev -size +10M -print | xargs ls -lS > /tmp/bigfiles.txt
```

In this example, the -xdev option prevents any mounted file systems, besides the root file system, from being searched. This is a good way to keep the find command from searching the /proc directory and any remotely mounted file systems, as well as other locally mounted file systems.

Using Other Commands to Find Files

Other commands for finding files include the whereis and which commands. Here are some examples of those commands:

```
$ whereis man
man: /usr/bin/man /etc/man.config /usr/local/man /usr/share/man
/usr/share/man/man1p/man1p.gz /usr/share/man/man1/man1.gz
/usr/share/man/man7/man.7.gz
$ which ls
alias ls='ls --color=tty'
     /bin/ls
```

The whereis command is useful because it not only finds commands, it also **finds man pages and configuration files associated with a command.** From the example of whereis for the word man, you can see the man executable, its configuration file, and the location of man pages for the man command. The which example shows that there is an alias set for the ls command and shows where the ls executable is (/bin/ls). The which command is useful when you're looking for the actual location of an executable file in your PATH, as in this example:

```
$ rpm -qif `which ps`
```

Finding Out More About Files

Now that you know how to find files, you can get more information about those files. Using less-common options to the ls command lets you list information about a file that you won't see when you run ls without options. Commands such as file help you identify a file's type. With md5sum and sha1sum, you can verify the validity of a file.

Listing Files

Although you are probably quite familiar with the ls command, you may not be familiar with many of the useful options for ls that can help you find out a lot about the files on your system. Here are some examples of **using ls to display long lists** (-l) of files and directories:

```
$ ls -l      Files and directories in current directory
$ ls -la     Includes files/directories beginning with dot (.)
$ ls -lt     Orders files by time recently changed
$ ls -lu     Orders files by time recently accessed
$ ls -lS     Orders files by size
$ ls -li     Lists the inode associated with each file
$ ls -ln     List numeric user/group IDs, instead of names
$ ls -lh     List file sizes in human-readable form (K, M, etc.)
$ ls -lR     List files recursively, from current directory and subdirectories
```

When you list files, there are also ways to **have different types of files appear differently** in the listing:

```
$ ls -F                     Add a character to indicate file type
FC7@    FC8/   memo.txt   pipefile|   script.sh*  xpid.socket=
$ ls --color=always    Show file types as different colors
$ ls -C                     Show file listing in columns
```

In the -F example, the output shows several different file types. The FC7@ indicates a symbolic link to a directory, FC8/ is a regular directory, memo.txt is a regular file (no extra characters), pipefile| is a named pipe (created with mkfifo), script.sh* is an executable file, and xpid.socket= is a socket. The next two examples display different file types in different colors and lists output in columns, respectively.

Verifying Files

When files such as software packages and CD or DVD images are shared over the Internet, often a SHA1SUM or MD5SUM file is published with it. Those files contain checksums that can be used to make sure that the file you downloaded is exactly the one that the repository published.

The following are examples of the md5sum and sha1sum commands being used to **produce checksums of files**:

```
$ md5sum FC-6-i386-rescuecd.iso
54881969da026da24a92db4aab1dcc69  FC-6-i386-rescuecd.iso
$ sha1sum FC-6-i386-rescuecd.iso
834fd761b9c0a5dc550d10d97307dac998103a68  FC-6-i386-rescuecd.iso
```

Which command you choose depends on whether the provider of the file you are checking distributed md5sum or sha1sum information. For example, here is what the SHA1SUM file for the Fedora 6 distribution looked like:

```
-----BEGIN PGP SIGNED MESSAGE-----
Hash: SHA1


834fd761b9c0a5dc550d10d97307dac998103a68  FC-6-i386-rescuecd.iso
cc503d99c9d736af9052904a6ab14931b0850078  FC-6-i386-disc1.iso
3051710e6b2f1d17a14ede0ebb74761c29cda954  FC-6-i386-disc2.iso
5357ce21f8766db385b25923216a430b694bca5d  FC-6-i386-disc3.iso
d6133ab5ccf19431c14fd2ad85bce03c9834ef87  FC-6-i386-disc4.iso
6722f95b97e5118fa26bafa5b9f622cc7d49530c  FC-6-i386-DVD.iso
22327af62d6376916e209b0c4934540e14d5664a  FC-6-i386-disc5.iso
-----BEGIN PGP SIGNATURE-----
Version: GnuPG v1.2.6 (GNU/Linux)


iD8DBQFFNo/utEJp0E8qb9IRAsf7AJ9ZqiDlKqJfAh8g5QHyDMmP0zNbTACfbyGw
hB8bkLBT+6ANW6y8iBmlxz8=
=O/Le
-----END PGP SIGNATURE-----
```

With all the ISO files listed in this SHA1SUM file contained in the current directory, you can **verify them all at once** using the -c option to sha1sum. Here is an example:

```
$ sha1sum -c SHA1SUM
FC-6-i386-rescuecd.iso: OK
FC-6-i386-disc1.iso: OK
FC-6-i386-disc2.iso: OK
FC-6-i386-disc3.iso: OK
FC-6-i386-disc4.iso: OK
FC-6-i386-DVD.iso: OK
FC-6-i386-disc5.iso: OK
```

To **verify only one of the files listed** in the SHA1SUM file, you could do something like the following:

```
$ cat SHA1SUM | grep rescuecd |sha1sum -c
FC-6-i386-rescuecd.iso: OK
```

If you had an MD5SUM file instead of a SHA1SUM file to check against, you could use the md5sum command in the same way. By combining the find command described earlier in this chapter with the md5sum command, you can verify any part of your file system. For example, here's how to **create an MD5 checksum for every file in the /etc directory** so they can be checked later to see if any have changed:

```
# find /etc -type f -exec md5sum {} \; 2>/dev/null > /tmp/md5.list
```

The result of the previous command line is a /tmp/md5.list file that contains a 128-bit checksum for every file in the /etc directory. Later, you could type the following command to see if any of those files have changed:

```
# cd /etc
# md5sum -c /tmp/md5.list | grep -v 'OK'
./hosts.allow: FAILED
md5sum: WARNING: 1 of 1668 computed checksums did NOT match
```

As you can see from the output, only one file changed (hosts.allow). So the next step is to check the changed file and see if the changes to that file were intentional.

Summary

There are dozens of commands for exploring and working with files in Linux. Commands such as chmod can change the permissions associated with a file, whereas commands that include lsattr and chattr can be used to list and change file attributes that are associated with ext2 and ext3 file system types.

To move around the file system, people use the cd command most often. However, to move repeatedly among the same directories, you can use the pushd and popd commands to work with a stack of directories.

Copying files is done with the cp command. However, the dd command can be used to copy files (such as disk images) from a device (such as a CD-ROM drive). For creating directories, you can use the mkdir command.

Instead of keeping multiple copies of a file around on the file system, you can use symbolic links and hard links to have multiple file names point to the same file or directory. Symbolic links can be anywhere in the file system, whereas hard links must exist on the same partition that the original file is on.

To search for files, Linux offers the locate and find commands. To verify the integrity of files you download from the Internet, you can use the md5sum and sha1sum commands.

5

Manipulating Text

With only a shell available on the first UNIX systems (on which Linux was based), using those systems meant dealing primarily with commands and plain text files. Documents, program code, configuration files, e-mail, and almost anything you created or configured was represented by text files. To work with those files, early developers created many text manipulation tools.

Despite having graphical tools for working with text, most seasoned Linux users find command line tools to be more efficient and convenient. Text editors such as vi (Vim), Emacs, JOE, nano, and Pico are available with most Linux distributions. Commands such as grep, sed, and awk can be used to find, and possibly change, pieces of information within text files.

This chapter shows how to use many popular commands for working with text files in Fedora. It also explores some of the less common uses of text manipulation commands that you might find interesting.

Matching Text with Regular Expressions

Many of the tools for working with text enable you to use *regular expressions*, sometimes referred to as *regex*, to identify the text you are looking for based on some pattern. You can use these strings to find text within a text editor or use them with search commands to scan multiple files for the strings of text you want.

A regex search pattern can include a specific string of text (as in a word such as *Linux*) or a location (such as the end of a line or the beginning of a word). It can also be specific (find just the word *hello*) or more inclusive (find any word beginning with *h* and ending with *o*).

Appendix C includes reference information for shell metacharacters that can be used in conjunction with regular expressions to do the exact kinds of matches you are look-ing for. This section shows examples of using regular expressions with several differ-ent tools you encounter throughout this chapter.

Table 5-1 shows some examples using basic regular expressions to match text strings.

Many examples of regular expressions are used in examples throughout this chapter. Keep in mind that not every command that incorporates regex uses its features the same way.

Table 5-1: Matching Using Regular Expressions

Expression	Matches
`a*`	a, ab, abc, and aecjejich
`^a`	Any "a" appearing at the beginning of a line
`*a$`	Any "a" appearing at the end of a line
`a.c`	Three-character strings that begin with a and end with c
`[bcf]at`	bat, cat, or fat
`[a-d]at`	aat, bat, cat, dat, but not Aat, Bat, and so on
`[A-D]at`	Aat, Bat, Cat, and Dat, but not aat, bat, and so on
`1[3-5]7`	137, 147, and 157
`\tHello`	A tab character preceding the word Hello
`\.[tT][xX][Tt]`	.txt, .TXT, .TxT, or other case combinations

Editing Text Files

There are many text editors in the Linux/UNIX world. The editor that is most common is vi, which can be found virtually on any UNIX system available today. That is why knowing how to at least make minor file edits in vi is a critical skill for any Linux administrator. One day, if you find yourself in a minimalist, foreign Linux environment trying to bring a server back online, vi is the tool that will almost always be there.

On Fedora, make sure you have the vim-enhanced package installed. Vim (Vi IMproved) with the vim-enhanced package will provide the most up-to-date, feature-rich, and user-friendly vi editor. For more details about using vi, refer to Appendix A.

Traditionally, the other popular UNIX text editor has been Emacs and its more graphical variant, XEmacs. Emacs is a powerful multi-function tool that can also act as a mail/news reader or shell, and perform other functions. Emacs is also known for its very complex series of keyboard shortcuts that require three arms to execute properly.

In the mid-90s, Emacs was ahead of vi in terms of features. Now that Vim is widely available, both can provide all the text editing features you'll ever need. If you are not already familiar with either vi or Emacs, we recommend you start by learning vi.

There are many other command line and GUI text editors available for Linux. Text-based editors that you may find to be simpler than vi and Emacs include JED, JOE, and nano. Start any of those editors by typing its command name, optionally followed by the file name you want to edit. The following sections offer some quick descriptions of how to use each of those editors.

Using the JOE Editor

If you have used classic word processors such as WordStar that worked with text files, you might be comfortable with the JOE editor. To use JOE, install the joe package. To use the spell checker in JOE, install the aspell package. With JOE, instead of entering a command or text mode, you are always ready to type. To move around in the file, you can use control characters or the arrow keys. To **open a text file for editing**, just type **joe** and the file name or use some of the following options:

```
$ joe memo.txt                        Open memo.txt for editing
$ joe -wordwrap memo.txt              Turn on wordwrap while editing
$ joe -lmargin 5 -tab 5 memo.txt      Set left margin to 5 and tab to 5
$ joe +25 memo.txt                    Begin editing on line 25
```

To **add text**, just begin typing. You can **use keyboard shortcuts** for many functions. Use arrow keys to move the cursor left, right, up, or down. Use the Delete key to delete text under the cursor or the Backspace key to erase text to the left of the cursor. Press Enter to add a line break. Press Ctrl+k+h to see the help screen. Some commands have slightly different key bindings on Fedora. Table 5-2 shows the most commonly used control keys for editing in JOE.

Table 5-2: Control Keys for Editing with JOE

Key Combo	Result
Cursor	
Ctrl+b	Left
Ctrl+p	Up
Ctrl+f	Right
Ctrl+n	Down
Ctrl+z	Previous word
Ctrl+x	Next word
Search	
Ctrl+k+f	Find text
Ctrl+l	Find next
Block	
Ctrl+k+b	Begin
Ctrl+k+k	End
Ctrl+k+m	Move block
Ctrl+k+c	Copy block
Ctrl+k+w	Write block to file
Ctrl+k+y	Delete block
Ctrl+k+/	Filter
Misc	
Ctrl+k+a	Center line
Ctrl+t	Options
Ctrl+r	Refresh
File	
Ctrl+k+e	Open new file to edit

Table 5-2: Control Keys for Editing with JOE (*continued*)

Key Combo	Result
File (*continued*)	
Ctrl+k+r	Insert file at cursor
Ctrl+k+d	Save
Goto	
Ctrl+u	Previous screen
Ctrl+v	Next screen
Ctrl+a	Line beginning
Ctrl+e	End of line
Ctrl+k+u	Top of file
Ctrl+k+v	End of file
Ctrl+k+l	To line number
Delete	
Ctrl+d	Delete character
Ctrl+y	Delete line
Ctrl+w	Delete word right
Ctrl+o	Delete word left
Ctrl+j	Delete line to right
Ctrl+-	Undo
Ctrl+6	Redo
Exit	
Ctrl+k+x	Save and quit
Ctrl+c	Abort
Ctrl+k+z	Shell

Continued

Table 5-2: Control Keys for Editing with JOE (*continued*)

Key Combo	Result
Spell	
Ctrl+[+n	Word
Ctrl+[+l	File

Using the pico and nano Editors

Pico is a popular, very small text editor, distributed as part of the Pine e-mail client. Although Pico is free, it is not truly open source. Therefore, many Linux distributions, including Fedora, don't offer Pico. Instead, they offer an open source clone of Pico called nano (*n*ano's *a*nother editor). This section describes the nano editor.

Nano (represented by the nano command) is a compact text editor that runs from the shell, but is screen-oriented (owing to the fact that it is based on the curses library). Nano is popular with those who formerly used the Pine e-mail client because nano's editing features are the same as those used by Pine's Pico editor. On the rare occasion that you don't have the vi editor available on a Linux system (such as when installing a minimal Gentoo Linux), nano may be available. On Fedora, nano is part of the nano package and relies on the aspell package for spell checking.

As with the JOE editor, instead of having command and typing modes, you can just begin typing. To **open a text file for editing**, just type **nano** and the file name or use some of the following options:

```
$ nano memo.txt        Open memo.txt for editing
$ nano -B memo.txt     When saving, back up previous to ~.filename
$ nano -m memo.txt     Turn on mouse to move cursor (if supported)
$ nano +83 memo.txt    Begin editing on line 83
```

As with JOE, to **add text,** just begin typing. Use arrow keys to move the cursor left, right, up, or down. Use the Delete key to delete text under the cursor or the Backspace key to erase text to the left of the cursor. Press Enter to add a line break. Press Ctrl+g to read help text. Table 5-3 shows the control codes for nano that are described on the help screen.

Table 5-3: Control Keys for Editing with nano

Control Code	Function Key	Description
Ctrl+g	F1	Show help text. (Press Ctrl+X to exit help.)
Ctrl+x	F2	Exit nano (or close the current file buffer).

Table 5-3: Control Keys for Editing with nano (*continued*)

Control Code	Function Key	Description
Ctrl+o	F3	Save the current file.
Ctrl+j	F4	Justify the current text in the current paragraph.
Ctrl+r	F5	Insert a file into the current file.
Ctrl+w	F6	Search for text.
Ctrl+y	F7	Go to the previous screen.
Ctrl+v	F8	Go to the next screen.
Ctrl+k	F9	Cut (and store) the current line or marked text.
Ctrl+u	F10	Uncut (paste) the previously cut line into file.
Ctrl+c	F11	Display the current cursor position.
Ctrl+t	F12	Start spell checking.
Ctrl+-		Go to selected line and column numbers.
Ctrl+\		Search and replace text.
Ctrl+6		Mark text, starting at the cursor (Ctrl+6 to unset mark).
Ctrl+f		Go forward one character.
Ctrl+b		Go back one character.
Ctrl+Space		Go forward one word.
Alt+Space		Go backward one word.
Ctrl+p		Go to the previous line.
Ctrl+n		Go to the next line.
Ctrl+a		Go to the beginning of the current line.
Ctrl+e		Go to the end of the current line.
Alt+(		Go to the beginning of the current paragraph.
Alt+)		Go to the end of the current paragraph.

Continued

Table 5-3: Control Keys for Editing with nano (*continued*)

Control Code	Function Key	Description
Alt+\		Go to the first line of the file.
Alt+/		Go to the last line of the file.
Alt+]		Go to the bracket matching current bracket.
Alt+=		Scroll down one line.
Alt+-		Scroll up one line.

Graphical Text Editors

Just because you are editing text doesn't mean you have to use a text-based editor. The main advantages of using a graphical text editor is that you can use a mouse to select menus, highlight text, cut and copy text, or run special plug-ins.

You can expect to have the GNOME text editor (gedit) if your Linux system has the GNOME desktop installed. Features in gedit enable you to check spelling, list document statistics, change display fonts and colors, and print your documents. The KDE desktop also has its own KDE text editor (kedit in the kdeutils package). It includes similar features to the GNOME text editor, along with a few extras, such as the ability to send the current document with kmail or another user-configurable KDE component.

Vim itself comes with an X GUI version. It is launched with the gvim command, which is part of the vim-X11 package. If you'd like to turn GUI Vim into a more user-friendly text editor, you can download a third-party configuration called Cream from http://cream.sourceforge.net/.

Other text editors you can install include nedit (with features for using macros and executing shell commands) and leafpad (which is similar to the Windows Notepad text editor). The Scribes text editor (scribes) includes some advanced features for automatic correction, replacement, indentation, and word completion.

Listing, Sorting, and Changing Text

Instead of just editing a single text file, you can use a variety of Linux commands to display, search, and manipulate the contents of one or more text files at a time.

Listing Text Files

The most basic method to display the contents of a text file is with the `cat` command. The `cat` command con*cat*enates (in other words, outputs as a string of characters) the contents of a text file to your display (by default). You can then use different shell metacharacters to **direct the contents of that file in different ways**. For example:

```
$ cat myfile.txt                    Send entire file to the screen
$ cat myfile.txt > copy.txt         Direct file contents to another file
$ cat myfile.txt >> myotherfile.txt Append file contents to another file
$ cat -s myfile.txt                 Display consecutive blank lines as one
$ cat -n myfile.txt                 Show line numbers with output
$ cat -b myfile.txt                 Show line numbers only on non-blank lines
```

However, if your block of text is more than a few lines long, using `cat` by itself becomes impractical. That's when you need better tools to look at the beginning or the end, or page through the entire text.

To **view the top of a file**, use `head`:

```
$ head myfile.txt
$ cat myfile.txt | head
```

Both of these command lines use the `head` command to output the top 10 lines of the file. You can specify the line count as a parameter to display any number of lines from the beginning of a file. For example:

```
$ head -n 50 myfile.txt    Show the first 50 lines of a file
$ ps auwx | head -n 15     Show the first 15 lines of ps output
```

This can also be done using this obsolete (but shorter) syntax:

```
$ head -50 myfile.txt
$ ps auwx | head -15
```

You can use the `tail` command in a similar way to **view the end of a file**:

```
$ tail -n 15 myfile.txt    Display the last 15 lines in a file
$ tail -15 myfile.txt      Display the last 15 lines in a file
$ ps auwx | tail -n 15     Display the last 15 lines of ps output
```

The `tail` command can also be used to **continuously watch the end of a file** as the file is written to by another program. This is very useful for reading live log files when troubleshooting apache, sendmail, or many other system services:

```
# tail -f /var/log/messages         Watch system messages live
# tail -f /var/log/maillog          Watch mail server messages live
# tail -f /var/log/httpd/access_log Watch web server messages live
```

Paging Through Text

When you have a large chunk of text and need to get to more than just its beginning or end, you need a tool to **page through the text**. The original Unix system pager was the `more` command:

```
$ ps auwx | more      Page through the output of ps (press spacebar)
$ more myfile.txt      Page through the contents of a file
```

However, `more` has some limitations. For example, in the line with `ps` above, `more` could not scroll up. The `less` command was created as a more powerful and user-friendly `more`. The common saying when `less` was introduced was: "What is `less`? `less` is more!" We recommend you no longer use `more`, and use `less` instead.

> **NOTE** The `less` command has another benefit worth noting. Unlike text editors such as vi, it does not read the entire file when it starts. This results in faster start-up times when viewing large files.

The `less` command can be used with the same syntax as `more` in the examples above:

```
$ ps auwx | less           Page through the output of ps
$ cat myfile.txt | less     Page through the contents of a file
$ less myfile.txt           Page through a text file
```

The `less` command enables you to **navigate** using the up and down arrow keys, PageUp, PageDown, and the spacebar. If you are using `less` on a file (not standard input), press v to open the current file in `vi`. As in `vi`, Shift+g takes you to the end of the file. Shift+f takes you to the end of the file, and then scrolls the file as new input is added, similar to a `tail -f`.

Press Ctrl+c to interrupt that mode. As in `vi`, while viewing a file with `less`, you can **search for a string** by pressing / (forward slash) followed by the string and Enter. To search for further occurrences, press / and Enter repeatedly.

To **scroll forward and back** while using `less`, use the f and b keys, respectively. For example, 10f scrolls forward 10 lines and 15b scrolls back 15 lines. Type **d** to scroll down half a screen and **u** to scroll up half a screen.

Paginating Text Files with pr

The `pr` command provides a quick way to format a bunch of text into a form where it can be printed. This can be particularly useful if you want to print the results of some commands, without having to open up a word processor or text editor. With `pr`, you can **format text into pages with header information** such as date, time, file name, and page number. Here is an example:

```
$ rpm -qa | sort | pr --column=2 | less    Paginate package list in 2 cols
```

In this example, the `rpm -qa` command lists all software packages installed on your system and pipes that list to the `sort` command, to be sorted alphabetically. Next that list is piped to the `pr` command, which converts the single-column list into two columns (`--columns=2`) and paginates it. Finally, the `less` command enables you to page through the text.

Instead of paging through the output, you can **send the output to a file or to a printer.** Here are examples of that:

```
$ rpm -qa | sort | pr --column=2 > pkg.txt   Send pr output to a file
$ rpm -qa | sort | pr --column=2 | lpr       Send pr output to printer
```

Other **text manipulation** you can do with the `pr` command includes double-spacing the text (`-d`), showing control characters (`-c`), or offsetting the text a certain number of spaces from the left margin (for example, `-o 5` to indent five spaces from the left).

Searching for Text with grep

The `grep` command comes in handy when you need to **perform more advanced string searches in a file.** In fact, the phrase *to grep* has actually entered the computer jargon as a verb, just as *to Google* has entered the popular language. Here are examples of the `grep` command:

```
$ grep francois myfile.txt              Show lines containing francois
# grep 404 /var/log/httpd/access_log    Show lines containing 404
$ ps auwx | grep init                   Show init lines from ps output
$ ps auwx | grep "\[*\]"                Show bracketed commands
$ dmesg | grep "[ ]ata\|^ata"           Show ata kernel device information
```

These command lines have some particular uses, beyond being examples of the `grep` command. By searching `access_log` for `404` you can see requests to your web server for pages that were not found (these could be someone fishing to exploit your system, or a web page you moved or forgot to create). Displaying bracketed commands that are output from the `ps` command is a way to see commands for which `ps` cannot display options. The last command checks the kernel buffer ring for any ATA device information, such as hard disks and CD-ROM drives.

The `grep` command can also **recursively search a few or a whole lot of files at the same time.** The following command recursively searches files in the /etc/httpd/conf and /etc/httpd/conf.d directories for the string `VirtualHost`:

```
$ grep -R VirtualHost /etc/httpd/conf*
```

Add line numbers (`-n`) to your `grep` command to **find the exact lines** where the search terms occur:

```
$ grep -Rn VirtualHost /etc/httpd/conf*
```

To colorize the searched term in the search results, add the `--color` option:

```
# grep --color -Rn VirtualHost /etc/httpd/conf*
```

By default, in a multifile search, the file name is displayed for each search result. Use the `-h` option to **disable the display of file names**. This example searches for the string `sshd` in the files `secure`, `secure.1`, `secure.2`, and so on:

```
# grep -h sshd /var/log/secure*
```

If you want to **ignore case** when you search messages, use the `-i` option:

```
# grep -i selinux /var/log/messages    Search file for selinux (any case)
```

To **display only the name of the file** that includes the search term, add the `-l` option:

```
$ grep -Rl VirtualHost /etc/httpd/conf*
```

To **display all lines that do *not* match the string,** add the `-v` option:

```
# grep -v " 200 " /var/log/httpd/access_log*   Show lines without " 200 "
```

> **NOTE**   When piping the output of ps into grep, here's a trick to prevent the grep process from appearing in the grep results:
>
> ```
> # ps auwx | grep "[i]nit"
> ```

Checking Word Counts with wc

There are times when you need to know the number of lines that match a search string. The wc command can be used to **count the lines** that it receives. For example, the following command lists how many hits in an Apache log file come from a specific IP address:

```
$ grep 192.198.1.1 /var/log/httpd/access-log | wc -l
```

The wc command has other uses as well. By default, wc **prints the number of lines, words, and bytes in a file:**

```
$ wc /etc/httpd/conf.d/README          List counts for a single file
9 58 392  /etc/httpd/conf.d/README
$ wc /etc/httpd/conf.d/*               List single/totals for many files
  20   83  566 /etc/httpd/conf.d/proxy_ajp.conf
   9   58  392 /etc/httpd/conf.d/README
  11   45  299 /etc/httpd/conf.d/welcome.conf
  40  186 1257 total
```

Sorting Output with sort

It can also be useful to **sort the content of a file or the output of a command**. This can be helpful in bringing order to disorderly output. The following examples list the names of all RPM packages currently installed, grabs any with *kernel* in the name, and sorts the results in alphanumeric order (forward and reverse):

```
$ rpm -qa | grep kernel | sort        Sort in alphanumeric order
$ rpm -qa | grep kernel | sort -r     Sort in reverse alphanumeric order
```

The following command **sorts processes based on descending memory usage** (fourth field of ps output). The -k option specifies the key field to use for sorting. 4,4 indicates that the fourth field, and only the fourth field, is a key field.

```
$ ps auwx | sort -r -k 4,4
```

The following command line **sorts loaded kernel modules in increasing size order**. The n option tells sort to treat the second field as a number and not a string:

```
# lsmod | sort -k 2,2n
```

Finding Text in Binaries with Strings

Sometimes you need to read the ASCII text that is inside a binary file. Occasionally, you can learn a lot about an executable that way. For those occurrences, use strings to **extract all the human-readable ASCII text**. The strings command is part of the binutils package. Here are some examples:

```
$ strings /bin/ls | grep -i libc    Find occurrences of libc in ls
$ cat /bin/ls | strings             List all ASCII text in ls
$ strings /bin/ls                   List all ASCII text in ls
```

Replacing Text with sed

Finding text within a file is sometimes the first step towards replacing text. Editing streams of text is done using the sed command. The sed command is actually a full-blown scripting language. For the examples in this chapter, we cover basic text replacement with the sed command.

If you are familiar with text replacement commands in vi, sed has some similarities. In the following example, you would **replace only the first occurrence per line** of *francois* with *chris*. Here, sed takes its input from a pipe, while sending its output to stdout (your screen):

```
$ cat myfile.txt | sed s/francois/chris/
```

Adding a g to the end of the substitution line, as in the following command, causes every occurrence of *francois* to be changed to *chris*. Also, in the following example, input is directed from the file myfile.txt and output is directed to mynewfile.txt:

```
$ sed s/francois/chris/g < myfile.txt > mynewfile.txt
```

The next example replaces the first occurrences of /var/www on each line in the /etc/httpd/conf/httpd.conf file with /home/www. Here, we have to use quotes and backslashes to escape the forward slashes so they are not interpreted as delimiters:

```
$ sed 's/\/var\/www\//\/home\/www\//' < /etc/httpd/conf/httpd.conf
```

Although the forward slash is the sed command's default delimiter, you can **change the delimiter** to any other character of your choice. Changing the delimiter can make your life easier when the string contains slashes. For example, the previous command line that contains a path could be replaced with either of the following commands:

```
$ sed 's-/var/www/-/home/www/-' < /etc/httpd/conf/httpd.conf
$ sed 'sD/var/www/D/home/www/D' < /etc/httpd/conf/httpd.conf
```

In the first line shown, a dash (-) is used as the delimiter. In the second case, the letter D is the delimiter.

The sed command can **run multiple substitutions at once**, by preceding each one with -e. Here, in the text streaming from myfile.txt, all occurrences of *francois* are changed to *FRANCOIS* and occurrences of *chris* are changed to *CHRIS*:

```
$ sed -e s/francois/FRANCOIS/g -e s/chris/CHRIS/g < myfile.txt
```

You can use sed to **add newline characters to a stream of text**. Where Enter appears, press the Enter key. The > on the second line is generated by bash, not typed in.

```
$ echo aaabccc | sed 's/b/\Enter
> /'
aaa
ccc
```

The trick just shown does not work on the left side of the sed substitution command. When you need to substitute newline characters, it's easier to use the tr command.

Translating or Removing Characters with tr

The tr command is an easy way to **do simple character translations on the fly**. In the following example, new lines are replaced with spaces, so all the files listed from the current directory are output on one line:

```
$ ls | tr '\n' ' '                  Replace newline characters with spaces
```

The `tr` command can be used to **replace one character with another**, but does not work with strings like `sed` does. The following command replaces all instances of the lowercase letter f with a capital F.

```
$ tr f F < myfile.txt          Replace every f in the file with F
```

You can also use the `tr` command to simply **delete characters**. Here are two examples:

```
$ ls | tr -d '\n'              Delete new lines (resulting in one line)
$ tr -d f < myfile.txt         Delete every letter f from the file
```

The `tr` command can do some nifty tricks when you **specify ranges of characters** to work on. Here's an example of capitalizing lowercase letters to uppercase letters:

```
$ echo chris | tr a-z A-Z      Translate chris into CHRIS
CHRIS
```

The same result can be obtained with the following syntax:

```
$ echo chris | tr '[:lower:]' '[:upper:]'      Translate chris into CHRIS
```

Checking Differences Between Two Files with diff

When you have two versions of a file, it can be useful to **know the differences between the two files**. For example, when upgrading an RPM, your old configuration file is typically left in place and the configuration file for the new version is created as `file.rpmnew`. When that occurs, you can use the `diff` command to discover which lines differ between your configuration and the new configuration, in order to merge the two. For example:

```
$ diff /etc/named.conf.rpmnew /etc/named.conf
```

You can change the output of `diff` to what is known as *unified format*. Unified format can be easier to read by human beings. It adds three lines of context before and after each block of changed lines that it reports, and then uses + and - to show the difference between the files. The following set of commands creates a file (`f1.txt`) containing a sequence of numbers (1–7), creates a file (`f2.txt`) with one of those numbers changed (using `sed`), and compares the two files using the `diff` command:

```
$ seq 1 7 > f1.txt             Send a sequence of numbers to f1.txt
$ cat f1.txt                   Display contents of f1.txt
1
2
3
4
5
6
7
```

```
$ sed s/4/FOUR/ < f1.txt > f2.txt    Change 4 to FOUR and send to f2.txt
$ diff f1.txt f2.txt
4c4                                  Shows line 4 was changed in file
< 4
- -
> FOUR
$ diff -u f1.txt f2.txt              Display unified output of diff
- - f1.txt 2007-09-07 18:26:06.000000000 -0500
+++ f2.txt 2007-09-07 18:26:39.000000000 -0500
@@ -1,7 +1,7 @@
1
2
3
-4
+FOUR
5
6
7
```

The diff -u output just displayed adds information such as modification dates and times to the regular diff output. The sdiff command can be used to give you yet another view. The sdiff command can **merge the output of two** files interactively, as shown in the following output:

```
$ sdiff f1.txt f2.txt
1                                               1
2                                               2
3                                               3
4                                             | FOUR
5                                               5
6                                               6
7                                               7
```

Another variation on the diff theme is vimdiff, which opens the two files side by side in Vim and outlines the differences in color. Similarly, gvimdiff opens the two files in gVim.

The output of diff -u can be fed into the patch command. The patch command takes an old file and a diff file as input and **outputs a patched file.** Following on the example above, we use the diff command between the two files to generate a patch and then apply the patch to the first file:

```
$ diff -u f1.txt f2.txt > patchfile.txt
$ patch f1.txt < patchfile.txt
patching file f1.txt
$ cat f1.txt
1
2
3
FOUR
```

5
6
7

That is how many OSS developers (including kernel developers) distribute their code patches. The `patch` and `diff` commands can also be run on entire directory trees. However, that usage is outside the scope of this book.

Using awk and cut to Process Columns

Another massive text processing tool is the `awk` command. The `awk` command is a full-blown programming language. Although there is much more you can do with the `awk` command, the following examples show you a few tricks related to extracting columns of text:

```
$ ps auwx | awk '{print $1,$11}'              Show columns 1, 11 of ps
$ ps auwx | awk '/francois/ {print $11}'      Show francois' processes
$ ps auwx | grep francois | awk '{print $11}' Same as above
```

The first example displays the contents of the first column (user name) and eleventh column (command name) from currently running processes output from the ps command (ps auwx). The next two commands produce the same output, with one using the awk command and the other using the grep command to find all processes owned by the user named francois. In each case, when processes owned by francois are found, column 11 (command name) is displayed for each of those processes.

By default, the awk command assumes the delimiter between columns is spaces. You can specify a different delimiter with the -F option as follows:

```
$ awk -F: '{print $1,$5}' /etc/passwd  Use colon delimiter to print cols
```

You can get similar results with the cut command. As with the previous awk example, we specify a colon (:) as the column delimiter to process information from the /etc/passwd file:

```
$ cut -d: -f1,5 /etc/passwd         Use colon delimiter to print cols
```

The cut command can also be used with ranges of fields. The following command prints columns 1 thru 5 of the /etc/passwd file:

```
$ cut -d: -f1-5 /etc/passwd         Show columns 1 through 5
```

Instead of using a dash (-) to indicate a range of numbers, you can use it to print all columns from a particular column number and above. The following command displays all columns from column 5 and above from the /etc/passwd file:

```
$ cut -d: -f5- /etc/passwd          Show columns 5 and later
```

We prefer to use the `awk` command when columns are separated by a varying number of spaces, such as the output of the `ps` command. And we prefer the `cut` command when dealing with files delimited by commas (,) or colons (:), such as the /etc/password file.

Converting Text Files to Different Formats

Text files in the Unix world use a different end-of-line character (\n) than those used in the DOS/Windows world (\r\n). You can view these special characters in a text file with the `od` command:

```
$ od -c -t x1 myfile.txt
```

So they will appear properly when copied from one environment to the other, it is necessary to **convert the files**. Here are some examples:

```
$ unix2dos < myunixfile.txt > mydosfile.txt
$ cat mydosfile.txt | dos2unix > myunixfile.txt
```

The `unix2dos` example just shown above converts a Linux or Unix plain text file (`myunixfile.txt`) to a DOS or Windows text file (`mydosfile.txt`). The dos2unix example does the opposite by converting a DOS/Windows file to a Linux/Unix file.

Summary

Linux and Unix systems traditionally use plain text files for system configuration, documentation, output from commands, and many forms of stored information. As a result, many commands have been created to search, edit, and otherwise manipulate plain text files. Even with today's GUI interfaces, the ability to manipulate plain text files is critical to becoming a power Linux user.

This chapter explores some of the most popular commands for working with plain text files in Linux. Those commands include text editors (such as vi, nano, and JOE), as well as commands that can edit streaming data (such as `sed` and `awk` commands). There are also commands for sorting text (`sort`), counting text (`wc`), and translating characters in text (`tr`).

6

Playing with Multimedia

There's no need to go to a GUI tool, if all you need to do is play a song or convert an image or audio file to a different form. There are commands for working with multimedia files (audio or images) that are quick and efficient if you find yourself working from the shell. And if you need to manipulate batches of multimedia files, the same command you use to transform one file can be added to a script to repeat the process on many files.

This chapter focuses on tools for working with audio and digital image files from the shell.

Working with Audio

There are commands available for Linux systems that can manipulate files in dozens of audio formats. Commands such as ogg123, mpg321, and play can be used to listen to audio files. There are commands for ripping songs from music CDs and encoding them to store efficiently. There are even commands to let you stream audio so anyone on your network can listen to your playlist.

Playing Music

Depending on the audio format you want to play, there are several command line players available for Linux. The play command (based on the sox facility, described later), can play audio files in multiple, freely available formats. You can use ogg123 to play popular open source music formats, including Ogg Vorbis, Free Lossless Audio Codec (FLAC), and Speex files. The mpg321 player, which is available via third-party RPM repositories, is popular for playing MP3 music files.

IN THIS CHAPTER

Playing music with play, ogg123, and mpg321

Adjusting audio with alsamixer and aumix

Ripping music CDs with cdparanoia

Encoding music with oggenc, flac, and lame

Streaming music with icecast and ices

Converting audio files with sox

Transforming digital images with convert

Type `play -h` to **see audio formats and effects** available to use with `play`:

```
$ play -h
   ...
SUPPORTED FILE FORMATS: 8svx aif aifc aiff aiffc al alsa au auto avr cdda cdr
cvs cvsd dat dvms fssd gsm hcom ima ircam la lu maud nist nul null ogg ossdsp
prc raw s3 sb sf sl smp snd sndt sou sph sw txw u3 u4 ub ul uw vms voc vorbis
vox wav wve xa

SUPPORTED EFFECTS: allpass band bandpass bandreject bass chorus compand dcshift
deemph dither earwax echo echos equalizer fade filter flanger highpass lowpass
mcompand mixer noiseprof noisered pad pan phaser pitch polyphase repeat resample
reverb reverse silence speed stat stretch swap synth treble tremolo trim vibro
vol
```

Here are some examples of playing files using `play`:

```
$ play inconceivable.wav      Play WAV file (may be ripped from CD)
$ play *.wav                  Play all WAV files in directory (up to 32)
$ play hi.au vol .6           AU file, lower volume (can lower distortion)
$ play -r 14000 short.aiff    AIFF, sampling rate of 14000 hertz
```

Here are examples for playing Ogg Vorbis (`www.vorbis.com`) files with `ogg123`:

```
$ ogg123 mysong.ogg                              Play ogg file
$ ogg123 http://vorbis.com/music/Lumme-Badloop.ogg    Play web address
$ ogg123 -z *.ogg                                Play files in pseudo-random order
$ ogg123 -Z *.ogg                                Same as -z, but repeat forever
$ ogg123 /var/music/                             Play songs in /var/music and sub dirs
$ ogg123 -@ myplaylist                           Play songs from playlist
```

A playlist is simply a list of directories or individual Ogg files to play. When a directory is listed, all Ogg files are played from that directory or any of its subdirectories. When playing multiple files, press `Ctrl+c` to **skip to the next song**. Press `Ctrl+c` twice to **quit**.

To use the `mpg321` player to play MP3 files, you need to install the mpg321 package from the `rpm.livna.org` repository (see Chapter 2 for information on installing from third-party repositories). Here are examples for playing MP3 audio files with `mpg321`:

```
$ mpg321 yoursong.mp3          Play MP3 file
$ mpg321 -@ mp3list            Play songs from playlist of MP3s
$ cat mp3list | mpg321 -@ -    Pipe playlist to mpg321
$ mpg321 -z *.mp3             Play files in pseudo-random order
$ mpg321 -Z *.mp3             Same as -z, but repeat forever
```

An mpg321 playlist is simply a list of files. You can produce the list using a simple `ls` command and directing the output to a file. Use full paths to the files, unless you plan to use the list from a location from which relative paths make sense.

Adjusting Audio Levels

The command line audio tools you use to enable audio devices and adjust audio levels depend on the type of audio system you use. Advanced Linux Sound Architecture (ALSA) is the sound system used by most Linux systems these days. The Open Source Sound System (OSS) has been around longer and is still used on older hardware. In general, you can use `alsamixer` to adjust sound when ALSA is used and `aumix` with OSS.

ALSA is the default sound system for many Linux systems. By adding loadable modules that enable OSS device interfaces to work as well, audio applications that require the OSS device interface can work with ALSA as well. To see if **OSS modules are loaded**, including `snd-pcm-oss` (emulates `/dev/dsp` and `/dev/audio`), `snd-mixer-oss` (emulates `/dev/mixer`), and `snd-seq-oss` (emulates `/dev/sequencer`), type:

```
# lsmod | grep snd
```

If the modules are loaded, you can use `alsamixer` to adjust audio levels for OSS sound applications. **Start alsamixer** as follows:

```
$ alsamixer              Show alsamixer screen with playback view
$ alsamixer -V playback  Show only playback channels (default)
$ alsamixer -V all       Show with playback and capture views
$ alsamixer -c 1         Use alsamixer on second (1) sound card
```

Volume bars appear for each volume channel. Move the right and left arrow keys to **highlight different channels** (Master, PCM, Headphone, and so on). Use the up and down arrow keys to raise and lower the volume on each channel. With a channel highlighted, press m to **mute or unmute** that channel. Press the spacebar on a highlighted input channel (Mic, Line, and so on) to **assign the channel as the capture channel** (to record audio input). To **quit alsamixer**, press Alt+q or the Esc key. Press Tab to cycle through settings for Playback, Capture, and All.

The `aumix` audio mixing application (aumix packages) can operate in screen-oriented or plain command mode. In plain text you use options to **change or display settings.** Here are examples of `aumix` command lines:

```
$ aumix -q               Show left/right volume and type for all channels
$ aumix -l q -m q        List current settings for line and mic only
$ aumix -v 80 -m 0       Set volume to 70% and microphone to 0
$ aumix -m 80 -m R -m q  Set mic to 80%, set it to record, list mic
$ aumix                  With no options, aumix runs screen-oriented
```

When run screen-oriented, `aumix` displays all available audio channels. In screen-oriented mode, **use keys to highlight and change displayed audio settings.** Use PageUp, Page-Down, and the up arrow and down arrow keys to select channels. Use the right or left arrow key to increase or decrease volume. Type **m** to mute the current channel. Press the spacebar to select the current channel as the recording device. If a mouse is available, you can use it to select volume levels, balance levels, or the current recording channel.

Ripping CD Music

To be able to play your personal music collection from Linux, you can use tools such as cdparanoia to rip tracks from music CDs to WAV files on your hard disk. The ripped files can then be encoded to save disk space, using tools such as oggenc (Ogg Vorbis), flac (FLAC), or lame (MP3).

> **NOTE** *There are some excellent graphical tools for ripping and encoding CDs, such as* grip *and* sound-juicer. *Because they are CDDB-enabled, those tools can also use information about the music on the CD to name the output files (artist, album, song, and so on). This section, however, describes how to use some of the underlying commands to rip and encode CD music manually.*

Using cdparanoia, you can check that your CD drive is capable of ripping Compact Disc Digital Audio (CDDA) CDs, retrieve audio tracks from your CDs drive, and copy them to hard disk. Start by inserting a music CD in your drive and typing the following:

```
$ cdparanoia -vsQ
   ...
Checking /dev/cdrom for cdrom...
Checking for SCSI emulation...
Checking for MMC style command set...
Verifying CDDA command set...
   ...
Table of contents (audio tracks only):
track        length                begin          copy pre ch
===========================================================
  1.    18295 [04:03.70]        0 [00:00.00]    no   no  2
  2.    16872 [03:44.72]    18295 [04:03.70]    no   no  2
  ...
 11.    17908 [03:58.58]   174587 [38:47.62]    no   no  2
 12.    17342 [03:51.17]   192495 [42:46.45]    no   no  2
TOTAL  209837 [46:37.62]     (audio only)
```

The snipped output shows cdparanoia checking the capabilities of /dev/cdrom, looking for SCSI emulations and MMC command set support, and verifying that the drive can handle CDDA information. Finally, it prints information about each track. Here are examples of cdparanoia command lines for **ripping a CD to hard drive**:

```
$ cdparanoia -B                 Rip tracks as WAV files by track name
$ cdparanoia -B -- "5-7"         Rip tracks 5-7 into separate files
$ cdparanoia -- "3-8" abc.wav    Rip tracks 3-8 to one file (abc.wav)
$ cdparanoia -- "1:[40]-"        Rip tracks 1 from 40 secs in to end
$ cdparanoia -f -- "3"           Rip track 3 and save to AIFF format
$ cdparanoia -a -- "5"           Rip track 5 and save to AIFC format
$ cdparanoia -w -- "1" my.wav    Rip track 1 and name it my.wav
```

Encoding Music

After a music file is ripped from CD, encoding that file to save disk space is usually the next step. Popular encoders include `oggenc`, `flac`, and `lame`, for encoding to Ogg Vorbis, FLAC, and MP3 formats, respectively.

With `oggenc`, you can start with audio files or streams in WAV, AIFF, FLAC, or raw format and convert them to Ogg Vorbis format. Although Ogg Vorbis is a lossy format, the default encoding from WAV files still produces very good quality audio and can result in a file that's about one-tenth the size. Here are some examples of `oggenc`:

```
$ oggenc mysong.wav              Encodes WAV to Ogg (mysong.ogg)
$ oggenc ab.flac -o new.ogg      Encodes FLAC to Ogg (new.ogg)
$ oggenc ab.wav -q 9             Raises encoding quality to 9
```

By default, the quality (-q) of the `oggenc` output is set to 3. You can **set the quality** to any number from -1 to 10 (including fractions such as 5.5).

```
$ oggenc NewSong.wav -o NewSong.ogg \
    -a Bernstein -G Classical       \
    -d 06/15/1972 -t "Simple Song"  \
    -l "Bernsteins Mass"            \
    -c info="From Kennedy Center"
```

The command just shown converts `MySong.wav` to `MySong.ogg`. The artist name is Bernstein and the music type is Classical. The date is June 15, 1972, the song title is Simple Song and the album name is Bernsteins Mass. A comment is From Kennedy Center. The backslashes aren't needed if you just keep typing the whole command on one line. However, if you do add backslashes, make sure there are no spaces after the backslash.

The preceding example adds information to the header of the resulting Ogg file. You can **see the header information**, with other information about the file, using `ogginfo`:

```
$ ogginfo NewSong.ogg
Processing file "NewSong.ogg"...

      ...
Channels: 2
Rate: 44100
Nominal bitrate: 112.000000 kb/s
User comments section follows...
        info=From Kennedy Center
        title=Simple Song
        artist=Bernstein
        genre=Classical
        date=06/15/1972
        album=Bernsteins Mass
```

```
Vorbis stream 1:
        Total data length: 3039484 bytes
        Playback length: 3m:25.240s
        Average bitrate: 118.475307 kb/s
Logical stream 1 ended
```

Here you can see that comments were added during encoding. The -c option was used to set an arbitrary field (in this case, info) with some value to the header. Besides the comments information, you can see that this file has two channels and was recorded at a 44100 bitrate. You can also see the data length, playback time, and average bitrate.

The flac command is an encoder similar to oggenc, except that the WAV, AIFF, RAW, FLAC, or Ogg file is encoded to a FLAC file. Because flac is a free lossless audio codec, it is a popular encoding method for those who want to save some space, but still want top-quality audio output. Using default values, our encoding from WAV to FLAC resulted in files one-half the size, as opposed to one-tenth the size with oggenc. Here is an example of the flac command:

```
$ flac now.wav                       Encodes WAV to FLAC (now.flac)
$ sox now.wav now.aiff               Encodes WAV to AIFF (now.aiff)
$ flac now.aiff -o now2.flac         Encodes AIFF to FLAC (now.flac)
$ flac -8 top.wav -o top.flac        Raises compression level to 8
```

The compression level is set to -5 by default. A range from -0 to -8 can be used, with the highest number giving the greatest compression and the lower number giving faster compression time. The flac command can also be used to **add an image to the FLAC file**. Here's an example:

```
$ flac hotsong.wav -o hotsong.flac \   Encodes WAV to FLAC (now.flac)
        --picture=cover.jpg            Adds cover.jpg to FLAC file
```

With an image embedded into the FLAC audio file, music players such as Rhythmbox can display the embedded image when the song is playing. So, a CD cover or image from a music video can be used in the FLAC file.

To **convert files to MP3 format** using the lame command, you must first install the lame package. Because lame is not included with Fedora, you must get it from a third-party software repository. See Chapter 2 for information on installing from the rpm.livna.org repository. Here are some examples of the lame command to encode from WAV and AIFF files:

```
$ lame in.wav                        Encodes WAV to MP3 (in.wav.mp3)
$ lame in.wav --preset standard      Encodes to MP3 with std presets
$ lame tune.aiff -o tune.mp3         Encodes AIFF to MP3 (tune.mp3)
$ lame -h -b 64 -m m in.wav out.mp3  High quality, 64-bit, mono mode
$ lame -q 0 in.wav -o abcHQ.mp3      Encodes with quality set to 0
```

With lame, you can set the quality from 0 to 9 (5 is the default). Setting the quality to 0 uses the best encoding algorithms, while setting it to 9 disables most algorithms (but the encoding process moves much faster). As with `oggenc`, you can **add tag information to your MP3 file** that can be used later when you play back the file. Here's an example:

```
$ lame NewSong.wav NewSong.mp3     \
   --ta Bernstein --tg Classical \
   --ty 1972 --tt "Simple Song"   \
   --tl "Bernsteins Mass"         \
   --tc "From Kennedy Center"
```

Like the wav-to-ogg example shown earlier in this chapter, the command just shown converts `MySong.wav` to `MySong.mp3`. As before, the artist name is Bernstein and the music type is Classical. The year is 1972, the song title is Simple Song, and the album name is Bernsteins Mass. A comment is From Kennedy Center. The backslashes aren't needed if you just keep typing the whole command on one line. However, if you do add backslashes, make sure there are no spaces after the backslash.

The tag information appears on the screen in graphical MP3 players (such as Rhythmbox and Totem, when they have been enabled to play MP3 format). You can also see tag information when you use command line players, such as the following `mpg321` example:

```
$ mpg123 NewSong.mp3
High Performance MPEG 1.0/2.0/2.5 Audio Player for Layer 1, 2, and 3.
    . . .
Title  : Simple Song              Artist: Bernstein
Album  : Bernsteins Mass          Year  : 1972
Comment: From Kennedy Center      Genre : Classical

Playing MPEG stream from NewSong.mp3 ...
MPEG 1.0 layer III, 128 kbit/s, 44100 Hz joint-stereo
```

Streaming Music

If your music is on one machine, but you're working from another machine, **setting up a streaming music server** is a quick way to broadcast your music so it can be picked up from one or more computers on your network. The icecast streaming media server and ices audio source client can be installed in Fedora by typing:

```
# yum install icecast ices
```

Here's a quick and dirty procedure for setting up icecast and ices to stream your music. Perform this task on the computer that contains the music you want to serve:

1. Edit the `/etc/icecast.xml` file to change all passwords listed. Search for hackme to find the current passwords. You probably want different user and administrative passwords, especially if you allow others to stream music to the server. Remember the passwords you set for later. You may want to change other settings in this file as well, such as hostname.

2. If you have a firewall, check that TCP port 8000 is accessible.

3. Start the icecast server as root user by typing the following (the server will actually run as the icecast user):

```
# service icecast start
```

4. Use the ices user account to create your playlist. The ices user account is created when you install the ices package, However, you need to modify the account to be able to log in as the ices user and save files to that user's home directory. As root user, type the following:

```
# usermod -m -d /home/ices -s /bin/bash
# passwd ices
Changing password for user ices.
New UNIX password: ********
```

5. Log in as the ices user.

6. Create a playlist using any text edit or by directing a listing of your music to a file. For example, if all your Ogg music files are in /var/music subdirectories, type the following:

```
$ find /var/music -name *.ogg > /home/ices/playlist.txt
```

With the playlist file created, use any text editor to remove or add files or directories to make your playlist as you would like it. (If you want some files to try out for your playlist, download some from http://vorbis.com/music.)

7. As root user, edit the /etc/ices.conf file so it will play from your playlist and feed that music to your running icecast server. In particular, you want to modify the metadata, input, and instance modules. (Be sure to change /home/foo/playlist.txt to the path where you put your playlist.txt file.)

```
<metadata>
    <name>My Music Server</name>
    <genre>Different music styles</genre>
    <description>Mix of my personal music</description>
</metadata>
<input>
    <module>playlist</module>
    <param name="type">basic</param>
    <param name="file">/home/ices/playlist.txt</param>
    <!— random play —>
    <param name="random">1</param>
            . . .
</input>
<instance>
    <hostname>localhost</hostname>
    <port>8000</port>
    <password>MIcePw</password>
    <mount>/mymusic.ogg</mount>
            . . .
</instance>
```

Of the values just shown (in bold), the most critical are the location of your playlist and the information about the instance of your icecast server. The password must match the source password you added to your `/etc/icecast.xml` file.

8. Launch the ices audio feed by typing the following:

```
# service ices start
```

9. Test that you can play music from the local computer as follows:

```
$ ogg123 http://localhost:8000/mymusic.ogg
```

10. If that test works, try playing the icecast stream from another computer on your network by replacing localhost with the server's IP address or host name.

11. If there are problems, check `/var/log/icecast` and `/var/log/ices` log files. Recheck your passwords and locations of configuration files.

12. When you are done, just kill the ices and icecast services:

```
# service ices stop
# service icecast stop
```

When the icecast and ices servers are running, you should have access to that streaming music from any computer that can access your server computer. Use any music player that can play from an HTTP address (ogg123, Rhythmbox, XMMS, and so on). Windows music players that can support the type of content you are serving should work as well.

NOTE *If you want to skip a song, type this from the server:* `killall -HUP ices.`

Converting Audio Files

The sox utility is an extremely versatile tool for working with audio files in different freely available formats. Here are a few examples of things you can do with sox:

The following command **concatenates two WAV files to a single output file**:

```
$ sox head.wav tail.wav output.wav
```

This command **mixes two WAV files**:

```
$ soxmix sound1.wav sound2.wav output.wav
```

To use sox to **display information about a file**, use the stat effect as follows:

```
$ sox sound1.wav -e stat
Samples read:             208512
Length (seconds):       9.456327
Scaled by:         2147483647.0
Maximum amplitude:      0.200592
```

```
Minimum amplitude:     -0.224701
Midline amplitude:     -0.012054
Mean    norm:           0.030373
Mean    amplitude:      0.000054
RMS     amplitude:      0.040391
Maximum delta:          0.060852
Minimum delta:          0.000000
Mean    delta:          0.006643
RMS     delta:          0.009028
Rough   frequency:          784
Volume adjustment:        4.450
```

Use trim to **delete seconds of sound** from an audio file. For example:

```
$ sox sound1.wav output.wav trim 4       Trim 4 seconds from start
$ sox sound1.wav output.wav trim 2 6     Keep from 2-6 seconds of file
```

The first example deletes the first 4 seconds from sound1.wav and writes the results to output.wav. The second example takes sound1.wav, keeps the section between second 2 and second 6 and deletes the rest, and writes to output.wav.

Transforming Images

With directories full of digital images, the ability to manipulate images from the command line can be a huge time saver. The ImageMagick package (available with Fedora) comes with some very useful tools for transforming your digital images into forms you can work with. This section shows some commands for manipulating digital images, and provides examples of simple scripts for making those changes in batches.

Getting Information about Images

To **get information about an image,** use the identify command, as follows:

```
$ identify p2090142.jpg
p2090142.jpg JPEG 2048x1536+0+0 DirectClass 8-bit 402.037kb
$ identify -verbose p2090142.jpg | less
   Standard deviation: 61.1665 (0.239869)
   Colors: 205713
   Rendering intent: Undefined
   Resolution: 72x72
   Units: PixelsPerInch
   Filesize: 402.037kb
   Interlace: None
   Background color: white
   Border color: rgb(223,223,223)
   Matte color: grey74
```

```
Transparent color: black
Page geometry: 2048x1536+0+0
Compression: JPEG
Quality: 44
   ...
```

The first command in the preceding example displays basic information about the image (its file name, format, geometry, class, channel depth, and file size). The second command shows every bit of information it can extract from the image. In addition to the information you see in the example, the verbose output also shows creation times, the type of camera used, aperture value, and ISO speed rating.

Converting Images

The `convert` command is a Swiss Army knife of file converters. Here are some ways to manipulate images using the `convert` command. The following examples **convert image files from one format to another:**

```
$ convert tree.jpg tree.png      Convert a JPEG to a PNG file
$ convert icon.gif icon.bmp      Convert a GIF to a BMP file
$ convert photo.tiff photo.pcx   Convert a TIFF to a PCX file
```

Image types that `convert` supports include JPG, BMP, PCX, GIF, PNG, TIFF, XPM, and XWD. Here are examples of `convert` being used to **resize images:**

```
$ convert -resize 1024x768 hat.jpg hat-sm.jpg
$ convert -sample 50%x50% dog.jpg dog-half.jpg
```

The first example creates an image (`hat-sm.jpg`) that is 1024 × 768 pixels. The second example reduced the image `dog.jpg` in half (`50%x50%`) and saves it as `dog-half.jpg`.

You can **rotate images** from 0 to 360 degrees. Here are examples:

```
$ convert -rotate 270 sky.jpg sky-final.jpg      Rotate image 270 degrees
$ convert -rotate 90 house.jpg house-final.jpg   Rotate image 90 degrees
```

You can **add text to an image** using the `-draw` option:

```
$ convert -fill black -pointsize 60 -font helvetica   \
    -draw 'text 10,80 "Copyright NegusNet Inc."'   \
    p10.jpg p10-cp.jpg
```

The previous example adds copyright information to an image, using 60 point black Helvetica font to write text on the image. The text is placed 10 points in and 80 points down from the upper left corner. The new image name is `p10-cp.jpg`, to indicate that the new image had copyright information added.

Here are some interesting ways to **create thumbnails** with the `convert` command:

```
$ convert -thumbnail 120x120 a.jpg a-a.png
$ convert -thumbnail 120x120 -polaroid 8 a.jpg a-b.png
$ convert -thumbnail 120x120 -polaroid 8 -rotate 8 a.jpg a-c.png
```

All three examples create a 120×120 thumbnail. The second adds the -polaroid option to put a border around the thumbnail, so it looks like a Polaroid picture. The last example sets the -polaroid angle to 8 so that the image looks slightly askew. Figure 6-1 shows the results of these three examples.

Figure 6-1: Use convert to create a thumbnail, Polaroid, and angled Polaroid.

Besides the things you can do to make images useful and manageable, there are also ways of **making your images fun and even weird**. Here are some examples:

```
$ convert -sepia-tone 75% house.jpg oldhouse.png
$ convert -charcoal 5 house.jpg char-house.png
$ convert -colorize 175 house.jpg color-house.png
```

The -sepia-tone option gives the image an "old west" sort of look. The -charcoal option makes the image look as if the picture was hand-drawn using charcoal. By using the -colorize option, every pixel in the image is modified using the colorize number provided (175 in this case). Figure 6-2 shows the original house picture in the upper-left corner, the sepiatone in the upper-right, the charcoal in the lower left, and the colorized house in the lower right.

If you are looking for one more example of weird image conversions, try swirling your image. For example:

```
$ convert -swirl 300 photo.pcx weird.pcx
```

Converting Images in Batches

Most of the image conversions described in this chapter can be done quite easily using a graphical image manipulation tool such the GIMP. However, where the `convert` commands we described can really shine are when you use them in scripts. So, instead of resizing, rotating, writing on, or colorizing a single file, you can do any (or all) of those things to a whole directory of files.

Figure 6-2: Start with a normal image and sepiatone, charcoal, and colorize it.

You may want to create thumbnails for your duck decoy collection images. Or perhaps you want to reduce all your wedding photos so they can play well on a digital photo frame. You might even want to add copyright information to every image in a directory before you share them on the Web. All these things can be done quite easily with the convert commands already described and some simple shell scripts.

Here's an example of a script you can run to **resize an entire directory of photos** to 1024×768 pixels to play on a digital photo frame:

```
$ cd $HOME/myimages
$ mkdir small
$ for pic in `ls *.png`
do
    echo "converting $pic"
    convert -resize 1024x768 $pic small/sm-$pic
done
```

Before running the script, this procedure changes to the $HOME/myimages directory (which happens to contain a set of high-resolution images). Then it creates a subdirectory to hold the reduced images called small. The script itself starts with a for loop that lists each file ending in .png in the current directory (you might need to make that .jpg or other image suffix). Then, each file is resized to 1024×768 and copied to the small directory, with sm- added to each file name.

101

Using that same basic script, you can use any of the convert command lines shown earlier, or make up your own to suit your needs. You might be able to convert a whole directory of images in a few minutes that would have taken you hours of clicking in the GUI.

Summary

The shell can provide a quick and efficient venue for working with your audio and digital image files. This chapter describes ways of playing, ripping, encoding, converting, and streaming audio files from the command line. As for digital images, we provide many examples of using the convert command for resizing, rotating, converting, writing on, and otherwise manipulating those images.

7

Administering File Systems

File systems provide the structures in which files, directories, devices, and other elements of the system are accessed from Linux. Linux supports many different types of file systems (ext3, VFAT, ISO9660, NTFS, and so on) as well as many different types of media on which file systems can exist (hard disks, CDs, USB flash drives, ZIP drives, and so on).

Creating and managing disk partitions and the file systems on those partitions are among the most critical jobs in administering a Linux system. That's because if you mess up your file system, you might very well lose the critical data stored on your computer's hard disk or removable media.

This chapter contains commands for partitioning storage media, creating file systems, mounting and unmounting partitions, and checking file systems for errors and disk space.

Understanding File System Basics

Even though there are a lot of different file system types available in Linux, there are not many that you need to set up a basic Linux system. For a basic Linux system, your computer hard disk may contain only three partitions: a swap partition (used to handle the overflow of information in RAM), a boot partition that contains the boot loader and kernel, and a root file system partition. The boot and root file system partitions are usually an ext3 file system type.

The ext3 file system type is based on the ext2 file system type, adding a feature called *journaling* to its predecessor. Journaling can improve data integrity and recovery, especially after unclean system shutdowns. Time-consuming file system checks are avoided during the next reboot after an unclean shutdown, because the changes that occurred since the most recent write to disk are saved and ready to be restored.

Most of the examples in this chapter use ext3 files systems to illustrate how a file system is created and managed. However, there are times when you might want to use other file system types. Table 7-1 lists different file system types and describes when you might want to use them.

Table 7-1: File System Types Supported in Linux

File System Type	Description
ext3	Most commonly used file system with Linux. Contains journaling features for safer data and fast reboots after unintended shutdowns.
ext2	Predecessor of ext3, but doesn't contain journaling.
iso9660	Evolved from the High Sierra file system (which was the original standard used on CD-ROM). May contain Rock Ridge extensions to allow iso9660 file systems to support long file names and other information (file permissions, ownership, and links).
Jffs2	Journaling Flash File System version 2 (JFFS2) that is designed for efficient operations on USB flash drives. Successor to JFFS.
jfs	JFS file system that IBM used for OS/2 Warp. Tuned for large file systems and high-performance environments.
msdos	MS-DOS file system. Can be used to mount older MS-DOS file systems, such as those on old floppy disks.
ntfs	Microsoft New Technology File System (NTFS). Useful when file systems need to share files with newer Windows systems (as with dual booting or removable drives).
reiserfs	Journaling file system that used to be used by default on some SUSE, Slackware, and other Linux systems. Reiserfs is not well-supported in Fedora or RHEL.
squashfs	Compressed, read-only file system used on many Linux live CDs.
swap	Used on swap partitions to hold data temporarily when RAM is not currently available.

Table 7-1: File System Types Supported in Linux (*continued*)

File System Type	Description
ufs	Popular file system on Solaris and SunOS operating systems from Sun Microsystems.
vfat	Extended FAT (VFAT) file system. Useful when file systems need to share files with older Windows systems (as with dual booting or removable drives).
xfs	Journaling file system for high-performance environments. Can scale up to systems that include multiple terabytes of data that transfer data at multiple gigabytes per second.

Besides the file system types listed in the table, there are also what are referred to as *network shared file systems*. Locally, a network shared file system may be an ext3, ntfs, or other normal file system type. However, all or part of those file systems can be shared with network protocols such as Samba (smbfs or cifs file system type), NFS (nfs), and NetWare (ncpfs).

Many available file system types are either not useful for creating new file systems or not fully supported in every version of Linux. For example, file system types such as minix (for Minix systems), befs (for BeOS systems), and affs (for Amiga systems) are mostly useful if you need to mount and access old backup media from those systems. Even popular file systems may not be fully supported. For example, reiserfs file systems can't be used with Security Enhanced Linux (SELinux) in Fedora and RHEL.

Creating and Managing File Systems

Fedora and RHEL give you the option of either having the anaconda installer create a default partitioning and file system scheme or letting you set that all up manually when you first install Linux. The installer lets you choose to erase the entire hard disk, erase only Linux partitions, or only use free disk space to set up the partitions. To take the manual approach instead, you must choose to create a custom layout.

With the manual approach, the disk-partitioning tool (formerly called Disk Druid) lets you divide the hard disk into partitions as you choose. Later, there are a lot of command-line utilities you can use to change and work with your disk partitions and the file systems created on those partitions.

Partitioning Hard Disks

Historically, PC hard drives have used a 32-bit PC-BIOS partition table with a Master Boot Record (MBR). This limits partition sizes to 2TB and only allows four primary partitions per drive. The use of extended partitions is a way to overcome the four primary partition limit. In order to overcome the 2TB limit, PC-BIOS partition tables are being replaced with GPT (GUID Partition Tables).

The old standard command for working with disk partitions is `fdisk`. Because `fdisk` cannot work with GPT partitions, however, it is slowly being deprecated. A more powerful and actively supported tool is the `parted` command.

> **NOTE** *If you prefer to use graphical tools for partitioning, resizing, and otherwise manipulating your hard disk, you can try* gparted *or* qtparted *partitioning tools. The command names and package names are the same for those two tools.*

Changing Disk Partitions with fdisk

The `fdisk` command is a useful Linux tool for listing and changing disk partitions. Keep in mind that modifying or deleting partitions can cause valuable data to be removed, so be sure of your changes before writing them to disk. To use the `fdisk` command to **list information about the partitions on your hard disk**, type the following command as root user:

```
# fdisk -l                   List disk partitions for every disk
Disk /dev/sda: 82.3 GB, 82348277760 bytes
255 heads, 63 sectors/track, 10011 cylinders
Units = cylinders of 16065 * 512 = 8225280 bytes

   Device Boot      Start         End      Blocks   Id  System
/dev/sda1   *           1          13      104391   83  Linux
/dev/sda2              14        9881    79264710   83  Linux
/dev/sda3            9882       10011     1044225   82  Linux swap
```

This example is for an 80GB hard disk that is divided into three partitions. The first (`/dev/sda1`) is a small `/boot` partition that is configured as a Linux ext3 file system (`Id 83`). Note the asterisk (*), indicating that the first partition is bootable. The next partition is assigned to the root file system and is also ext3. The final partition is Linux swap.

> **NOTE** *In Fedora 7 and later, both IDE and SCSI disks use device names* /dev/sd?, *where the ? is replaced by a letter (a, b, or c, and so on). In RHEL5 and earlier versions of Fedora, only SCSI disks and USB flash drives used the* /dev/sd? *names. IDE hard drives used* /dev/hd? *instead.*

If multiple disks are present, `fdisk -l` will list them all unless you **indicate the specific disk** you want:

```
# fdisk -l /dev/sdb          List disk partitions for a specific disk
```

To **work with a specific disk** with the `fdisk` command, simply indicate the disk you want with no other options:

```
# fdisk /dev/sda             Start interactive fdisk session with disk 1
Command (m for help): m      Type m to list help text as shown
Command action
```

```
a    toggle a bootable flag
b    edit bsd disklabel
c    toggle the dos compatibility flag
d    delete a partition
l    list known partition types
m    print this menu
n    add a new partition
o    create a new empty DOS partition table
p    print the partition table
q    quit without saving changes
s    create a new empty Sun disklabel
t    change a partition's system id
u    change display/entry units
v    verify the partition table
w    write table to disk and exit
x    extra functionality (experts only)
Command (m for help):
```

With the prompt displayed, you can use any of the commands shown to work with your hard disk. In particular, you can use p (to print the same listing as fdisk -l), n (to create a new partition), d (to delete an existing partition), l (to list known file system types), or t (to change the file system type for a partition). The following examples show some of those fdisk commands in action:

```
Command (m for help): d                       Ask to delete a partition
Partition number (1-4): 4                     Type partition number to delete
Command (m for help): n                       Create a new disk partition
First cylinder (1-4983, default 1): 1         Select start (or Enter)
Last cylinder ... (default 4983): 4983        Select end (or Enter)
Command (m for help): a                       Make a partition bootable
Partition number (1-3): 1                     Type bootable partition number
Command (m for help): t                       Select a file system type
Partition number (1-3): 3                     Select partition to change
Hex code (type L to list codes): 82           Assign partition as swap
```

Unless you tell it otherwise, fdisk assumes the new partition is a Linux ext3 partition (83). You could have typed L to see the same listing of file system types and hex codes produced from the l command. As noted above, 82 can assign the partition as swap. Other Linux partitions that may interest you include Linux extended (85), Linux LVM (8e), Linux software raid (fd), and EFI/GTP (ee).

For Windows partitions, you can assign a partition as HPFS/NTFS (7), Windows 95 FAT32 (b), FAT 16 (6), or Windows 95 FAT32 LBA (c). Other Unix-type file systems include Minix (be or bf), BSD/OS (e4), FreeBSD (ee), OpenBSD (ef), NeXTSTEP (f0), Darwin UFS (f1), and NetBSD (f4). Any of these file system types might be useful if you have old backup media from those file systems that you want to restore.

So far, you have not made any permanent changes to your partition table. If you are now *very sure* that your new settings are correct, type w to write those changes to the partition table. To abandon your changes (or quit after writing your changes), type q to quit your fdisk session.

107

Copying Partition Tables with sfdisk

To **back up or replicate a disk's partition table**, use `sfdisk`:

```
# sfdisk -d /dev/sda > sda-table         Back up partition table to file
# sfdisk /dev/sda < sda-table            Restore partition table from file
# sfdisk -d /dev/sda | sfdisk /dev/sdb   Copy partition table from disk to disk
```

Changing Disk Partitions with parted

As with `fdisk`, `parted` can be used to list or change disk partitions. However, `parted` has a few other useful features as well. Here's how to **list partitions with parted**:

```
# parted -1
Model: ATA FUJITSU MPG3409A (scsi)
Disk /dev/sda: 41.0GB
Sector size (logical/physical): 512B/512B
Partition Table: msdos

Number   Start    End     Size    Type     File system   Flags
1        32.3kB   206MB   206MB   primary  ext3          boot
2        206MB    39.5GB  39.3GB  primary  ext3
3        39.5GB   41.0GB  1536MB  primary  linux-swap
```

This listing shows you if you have a classic msdos disk label (partition table), or a gpt one. In this case, the partition table is msdos.

To **run parted interactively**, type `parted` followed by the name of the storage device you want to work with (such as `/dev/sda`). Or, if you have only one storage device, simply type `parted`:

```
# parted
GNU Parted 1.8.6
Using /dev/sda
Welcome to GNU Parted! Type 'help' to view a list of commands.
(parted)
```

To use `parted` interactively, either type whole commands or start with a few letters and use the Tab key to complete the command (as you would in the bash shell). And if you're really efficient, you can just type enough letters to allow `parted` to guess your input, as you would with Cisco IOS: p for print, mkl for mklabel, and so on.

> **WARNING!** Unlike `fdisk`, `parted` *immediately incorporates changes you make to your partitions, without explicitly writing the changes to disk. So don't just assume you can back out of any changes by simply quitting* `parted`.

With each command in a `parted` session, you also have the option to enter the command with all the arguments (for example, `mkpart logical ext3 10.7GB 17.0GB`) or just enter the command (`mkpart`) and `parted` will guide you interactively:

```
(parted) mkpart                         Create a new partition
Partition type?  [logical]? primary
File system type?  [ext2]? ext3
Start? 17GB
End? 24GB
```

Avoid using `mkpartfs`. It cannot create ext3 partitions properly. Instead, `mkpart` an ext3 partition (as shown) and format it later outside of `parted` with the `mkfs.ext3` command. **Resizing common Linux partitions** can be useful if you need to make space for a new partition. Here is an example:

```
(parted) resize 2                       Resize a partition
Start? [1.2GB] 1.2GB
End? [24GB] 10GB
```

> **WARNING!**   *Unless you're using LVM, this will typically destroy your file system.*

To **resize NTFS partitions**, you can use the `ntfsresize` command. In Fedora, that command comes with the ntfsprogs package. That package also comes with commands for creating (`mkfs.ntfs`), fixing (`ntfsfix`), and getting information about (`ntfsinfo`) NTFS partitions.

Working with File System Labels

The term *label*, in regards to disk partitions, can refer to two different things. A *disk label* can be used as another name for a partition table, as seen in `parted` output. A *partition label* can also be the name of an individual partition. To **see a partition's label**, use the `e2label` command:

```
# e2label /dev/sda2
/
```

To **set the label on a partition:**

```
# e2label /dev/sda2 mypartition
```

Bear in mind that `/etc/fstab` sometimes uses the partition label to mount the partition as in the example below. Changing this label may render the system unbootable.

```
LABEL=/boot          /boot           ext3    defaults     1 2
```

To find a partition when you know only the label, type the following:

```
# findfs LABEL=mypartition
/dev/sda2
```

Formatting a File System

With your disk partitions in place, you can build a file system of your choice on each partition. Most Linux systems come with the commands needed to make and check file systems that are commonly used in Linux. Commands for formatting and checking file systems are `mkfs` and `fsck`, respectively.

The `mkfs` command serves as the front end for many different commands aimed at formatting particular file system types, such as `mkfs.ext2`, `mkfs.ext3`, `mkfs.cramfs`, `mkfs.msdos`, `mkfs.ntfs`, and `mkfs.vfat`. By adding packages that support other file systems, additional `mkfs` commands are available to seamlessly work with `mkfs`. These include `mkfs.bfs`, `mkfs.minix`, `mkfs.xfs`, and `mkfs.xiafs`. Use each command directly (as in `mkfs.vfat /dev/sdb1`) or via the `mkfs` command (as in `mkfs -t vfat /dev/sdb1`).

Creating a File System on a Hard Disk Partition

Basic software packages you need in Fedora to do file system creation and checking include util-linux (includes `mkfs` and other general utilities) and e2fsprogs (ext2/ext3-specific tools). Specific `mkfs` commands for different file system types are included in ntfsprogs (ntfs), dosfstools (msdos and vfat), xfsprogs (xfs), jfsutils (jfs), mtd-utils (jffs and jffs2), and reiserfs-utils (reiserfs).

Here are examples of the mkfs command to create file systems (be sure to add the `-t` option first):

```
# mkfs -t ext3 /dev/sdb1        Create ext3 file system on sba1
# mkfs -t ext3 -v -c /dev/sdb1  More verbose and scan for bad blocks
# mkfs.ext3 -c /dev/sdb1        Same result as previous command
```

If you would like to add a partition label to the new partition, use the `-L` option:

```
# mkfs.ext3 -c -L mypartition /dev/sdb1  Add mypartition label
```

Creating a Virtual File System

If you want to try out different file system types or simply make a file system that is more portable (in other words, not tied to a physical disk), you can create a *virtual file system*. A virtual file system is one that sits within a file on an existing file system. You can format it as any file system type you like, move it around, and use it from different computers.

Virtual file systems are useful for such things as creating live CDs or running dedicated virtual operating systems. In the example that follows, you create a blank 500MB disk image file, format it as a file system, and then mount it to access data on the file system:

```
$ dd if=/dev/zero of=mydisk count=2048000    Create zero-filled 1GB file
$ du -sh mydisk                              Check virtual file system size
1001M   mydisk
$ mkfs -t ext3 mydisk                        Create files system on mydisk
mydisk is not a block special device
Continue (y/n): y
$ mkdir /mnt/image                           Create a mount point
# mount -o loop mydisk /mnt/image            Mount mydisk on /mnt/image
```

In this procedure, the dd command creates an empty disk image file of 2048000 blocks (about 1GB). The mkfs command can create any file system type you choose (ext3 is done here). Because the file is not a block special device, as is the case when formatting disk partitions, mkfs will warn you before starting to make the file system. The only other trick, after creating the mount point, is to indicate that you are mounting the file (mydisk) as a loop device (-o loop). Note that the mount command is the only command shown above that requires root privilege.

When the virtual file system is mounted, you can access it as you would any file system. When you are done with the file system, leave it and unmount it:

```
# cd /mnt/image           Change to the mount point
# mkdir test              Create a directory on the file system
# cp /etc/hosts .         Copy a file to the file system
# cd                      Leave the file system
# umount /mnt/image       Unmount the file system
```

With the virtual file system unmounted, you could move it to another system or burn it to a CD to use a file system in another location. If you don't want the file system any more, simply delete the file.

Viewing and Changing File System Attributes

Using the tune2fs or dumpe2fs commands, you can view attributes of ext2 and ext3 file systems. The tune2fs command can also be used to change file system attributes. Use the swapfs command to create a swap partition. Here are examples (both commands produce the same output):

```
# tune2fs -l /dev/sda1          View tunable file system attributes
# dumpe2fs -h /dev/sda1         Same as tune2fs output
dumpe2fs 1.39 (29-May-2006)
Filesystem volume name:    /
Last mounted on:           <not available>
Filesystem UUID:           f5f261d3-3879-41d6-8245-f2153b003204
Filesystem magic number:   0xEF53
Filesystem revision #:     1 (dynamic)
```

```
Filesystem features:        has_journal ext_attr resize_inode dir_index filetype
    needs_recovery sparse_super large_file
Default mount options:      user_xattr acl
Filesystem state:           clean
Errors behavior:            Continue
Filesystem OS type:         Linux
Inode count:                7914368
Block count:                7907988
Reserved block count:       395399
Free blocks:                5916863
Free inodes:                7752077
First block:                0
Block size:                 4096
Fragment size:              4096
Reserved GDT blocks:        1022
Blocks per group:           32768
Fragments per group:        32768
Inodes per group:           32704
Inode blocks per group:     1022
Filesystem created:         Fri Jun 15 12:13:17 2007
Last mount time:            Tue Jul 24 06:47:35 2007
Last write time:            Tue Jul 24 06:47:35 2007
Mount count:                2
Maximum mount count:        29
Last checked:               Fri Jun 15 12:13:17 2007
Check interval:             0 (<none>)
Reserved blocks uid:        0 (user root)
Reserved blocks gid:        0 (group root)
First inode:                11
Inode size:   128
Journal inode:              8
First orphan inode:         988413
Default directory hash:     tea
Directory Hash Seed:        4137d20d-b398-467b-a47a-a9110416b393
Journal backup:             inode blocks
Journal size:               128M
```

The output shows a lot of information about the file system. For example, if you have a file system that needs to create many small files (such as a news server), you can check that you don't run out of inodes. Setting the Maximum mount count ensures that the file system is checked for errors after it has been mounted the selected number of times. You can also find dates and times for when a file system was created, last mounted, and last written to.

To **change settings on an existing ext2 or ext3 file system,** you can use the tune2fs command. The following command changes the number of mounts before a forced file system check:

```
# tune2fs -c 31 /dev/sda1        Sets # of mounts before check is forced
tune2fs 1.39 (29-May-2006)
Setting maximal mount count to 31
```

112

If you'd like to switch to forced **file system checks based on time interval** rather than number of mounts, disable mount-count checking by setting it to negative 1 (-1):

```
# tune2fs -c -1 /dev/sda1
tune2fs 1.39 (29-May-2006)
Setting maximal mount count to -1
```

Use the -i option to **enable time-dependent checking**. Here are some examples:

```
# tune2fs -i 10 /dev/sda1      Check after 10 days
# tune2fs -i 1d /dev/sda1      Check after 1 day
# tune2fs -i 3w /dev/sda1      Check after 3 weeks
# tune2fs -i 6m /dev/sda1      Check after 6 months
# tune2fs -i 0 /dev/sda1       Disable time-dependent checking
```

Be sure you always have either mount-count or time-dependent checking turned on.

Use the -j option to **turn an ext2 file system into ext3** (by adding a journal):

```
# tune2fs -j /dev/sda1         Add journaling to change ext2 to ext3
```

Creating and Using Swap Partitions

Swap partitions are needed in Linux systems to hold data that overflows from your system's RAM. If you didn't create a swap partition when you installed Linux, you can create it later using the mkswap command. You can **create your swap partition** either on a regular disk partition or in a file formatted as a swap partition. Here are some examples:

```
# mkswap /dev/sda1             Format sda1 as a swap partition
Setting up swapspace version 1, size = 205594 kB
```

To **check your swap area for bad blocks**, use the -c option to mkswap:

```
# mkswap -c /dev/sda1
```

If you don't have a spare partition, you can **create a swap area within a file**:

```
# dd if=/dev/zero of=/tmp/swapfile count=65536
65536+0 records in
65536+0 records out
33554432 bytes (34 MB) copied, 1.56578 s, 21.4 MB/s
# chmod 600 /tmp/swapfile
# mkswap /tmp/swapfile
Setting up swapspace version 1, size = 67104 kB
```

The dd command above creates a 32MB file named swapfile. The chmod command locks down the permissions on the file, to avoid getting a warning from the swapon command down the road. The mkswap command formats the /tmp/swapfile file to be a swap partition.

After you have created a swap partition or swap file, you need to **tell the system to use the swap area** you made using the `swapon` command. This is similar to what happens at boot time. Here are examples:

```
# swapon /dev/sda1          Turn swap on for /dev/sda1 partition
# swapon -v /dev/sda1        Increase verbosity as swap is turned on
swapon on /dev/sda1
# swapon -v /tmp/swapfile    Turn swap on for the /tmp/swapfile file
swapon on /tmp/swapfile
```

You can also use the `swapon` command to **see a list of your swap files and partitions:**

```
# swapon -s          View all swap files and partitions that are on
Filename            Type          Size      Used     Priority
/dev/sda5           partition     1020088   142764   -1
/tmp/swapfile       file          65528     0        -6
```

To **turn off a swap area,** you can use the `swapoff` command:

```
# swapoff -v /tmp/swapfile
swapoff on /tmp/swapfile
```

Swap areas are prioritized. The kernel will swap first to areas of high priorities, and then go down the list. Areas of the same priority get striped between. You can **specify the priority of your swap area** as you enable it using the `-p` option:

```
# swapon -v -p 1 /dev/sda1      Assign top swap priority to sda1
```

Mounting and Unmounting File Systems

Before you can use a regular, non-swap file system, you need to attach it to a directory in your computer's file system tree by *mounting* it. Your root file system (/) and other file systems you use on an ongoing basis are typically mounted automatically based on entries in your /etc/fstab file. Other file systems can be mounted manually as they are needed using the mount command.

Mounting File Systems from the fstab File

When you first install Linux, the /etc/fstab file is usually set up automatically to contain information about your root file systems and other file systems. Those file systems can then be set to mount at boot time or be ready to mount manually (with mount points and other options ready to use when a manual mount is done).

Here is an example of a /etc/fstab file:

```
/dev/VolGroup00/LogVol00    /           ext3    defaults          1 1
LABEL=/boot                 /boot       ext3    defaults          1 2
tmpfs                       /dev/shm    tmpfs   defaults          0 0
devpts                      /dev/pts    devpts  gid=5,mode=620 0 0
```

114

```
sysfs                       /sys          sysfs   defaults      0 0
proc                        /proc         proc    defaults      0 0
/dev/VolGroup00/LogVol01    swap          swap    defaults      0 0
/dev/sda1                   /mnt/windows  vfat    noauto        0 0
```

All the file systems are mounted automatically, except for /dev/sda1 (as indicated by the noauto option). The root (/) and swap hard disk partitions are configured as logical volume management (LVM) volumes. LVM volumes can make it easier to move or join physical partitions, while still retaining the volume ID. Pseudo file systems (not associated with a partition) include devpts (an interface to pty pseudo terminals), sysfs (information from 2.6 kernel), and proc (kernel information implemented prior to 2.6 kernel). The /dev/sda1 disk partition was added manually in this example to mount the Windows partition located on that device.

The /etc/fstab file no longer typically holds information about removable media. That's because the hardware abstraction layer (HAL) facility automatically detects removable media and mounts those media in appropriate mount points in the /media directory (based on such things as volume ID on the media).

Table 7-2 describes each field in the /etc/fstab file.

Table 7-2: Fields in /etc/fstab File

Field	Description
1	**The device name representing the file system.** Originally, this contained the device name of the partition to mount (such as /dev/sda1). It can now also contain a LABEL or universally unique identifier (UUID), instead of a device name.
2	**The mount point in the file system.** The file system contains all data from the mount point down the directory tree structure, unless another file system is mounted at some point beneath it.
3	**The file system type.** See Table 7-1 for a list of many common file system types.
4	**The mount command options.** Examples of mount options include noauto (to prevent the file system from mounting at boot time) and ro (to mount the file system read-only). To let any user mount a file system, you could add the user or owner option to this field. Commas must separate options. See the mount command manual page (under the -o option) for information on other supported options.
5	**Dump file system?** This field is only significant if you run backups with dump. A number 1 signifies that the file system needs to be dumped. A zero means that it doesn't.
6	**File system check?** The number in this field indicates whether or not the file system needs to be checked with fsck. A zero indicates that the file system should not be checked. A number 1 means that the file system needs to be checked first (this is used for the root file system). A number 2 assumes that the file system can be checked at any point after the root file system is checked.

You can create your own entries for any hard disk or removable media partitions you want in the /etc/fstab file. Remote file systems (NFS, Samba, and others) can also contain entries in the /etc/fstab file to automatically mount those file systems at boot time or later by hand.

Mounting File Systems with the mount Command

The mount command is used to view mounted file systems, as well as mount any local (hard disk, USB drive, CD, DVD, and so on) or remote (NFS, Samba, and so on) file systems. Here is an example of the mount command for **listing mounted file systems**:

```
$ mount                        List mounted remote and local file systems
/dev/sda7 on / type ext3 (rw)
proc on /proc type proc (rw)
sysfs on /sys type sysfs (rw)
devpts on /dev/pts type devpts (rw,gid=5,mode=620)
/dev/sda6 on /mnt/debian type ext3 (rw)
/dev/sda3 on /mnt/slackware type ext3 (rw)
tmpfs on /dev/shm type tmpfs (rw)
none on /proc/sys/fs/binfmt_misc type binfmt_misc (rw)
sunrpc on /var/lib/nfs/rpc_pipefs type rpc_pipefs (rw)
```

Use the -t option to **list only mounts of a specific file system type**:

```
$ mount -t ext3                 List mounted ext3 file systems
/dev/sda7 on / type ext3 (rw)
/dev/sda6 on /mnt/debian type ext3 (rw)
/dev/sda3 on /mnt/slackware type ext3 (rw)
```

To **display partition labels with mount information**, use the -l option:

```
$ mount -t ext3 -l              List mounted ext3 file systems and labels
/dev/sda7 on / type ext3 (rw) [/123]
/dev/sda6 on /mnt/debian type ext3 (rw) [/mnt/debian]
/dev/sda3 on /mnt/slackware type ext3 (rw) [/mnt/slackware]
```

Here is a simple mount command to mount the /dev/sda1 device on an existing directory named /mnt/mymount:

```
# mount /dev/sda1 /mnt/mymount/      Mount a local file system
# mount -v /dev/sda1 /mnt/mymount/   Mount file system, more verbose
mount: you didn't specify a filesystem type for /dev/sda1
I will try type ext3
/dev/sda1 on /mnt/mymount type ext3 (rw)
```

In the examples above, the mount command will either look for an entry for /dev/sda1 in the /etc/fstab file or try to guess the type of file system.

Use -t to **explicitly indicate the type of file system to mount**:

```
# mount -v -t ext3 /dev/sda1 /mnt/mymount/   Mount an ext3 file system
/dev/sda1 on /mnt/mymount type ext3 (rw)
```

You can also **display the label/name of the partition** that is mounted:

```
# mount -vl -t ext3 /dev/sda1 /mnt/mymount/  Mount file system/show label
```

If you're mounting something that is listed in your fstab file already, you only need to specify one item: mount point or device. For example, with the following fstab entry:

```
/dev/sda1          /mnt/mymount         ext3    defaults      1 2
```

you can do either of the following to mount the file system:

```
# mount -v /dev/sda1        Mount file system with device name only
/dev/sda1 on /mnt/mymount type ext3 (rw)
# mount -v /mnt/mymount/    Mount file system with mount point only
/dev/sda1 on /mnt/mymount type ext3 (rw)
```

You can **specify mount options** by adding -o and a comma-separated list of options. They are the same options you can add to field 4 of the /etc/fstab file. By default, partitions are mounted with read/write access. You can explicitly indicate to **mount a file system as read/write (rw) or read-only (ro)**:

```
# mount -v -t ext3 -o rw /dev/sda1 /mnt/mymount/   Mount read/write
/dev/sda1 on /mnt/mymount type ext3 (rw)
# mount -v -t ext3 -o ro /dev/sda1 /mnt/mymount/   Mount read-only
/dev/sda1 on /mnt/mymount type ext3 (ro)
```

A few other useful mount options you can use include:

❑ noatime — Does not update the access time on files. Good on file systems with a lot of I/O, such as mail spools and logs.

❑ noexec — Prevents execution of binaries located on this file system. Can be used to increase security, for example for /tmp in environments with untrusted users.

❑ remount — Change options on a mounted file system. With remount, you can unmount the file system and remount it with the new options in a single command. In this example, we change a previous read/write mount to read-only:

```
# mount -v -o remount,ro /dev/sda1
/dev/sda1 on /mnt/mymount type ext3 (ro)
```

❑ --bind — Mount an existing file system to another location in the tree. Assuming /dev/sda1 is already mounted on /mnt/mymount, type the following:

```
# mount --bind -v /mnt/mymount/ /tmp/mydir/
/mnt/mymount on /tmp/mydir type none (rw,bind)
```

Now the same file system is accessible from two locations. The new mount point has the same mount options as the original.

❑ --move — Move a file system from one mount point to another. Assuming /dev/sda1 is already mounted on /mnt/mymount, this moves the file system to /tmp/mydir:

```
# mount -v --move /mnt/mymount/ /tmp/mydir/
/mnt/mymount on /tmp/mydir type none (rw)
```

Just like you can swap to a file, you can create a file system in a file and then mount it in what is called a *loopback* mount. Creating and mounting such a file is described in the "Creating a Virtual File System" section earlier in this chapter. A common situation where you might want to **mount a file in loopback** is after downloading a Linux install CD or LiveCD. By mounting that CD image in loopback, you can view its contents or copy files from that image to your hard disk.

In the following example, the mount command is allowed to automatically pick an existing loopback device when mounting a CD image file (file system type iso9660). The command output shows /dev/loop0 was selected:

```
# mount -v -t iso9660 -o loop /tmp/myimage.iso /mnt/mymount/
mount: going to use the loop device /dev/loop0
/tmp/myimage.iso on /mnt/mymount type ext3 (rw,loop=/dev/loop0)
```

In the following example, we downloaded a Fedora USB flash drive boot image called diskboot.img to /tmp. Here is an example of how to **mount the boot image**:

```
# mount -v -o loop /tmp/diskboot.img /mnt/mymount
mount: going to use the loop device /dev/loop0
mount: you didn't specify a filesystem type for /dev/loop0
       I will try type vfat
/tmp/diskboot.img on /mnt/mymount type vfat (rw,loop=/dev/loop0)
```

To **see the status of the loopback devices**, use the losetup command:

```
# losetup -a                 List mounted loopback devices
/dev/loop0: [0807]:1009045 (/tmp/diskboot.img)
```

If a loopback mount gets "stuck" and you have problems during unmount, try detaching it as follows:

```
# losetup -d /dev/loop1    Force unmount of a mounted loopback device
```

> **NOTE** *The* mount *command can also be used to attach to NFS, or Samba/*
> *Windows CIFS shares. See Chapter 12 for information on mounting those*
> *remote file system types.*

Unmounting File Systems with umount

To **unmount a file system**, use the umount command. You can umount the file system using the device name or the mount point. You're better off umounting with the mount point, to avoid the confusion when using bind mounts (one device, multiple mount points). Here is an example of each, with verbosity on:

```
# umount -v /dev/sda1          Unmount by device name
/dev/sda1 umounted
# umount -v /mnt/mymount/       Unmount by mount point
/tmp/diskboot.img umounted
```

If the device is busy, the unmount will fail. A common reason for an unmount to fail is that you have a shell open with the current directory of a directory inside the mount:

```
# umount -v /mnt/mymount/
umount: /mnt/mymount: device is busy
umount: /mnt/mymount: device is busy
```

Sometimes, it's not obvious what makes the device busy. You can use lsof to list open files, then **search that list for the mount point** that interests you:

```
# lsof | grep mymount          Find open files on mymount partition
bash   9341  francois  cwd   DIR   8,1   1024    2 /mnt/mymount
```

You can see that a bash process run by francois with a PID of 9341 is preventing the mymount partition from being unmounted.

Another option when a file system is busy is to **perform a lazy unmount**:

```
# umount -vl /mnt/mymount/     Perform a lazy unmount
```

A *lazy unmount* unmounts the file system from the tree now, but waits for the device to no longer be busy before cleaning up everything. Unmounts of removable media can also be done with eject. This **unmounts a CD and ejects the CD** from the drive:

```
# eject /dev/cdrom     Unmount and eject a CD
```

Checking File Systems

In Linux, instead of just having the scandisk utility you have in Windows, you can scan a physical device for bad blocks at a physical level with the badblocks command

and scan a file system for errors at the logical level with the `fsck` command. Here's how to **scan for bad blocks**:

```
# badblocks /dev/sda1          Physically scan hard disk for bad blocks
# badblocks -v /dev/sda1       Add verbosity to hard disk scan
Checking blocks 0 to 200781
Checking for bad blocks (read-only test): done
Pass completed, 0 bad blocks found.
```

By default, `badblock` does a safe read-only test of the blocks. You can also perform a non-destructive read/write test. This is the slowest test, but the best one you can perform without destroying the data on the device. Add `-s` to **see the ongoing progress**:

```
# badblocks -vsn /dev/sda1          Check bad blocks, non-destructive
Checking for bad blocks in non-destructive read-write mode
From block 0 to 200781
Testing with random pattern: Pass completed, 0 bad blocks found.
```

The following command performs a faster, *destructive* read-write test:

> **WARNING!**   *This will erase all the data on the partition.*

```
# badblocks -vsw /dev/sda1          Check bad blocks, destructive
Checking for bad blocks in read-write mode
From block 0 to 200781
Testing with pattern 0xaa: done
Reading and comparing: done
Testing with pattern 0x55: done
Reading and comparing: done
Testing with pattern 0xff: done
Reading and comparing: done
Testing with pattern 0x00: done
Reading and comparing: done
Pass completed, 0 bad blocks found.
```

You can **perform multiple badblocks passes**; for example, this command line can be used to burn in a drive and screen for hard drive infant mortality:

```
# badblocks -vswp 2 /dev/sda1
```

Like the `mkfs` command, the `fsck` command is just a front end to file-system–specific utilities. You can **check an ext3 file system** by simply adding the device name of the disk partition you want to check to the `fsck` command:

```
# fsck /dev/sda1
fsck 1.39 (29-May-2006)
e2fsck 1.39 (29-May-2006)
mypart has gone 18 days without being checked, check forced.
Pass 1: Checking inodes, blocks, and sizes
Pass 2: Checking directory structure
Pass 3: Checking directory connectivity
```

```
Pass 4: Checking reference counts
Pass 5: Checking group summary information
mypart: 11/50200 files (9.1% non-contiguous), 12002/200780 blocks
```

You can **add other options to** fsck, such as -T (to not display the useless fsck version number) and -V (to be more verbose about what fsck actually does):

```
# fsck -TV /dev/sda1          Check file system (verbose and no version)
[/sbin/fsck.ext3 (1) -- /dev/sda1] fsck.ext3 /dev/sda1
e2fsck 1.39 (29-May-2006)
mypart: clean, 11/50200 files, 12002/200780 blocks
```

For any problem that fsck encounters, it will ask you if you want to repair it:

```
# fsck -TV /dev/sda1        Prompting to correct problems encountered
[/sbin/fsck.ext3 (1) -- /mnt/mymount] fsck.ext3 /dev/sda1
e2fsck 1.39 (29-May-2006)
Couldn't find ext2 superblock, trying backup blocks...
Resize inode not valid.  Recreate<y>? y
```

Unless you have a very in-depth knowledge of file systems, you're better off answering yes. This can be done automatically with the -y option:

```
# fsck -TVy /dev/sda1
[/sbin/fsck.ext3 (1) -- /mnt/mymount] fsck.ext3 -y /dev/sda1
e2fsck 1.39 (29-May-2006)
Couldn't find ext2 superblock, trying backup blocks...
Resize inode not valid.  Recreate? yes
mypart was not cleanly unmounted, check forced.
Pass 1: Checking inodes, blocks, and sizes
Pass 2: Checking directory structure
Pass 3: Checking directory connectivity
Pass 4: Checking reference counts
Pass 5: Checking group summary information
Free blocks count wrong for group #0 (3552, counted=3553).
Fix? yes
Free blocks count wrong (188777, counted=188778).
Fix? yes

mypart: ***** FILE SYSTEM WAS MODIFIED *****
mypart: 11/50200 files (0.0% non-contiguous), 12002/200780 blocks
```

Checking RAID Disks

Redundant Array of Independent Drives (RAID) disks let you duplicate or distribute data across multiple hard drives. Using RAID can improve reliability and performance of your storage media. The mdadm command, which is part of the mdadm package, can be used to **check softraid devices** on your computer. Here's an example:

```
# mdadm -Q /dev/md1
/dev/md1: 1498.13MiB raid1 2 devices, 0 spares.
```

```
        Use mdadm --detail for more detail.
/dev/md1: No md super block found, not an md component.
```

The message on the last line simply means that /dev/md1 is not a member of a RAID array. That is normal, since md1 is the array itself. Similarly, if you query a member of a RAID array, your output will look like this:

 # mdadm -Q /dev/sdb3
```
/dev/sdb3: is not an md array
/dev/sdb3: device 1 in 4 device active raid6 md0.  Use mdadm --examine for more
detail.
```

To obtain more detailed output, add the --detail option:

 # mdadm -Q --detail /dev/md1
```
/dev/md1:
          Version : 00.90.01
    Creation Time : Fri Dec  8 16:32:12 2006
       Raid Level : raid1
       Array Size : 1534080 (1498.38 MiB 1570.90 MB)
      Device Size : 1534080 (1498.38 MiB 1570.90 MB)
     Raid Devices : 2
    Total Devices : 2
  Preferred Minor : 1
      Persistence : Superblock is persistent

      Update Time : Sun Jun 17 02:06:01 2007
            State : clean
   Active Devices : 2
  Working Devices : 2
   Failed Devices : 0
    Spare Devices : 0

             UUID : 49c564cc:2d3c9a14:d93ce1c9:070663ca
           Events : 0.42

    Number   Major   Minor   RaidDevice State
       0       3       2        0        active sync   /dev/hda2
       1       3      66        1        active sync   /dev/hdb2
```

The mdadm command can also be used to manage your softraid devices. For more info, run the following:

 # mdadm --manage --help
$ man mdadm

> **NOTE** *If you use 3ware/AMCC hardware RAID controllers, which are our favorite for SATA RAID, make sure you install 3ware Disk Manager (3dm2), which is available in rpm form from ATrpms.net. The 3dm2 utility provides a monitoring daemon and a web GUI.*

Finding Out About File System Use

Running out of disk space can be annoying on your desktop system and potentially a disaster on your servers. To determine how much disk space is available and how much is currently in use, you can use the df command. To check how much space particular files and directories are consuming, use the du command.

The df command provides **utilization summaries of your mounted file systems**. Using the -h option, you can have the data (which is shown in bytes by default) converted to megabytes (M) and gigabytes (G), to make that output more human-readable:

```
$ df -h              Display space on file systems in human-readable form
Filesystem          Size    Used    Avail Use%  Mounted on
/dev/sda2           7.6G    3.4G    3.9G   47%   /
/dev/sda1           99M     14M     80M    15%   /boot
tmpfs               501M    0       501M   0%    /dev/shm
/dev/sda5           352G    197G    137G   59%   /home
//thompson/chris    9204796 5722608 3007068 66%  /mnt/mymount
```

Because ext file systems have only so many inodes created at mkfs time, if you have lots of small files, you can possibly run out of inodes before you run out of actual space. To **check inode utilization**, use the -i option:

```
$ df -hi
Filesystem          Inodes  IUsed   IFree IUse% Mounted on
/dev/sda2           2.0M    108K    1.9M   6% /
```

If you have network mounts (such as Samba or NFS), these will show up too in your df output. To **limit df output to local file systems**, type the following:

```
$ df -hl             Display disk space only for local file systems
```

To **add the file system type** to the listing, use the -T option:

```
$ df -hT             Add file system type information to listing
Filesystem   Type    Size  Used Avail Use% Mounted on
/dev/sda7    ext3    8.8G  5.5G  2.9G  66% /
```

To **check for disk space usage for particular files or directories in a file system**, use the du command. The following command was run as the user named francois:

```
$ du -h /home/        Show disk space usage for /home directory
du: `/home/chris': Permission denied
4.0K    /home/francois/Mail
52K     /home/francois
64K     /home/
```

The output shows that access to another home directory's disk use (in this case /home/chris) was denied for security reasons. So the next examples show how to avoid permission issues and get totals that are correct by using the root user account. This is clearly visible when we use -s to summarize.

```
$ du -sh /home    Regular user is denied space totals to others' homes
du: `/home/chris': Permission denied
du: `/home/horatio199': Permission denied
64K     /home
# du -sh /home    You can display summary disk use as root user
1.6G    /home
```

You can specify multiple directories with the -c option and total them up:

```
# du -sch /home /var    Show directory and total summaries
1.6G    /home
111M    /var
1.7G    total
```

You can exclude files that match a pattern from being counted using the exclude option. In the following example, disk image files (ending with the .iso suffix) are not used in totaling the disk space used:

```
# du -sh --exclude='*.iso' /home/chris    Exclude ISO images from totals
588M    /home/chris
```

You can specify what depth in the tree you want to summarize. Set --max-depth to a number larger than the 1 value shown, to dig deeper into disk space usage:

```
# du -h --max-depth=1 /home    Provide disk space use, to one level deep
1.6G    /home/chris
52K     /home/francois
1.6G    /home
# du -h --max-depth=2 /home    Dig two-levels deep for disk space use
...
4.0K    /home/francois/Mail
52K     /home/francois
1.6G    /home
```

Logical Volume Manager

Logical Volume Manager (LVM) is a feature designed to help you cope with the changing needs for disk space on your Linux systems. With your hard disks configured as LVM volumes, you have tremendous flexibility in growing, shrinking, and moving the storage space on your systems as your needs change. LVM also allows for snapshots, a feature typically found on expensive enterprise SANs.

Fedora incorporates LVM2 into its releases and uses it to define how disk partitions are allocated when you first install Fedora. Using LVM2, you define and manage volume groups (vg), logical volumes (lv), and physical volumes (pv). Each logical volume and physical volume is divided into logical extents and physical extents, respectively.

The basic business of using LVM is to create the volume groups and logical volumes you need, then assign the extents (small chunks of disk space) to those areas where they are needed. Unlike older disk partitioning schemes, where you might have to back up your data, change your partitioning, then return data to the resized partitions, you can simply add unused extents where they are needed.

In Fedora, the Logical Volume Management GUI (system-config-lvm package) lets you view and work with your LVM volumes. There is also a set of commands that comes with LVM itself (lvm2 package) that can be used to work with LVM volumes. Step through the procedure in the following section to learn about many of those LVM commands.

> **WARNING!** *To avoid messing up the hard disks your computer relies on as you learn LVM, we recommend you try the following examples on some non-critical storage device. For example, we used an inexpensive 32 MB USB flash drive (on /dev/sdb) to run the commands shown in this section.*

Creating LVM Volumes

To begin, use the fdisk command to **create physical partitions for the storage device** on which you want to create logical partitions. Here we have a 32 MB USB flash drive, located on device /dev/sdb.:

```
# fdisk /dev/sdb                    Start command to manage disk partitions
Command (m for help): p            Print current partitions (none exist)

Disk /dev/sdb: 32 MB, 32112128 bytes
1 heads, 62 sectors/track, 1011 cylinders
Units = cylinders of 62 * 512 = 31744 bytes

    Device Boot      Start         End      Blocks   Id  System

Command (m for help): n            Create a new partition
Command action
   e   extended
   p   primary partition (1-4)
p                                  Make it a primary partition
Partition number (1-4): 1          Assigned to partition 1
First cylinder (2-1011, default 2): Enter
Using default value 2
Last cylinder or +size or +sizeM or +sizeK (2-1011, default 1011): Enter
Using default value 1011

Command (m for help): t            Assign a partition type
Selected partition 1
Hex code (type L to list codes): 8E    Indicate 8E (LVM partition)
Changed system type of partition 1 to 8e (Linux LVM)
Command (m for help): p            Type p to see the new partition
Disk /dev/sdb: 32 MB, 32112128 bytes
1 heads, 62 sectors/track, 1011 cylinders
Units = cylinders of 62 * 512 = 31744 bytes
```

```
Device Boot       Start        End     Blocks   Id  System
/dev/sdb1         2            1011    31310    8e  Linux LVM
```

Before proceeding, make sure you have made the correct changes to the correct partition! If everything looks correct, write the new partition table, as follows:

```
Command (m for help): w
The partition table has been altered!
Calling ioctl() to re-read partition table.
Syncing disks.
#
```

Back at the shell prompt, use the sfdisk command to see the partitioning on the drive:

```
# sfdisk -l /dev/sdb       View the LVM partitions

Disk /dev/sdb: 1011 cylinders, 1 heads, 62 sectors/track
Units = cylinders of 31744 bytes, blocks of 1024 bytes, counting from 0

   Device Boot Start    End   #cyls   #blocks   Id  System
/dev/sdb1          1   1010    1010     31310   8e  Linux LVM
/dev/sdb2          0      -       0         0    0  Empty
/dev/sdb3          0      -       0         0    0  Empty
/dev/sdb4          0      -       0         0    0  Empty
```

Next, make /dev/sdb1 a new LVM physical volume and use the pvs command to view information about physical LVM volumes:

```
# pvcreate /dev/sdb1            Make sdb1 an LVM physical volume
  Physical volume "/dev/sdb1" successfully created
# pvs                          View physical LVM partitions
  PV         VG      Fmt  Attr PSize  PFree
  /dev/sdb1  vgusb   lvm2 a-   28.00M 20.00M
```

Next use vgcreate to create the vgusb volume group and list the active current volume groups:

```
$ vgcreate vgusb /dev/sdb1          Create vgusb volume group
  Volume group "vgusb" successfully created
$ vgs                              View current volume groups
  VG     #PV #LV #SN Attr   VSize  VFree
  vgusb    1   0   0 wz--n- 28.00M 28.00M
```

Use lvcreate to create a new LVM partition of 10M from the vgusb volume group. Then use lvs to see the logical volume and vgs to see that the amount of free space has changed:

```
$ lvcreate --size 10M --name lvm_u1 vgusb
  Rounding up size to full physical extent 12.00 MB
  Logical volume "lvm_u1" created
$ lvs                    View the logical volume information
```

126

```
LV          VG      Attr    LSize  Origin Snap%  Move Log Copy%
lvm_u1      vgusb   -wi-a-  12.00M
$ vgs                       See that you still have 16M free
VG      #PV #LV #SN Attr    VSize  VFree
vgusb    1   1   0 wz--n-   28.00M 16.00M
```

To create an ext3 file system on the lvm partition, use the mkfs.ext3 command as follows:

```
$ mkfs.ext3 /dev/mapper/vgusb-lvm_u1
mke2fs 1.38 (30-Jun-2005)
Filesystem label=
OS type: Linux
Block size=1024 (log=0)
Fragment size=1024 (log=0)
3072 inodes, 12288 blocks
614 blocks (5.00%) reserved for the super user
First data block=1
Maximum filesystem blocks=12582912
2 block groups
8192 blocks per group, 8192 fragments per group
1536 inodes per group
Superblock backups stored on blocks:
        8193

Writing inode tables: done
Creating journal (1024 blocks): done
Writing superblocks and filesystem accounting information: done

This filesystem will be automatically checked every 35 mounts or
180 days, whichever comes first.  Use tune2fs -c or -i to override.
```

The ext3 file system has now been created and the LVM volume is ready to use.

Using LVM Volumes

To use the new volume just created, represented by /dev/mapper/vgusb-lvm_u1, **create a mount point** (/mnt/u1) and **mount the volume**. Then use df to check the available space:

```
# mkdir /mnt/u1                                        Create mount point
# mount -t ext3 /dev/mapper/vgusb-lvm_u1 /mnt/u1       Mount volume
$ df -m /mnt/u1                                        Check disk space
Filesystem            1M-blocks      Used Available Use% Mounted on
/dev/mapper/vgusb-lvm_u1
                         12           2       10   11% /mnt/u1
```

At this point, the file system contains only the lost+found directory:

```
$ ls /mnt/u1
lost+found
```

Copy a large file to the new file system. For example, choose one of the kernel files from the /boot directory and copy it to /mnt/u1:

```
$ cp /boot/vmlinuz-* /mnt/u1/        Copy a large file to /mnt/u1
$ df -m /mnt/u1                       See that 4MB is used on /mnt/u1
Filesystem            1M-blocks     Used Available Use% Mounted on
/dev/mapper/vgusb-lvm_u1
                            12        4         9  27% /mnt/u1
```

Run md5sum on the file you copied and save the resulting checksum for later. For example:

```
$ md5sum /mnt/u1/vmlinuz-2.6.20-1.2316.fc5     Check md5sum
8d0dc0347d36ebd3f6f2b49047e1f525  /mnt/u1/vmlinuz-2.6.20-1.2316.fc5
```

Growing the LVM Volume

Say that you are running out of space and you want to **add more space to your LVM volume**. To do that, unmount the volume and use the lvresize command. After that, you must also check the file system with e2fsck and run resize2fs to resize the ext3 file system on that volume:

```
# umount /mnt/u1                              Unmount volume
# lvresize --size 16M /dev/vgusb/lvm_u1       Resize volume
  Extending logical volume lvm_u1 to 16.00 MB
  Logical volume lvm_u1 successfully resized
# e2fsck -f /dev/vgusb/lvm_u1
e2fsck 1.40 (12-Jul-2007)
Pass 1: Checking inodes, blocks, and sizes
Pass 2: Checking directory structure
Pass 3: Checking directory connectivity
Pass 4: Checking reference counts
Pass 5: Checking group summary information
/dev/vgusb/lvm_u1: 12/3072 files (25.0% non-contiguous), 3379/12288 blocks
# resize2fs /dev/vgusb/lvm_u1 16M             Resize file system
resize2fs 1.38 (30-Jun-2005)
Resizing the filesystem on /dev/vgusb/lvm_u1 to 16384 (1k) blocks.
The filesystem on /dev/vgusb/lvm_u1 is now 16384 blocks long.
```

In the example just shown, the volume and the file system are both resized to 16M. Next, mount the volume again and check the disk space and the md5sum you created earlier:

```
# mount -t ext3 /dev/mapper/vgusb-lvm_u1 /mnt/u1   Remount volume
$ df -m /mnt/u1                                      See 4MB of 16MB used
Filesystem            1M-blocks     Used Available Use% Mounted on
/dev/mapper/vgusb-lvm_u1
                            16        4        13  20% /mnt/u1
$ md5sum /mnt/u1/vmlinuz-2.6.20-1.2316.fc5          Recheck md5sum
8d0dc0347d36ebd3f6f2b49047e1f525  /mnt/u1/vmlinuz-2.6.20-1.2316.fc5
```

The newly mounted volume is now 16MB instead of 10MB in size.

Shrinking an LVM Volume

You can also use the `lvresize` command if you want to **take unneeded space from an existing LVM volume**. As before, unmount the volume before resizing it and run `e2fsck` (to check the file system) and `resize2fs` (to resize it to the smaller size):

```
# umount /mnt/u1
$ e2fsck -f /dev/vgusb/lvm_u1
fsck 1.38 (30-Jun-2005)
e2fsck 1.38 (30-Jun-2005)
The filesystem size (according to the superblock) is 16384 blocks
The physical size of the device is 8192 blocks
Pass 1: Checking inodes, blocks, and sizes
...
/dev/vgusb/lvm_u1: 12/3072 files (8.3% non-continguous,3531/16384 blocks
# resize2fs /dev/vgusb/lvm_u1 12M            Resize file system
resize2fs 1.38 (30-Jun-2005)
Resizing the filesystem on /dev/vgusb/lvm_u1 to 12288 (1k) blocks.
The filesystem on /dev/vgusb/lvm_u1 is now 12288 blocks long.
# lvresize --size 12M /dev/vgusb/lvm_u1
  WARNING: Reducing active logical volume to 12.00 MB
  THIS MAY DESTROY YOUR DATA (filesystem etc.)
Do you really want to reduce lvm_u1? [y/n]: y
  Reducing logical volume lvm_u1 to 8.00 MB
  Logical volume lvm_u1 successfully resized
# mount -t ext3 /dev/mapper/vgusb-lvm_u1 /mnt/u1  Remount volume
$ df -m /mnt/u1                               See 4MB of 12MB used
Filesystem          1M-blocks     Used Available Use% Mounted on
/dev/mapper/vgusb-lvm_u1
                         12        4         9  20% /mnt/u1
```

The newly mounted volume appears now as 12MB instead of 16MB in size.

Removing LVM Logical Volumes and Groups

To **remove an LVM logical volume from a volume group**, use the `lvremove` command as follows:

```
# lvremove /dev/vgusb/lvm_u1
Do you really want to remove active logical volume "lvm_u1"? [y/n]: y
  Logical volume "lvm_u1" successfully removed
```

To remove an existing LVM volume group, use the `vgremove` command:

```
# vgremove vgusb
  Volume group "vgusb" successfully removed
```

There are many more ways to work with LVM. Refer to the LVM HOWTO for further information (`http://tldp.org/HOWTO/LVM-HOWTO/`).

Summary

Creating and managing file systems in Linux is a critical part of Linux system administration. Linux contains support for several standard Linux file system types (ext2, ext3, reiserfs, and others). It can also create and manage Windows file system types (VFAT, NTFS, and so on) as well as legacy and specialty Linux and Unix file system types (such as minix, jfs, and xfs).

You can partition hard disks with commands such as `fdisk` and `parted`. Tools for working with file systems include those that create file systems (`mkfs`), view and modify file system attributes (`tune2fs` and `dumpe2fs`), mount/unmount file systems (`mount` and `umount`), and check for problems (`badblocks` and `fsck`). To see how much space has been used in file systems, use the `df` and `du` commands.

8

Backups and Removable Media

Data backups in Linux were traditionally done by running commands to archive and compress the files to back up, then writing that backup archive to tape. Choices for archive tools, compression techniques, and backup media have grown tremendously in recent years. Tape archiving has, for many, been replaced with techniques for backing up data over the network, to other hard disks, or to CDs, DVDs, or other low-cost removable media.

This chapter details some useful tools for backing up and restoring your critical data. The first part of the chapter details how to use basic tools such as tar, gzip, and rsync for backups.

Backing Up Data to Compressed Archives

If you are coming from a Windows background, you may be used to tools such as WinZip and PKZIP, which both archive and compress groups of files in one application. Linux offers separate tools for gathering groups of files into a single archive (such as tar) and compressing that archive for efficient storage (gzip, bzip2, and lzop). However, you can also do the two steps together by using additional options to the tar command.

Creating Backup Archives with tar

The tar command, which stands for *tape archiver*, dates back to early Unix systems. Although magnetic tape was the common medium that tar wrote to originally, today tar is most often used to create an archive file that can be distributed to a variety of media.

The fact that the `tar` command is rich in features is reflected in the dozens of options available with `tar`. The basic operations of `tar`, however, are used to create a backup archive (-c), extract files from an archive (-x), compare differences between archives (-d), and update files in an archive (-u). You can also append files to (-r or -A) or delete files from (-d) an existing archive, or list the contents of an archive (-t).

NOTE *Although the `tar` command is available on nearly all Unix and Linux systems, it behaves differently on many systems. For example, Solaris does not support -z to manage tar archives compressed in gzip format. The* `Star` *(ess-tar) command supports access control lists (ACLs) and file flags (for extended permissions used by Samba).*

As part of the process of creating a tar archive, you can add options that compress the resulting archive. For example, add -j to compress the archive in bzip2 format or -z to compress in gzip format. By convention, regular tar files end in .tar, while compressed tar files end in .tar.bz2 (compressed with bzip2) or .tar.gz (compressed with gzip). If you compress a file manually with `lzop` (see www.lzop.org), the compressed tar file should end in .tar.lzo.

Besides being used for backups, tar files are popular ways to distribute source code and binaries from software projects. That's because you can expect every Linux and Unix-like system to contain the tools you need to work with tar files.

NOTE *One quirk of working with the `tar` command comes from the fact that tar was created before there were standards regarding how options are entered. Although you can prefix `tar` options with a dash, it isn't always necessary. So you might see a command that begins `tar` xvf with no dashes to indicate the options.*

A classic example for using the `tar` command might combine old-style options and pipes for compressing the output; for example:

```
$ tar c *.txt | gzip -c > myfiles.tar.gz Make archive, zip it, and output
```

The example just shown illustrates a two-step process you might find in documentation for old Unix systems. The `tar` command creates (c) an archive from all .txt files in the current directory. The output is piped to the `gzip` command and output to stdout (-c), and then redirected to the `myfiles.tar.gz` file. Note that `tar` is one of the few commands which don't require that options be preceded by a dash (-).

New tar versions, on modern Linux systems, can **create the archive and compress the output** in one step:

```
$ tar czf myfiles.tar.gz *.txt    Create gzipped tar file of .txt files
$ tar czvf myfiles.tar.gz *.txt   Be more verbose creating archive
textfile1.txt
textfile2.txt
```

In the examples just shown, note that the new archive name (myfiles.tar.gz) must immediately follow the f option to tar (which indicates the name of the archive). Otherwise the output from tar will be directed to stdout (in other words, your screen). The z option says to do gzip compression, and v produces verbose descriptions of processing.

When you want to **return the files to a file system** (unzipping and untarring), you can also do that as either a one-step or two-step process, using the tar command and optionally the gunzip command:

```
$ gunzip -c myfiles.tar.gz | tar x          Unzips and untars archive
```

Or try the following command line instead:

```
$ gunzip myfiles.tar.gz ; tar xf myfiles.tar   Unzips then untars archive
```

To do that same procedure in one step, you could use the following command:

```
$ tar xzvf myfiles.tar.gz
textfile1.txt
textfile2.txt
```

The result of the previous commands is that the archived .txt files are copied from the archive to the current directory. The x option extracts the files, z uncompresses (unzips) the files, v makes the output, and f indicates that the next option is the name of the archive file (myfiles.tar.gz).

Using Compression Tools

Compression is an important aspect of working with backup files. It takes less disk space on your backup medium (CD, DVD, tape, and so on) or server to store compressed files. It also takes less time to transfer the archives to the media or download the files over a network.

While compression can save a lot of storage space and transfer times, it can significantly increase your CPU usage. You can consider using hardware compression on a tape drive (see www.amanda.org/docs/faq.html#id346016).

In the examples shown in the previous section, tar calls the gzip command. But tar can work with many compression tools. Out of the box on Fedora, tar will work with gzip and bzip2. A third compression utility we add to our toolbox is the lzop command, which can be used with tar in a different way. The order of these tools from fastest/least compression to slowest/most compression is: lzop, gzip, and bzip2.

If you are archiving and compressing large amounts of data, the time it takes to compress your backups can be significant. So you should be aware that, in general, bzip2 may take about 10 times longer than lzop and only give you twice the compression. However, with each compression command, you can choose different compression levels, to balance the need for more compression with the time that compression takes.

To use the tar command with **bzip2 compression**, use the -j option:

```
$ tar cjvf myfiles.tar.bz2 *.txt     Create archive, compress with bzip2
```

You can also **uncompress (-j) a bzip2 compressed file** as you extract files (-x) using the tar command:

```
$ tar xjvf myfiles.tar.bz2     Extract files, uncompress bzip2 compression
```

The lzop compression utility is a bit less integrated into tar. Before you can use lzop, you might need to install the lzop package. To do **lzop compression**, you need the --use-compress-program option:

```
# yum install lzop
$ tar --use-compress-program=lzop -cf myfiles.tar.lzo *.txt
$ tar --use-compress-program=lzop -xf myfiles.tar.lzo
```

In the previous examples, the command line reverses the old syntax of tar with a switch before the command. For normal use and in other examples, we used the modern syntax of tar with no switch.

> **NOTE** *You may encounter .rar compressed files in the RAR format. This format seems to be popular in the world of peer-to-peer networks. RAR is a proprietary format so there is no widespread compressing tool. The FreshRPMs.net repository has a rar RPM package for some versions of Fedora. The unrar command, on the other hand, is more widely available. The Livna.org repository has an unrar RPM package for Fedora.*

Compressing with gzip

As noted, you can **use any of the compression commands alone** (as opposed to within the tar command line). Here are some examples of the gzip command to create and work with gzip-compressed files:

```
$ gzip myfile               gzips myfile and renames it myfile.gz
```

The following command provides the same result, with verbose output:

```
$ gzip -v myfile            gzips myfile with verbose output
myfile: 86.0% -- replaced with myfile.gz
$ gzip -tv myfile.gz        Tests integrity of gzip file
myfile.gz:    OK
```

```
$ gzip -lv myfile.gz          Get detailed info about gzip file
method  crc    date time    compressed   uncompressed  ratio uncompressed_name
defla 0f27d9e4 Jul 10 04:48     46785       334045       86.0%  myfile
```

Use any one of the following commands to **compress all files in a directory**:

```
$ gzip -rv mydir              Compress all files in a directory
mydir/file1: 39.1% -- replaced with mydir/file1.gz
mydir/file2: 39.5% -- replaced with mydir/file2.gz
$ gzip -1 myfile       Fastest compression time, least compression
$ gzip -9 myfile       Slowest compression time, most compression
```

Add a dash before a number from 1 to 9 to set the compression level. As illustrated above, -1 is the fastest (least) and -9 is the slowest (most) compression. The default for gzip is level 6. The lzop command has fewer levels: 1, 3 (default), 7, 8, and 9. Compression levels for bzip2 behave differently.

To **uncompress a gzipped file**, you can use the gunzip command. Use either of the following examples:

```
$ gunzip -v myfile.gz         Unzips myfile.gz and renames it myfile
myfile.gz:       86.0% -- replaced with myfile
$ gzip -dv myfile.gz          Same as previous command line
```

Although the examples just shown refer to zipping regular files, the same options can be used to compress tar archives.

Compressing with bzip2

The **bzip2 command** is considered to provide the highest compression among the compression tools described in this chapter. Here are some examples of bzip2:

```
$ bzip2 myfile             Compresses file and renames it myfile.bz2
$ bzip2 -v myfile          Same as previous command, but more verbose
  myfile:  9.529:1, 0.840 bits/byte, 89.51% saved, 334045 in, 35056 out.
$ bunzip2 myfile.bz2       Uncompresses file and renames it myfile
$ bzip2 -d myfile.bz2      Same as previous command
$ bunzip2 -v myfile.bz2    Same as previous command, but more verbose
  myfile.bz2: done
```

Compressing with lzop

The lzop command behaves differently from gzip and bzip2. The lzop command is best in cases where compression speed is more important than the resulting compression ratio. When lzop compresses the contents of a file, it leaves the original file intact (unless you use -U), but creates a new file with a .lzo suffix. Use either of the following examples of the **lzop command to compress a file called myfile**:

```
$ lzop -v myfile          Leave myfile, create compressed myfile.lzo
compressing myfile into myfile.lzo
$ lzop -U myfile          Remove myfile, create compressed myfile.lzo
```

135

With **myfile.lzo** created, choose any of the following commands to **test, list, or uncompress** the file:

```
$ lzop -t myfile.lzo        Test the compressed file's integrity
$ lzop --info myfile.lzo    List internal header for each file
$ lzop -l myfile.lzo        List compression info for each file
method   compressed  uncompr. ratio uncompressed_name
LZO1X-1     59008      99468  59.3% myfile
$ lzop --ls myfile.lzo      Show contents of compressed file as ls -l
$ cat myfile | lzop > x.lzo Compress standin and direct to stdout
$ lzop -dv myfile.lzo       Leave myfile.lzo, make uncompressed myfile
```

Unlike gzip and bzip2, lzop has no related command for unlzopping. Always just use the -d option to lzop to uncompress a file. If fed a list of file and directory names, the lzop command will compress all files and ignore directories. The original file name, permission modes, and timestamps are used on the compressed file as were used on the original file.

Listing, Joining, and Adding Files to tar Archives

So far, all we've done with tar is create and unpack archives. There are also options for listing the contents of archives, joining archives, adding files to an existing archive, and deleting files from an archive.

To **list an archive's contents,** use the -t option:

```
$ tar tvf myfiles.tar            List files from uncompressed archive
-rw-r--r-- root/root        9584 2007-07-05 11:20:33 textfile1.txt
-rw-r--r-- root/root        9584 2007-07-09 10:23:44 textfile2.txt
$ tar tzvf myfiles.tgz           List files from gzip compressed archive
```

If the archive were a tar archive compressed with lzop and named myfile.tar.lzo, you could **list that tar/lzop file's contents** as follows:

```
$ tar --use-compress-program=lzop -tf myfiles.tar.lzo  List lzo archives
```

To **concatenate one tar file to another,** use the -A option. The following command results in the contents of archive2.tar being added to the archive1.tar archive:

```
$ tar -Af archive1.tar archive2.tar
```

Use the -r option to **add one or more files to an existing archive.** In the following example, myfile is added to the archive.tar archive file:

```
$ tar rvf archive.tar myfile     Add a file to a tar archive
```

You can use wildcards to **match multiple files to add** to your archive:

```
$ tar rvf archive.tar *.txt      Add multiple files to a tar archive
```

Deleting Files from tar Archives

If you have a tar archive file on your hard disk, you can delete files from that archive. Note that you can't use this technique to delete files from tar output on magnetic tape. Here is an example of **deleting files from a tar archive**:

```
$ tar --delete file1.txt -f myfile.tar     Delete file1.txt from myfile.tar
```

Backing Up Over Networks

After you have backed up your files and gathered them into a tar archive, what do you do with that archive? The primary reason for having a backup is in case something happens (such as a hard disk crash) where you need to restore files from that backup. Methods you can employ to keep those backups safe include:

❑ **Copying backups to removable media** such as tape, CD, or DVD (as described later in this chapter)

❑ **Copying them to another machine over a network**

Fast and reliable networks, inexpensive high-capacity hard disks, and the security that comes with moving your data off-site have all made network backups a popular practice. For an individual backing up personal data or a small office, combining a few simple commands may be all you need to create efficient and secure backups. This approach represents a direct application of the Unix philosophy: joining together simple programs that do one thing to get a more complex job done.

Although just about any command that can copy files over a network can be used to move your backup data to a remote machine, some utilities are especially good for the job. Using OpenSSH tools such as ssh and scp, you can set up secure password-less transfers of backup archives and encrypted transmissions of those archives.

Tools such as the rsync command can save resources by backing up only files (or parts of files) that have changed since the previous backup. With tools such as unison, you can back up files over a network from Windows, as well as Linux systems.

The following sections describe some of these techniques for backing up your data to other machines over a network.

> **NOTE** *A similar tool that might interest you is the* rsnapshot *command (*yum install rsnapshot*). The* rsnapshot *command (*www.rsnapshot.org/*) can work with* rsync *to make configurable hourly, daily, weekly, or monthly snapshots of a file system. It uses hard links to keep a snapshot of a file system, which it can then sync with changed files.*

Backing Up tar Archives Over ssh

OpenSSH (www.openssh.org/) provides tools to securely do remote login, remote execution, and remote file copy over network interfaces. By setting up two machines to share encryption keys, you can transfer files between those machines without entering passwords for each transmission. That fact lets you create scripts to back up your data from an SSH client to an SSH server, without any manual intervention.

From a central Linux system, you can **gather backups from multiple client machines** using OpenSSH commands. The following example runs the `tar` command on a remote site (to archive and compress the files), pipes the tar stream to standard output, and uses the `ssh` command to catch the backup locally (over `ssh`) with `tar`:

```
$ mkdir mybackup ; cd mybackup
$ ssh francois@server1 'tar cf - myfile*' | tar xvf -
francois@server1's password: ******
myfile1
myfile2
```

In the example just shown, all files beginning with `myfile` are copied from the home directory of francois on server1 and placed in the current directory. Note that the left side of the pipe creates the archive and the right side expands the files from the archive to the current directory. (Keep in mind that ssh will overwrite local files if they exist, which is why we created an empty directory in the example.)

To reverse the process and **copy files from the local system to the remote system,** we run a local `tar` command first. This time, however, we add a `cd` command to put the files in the directory of our choice on the remote machine:

```
$ tar cf - myfile* | ssh francois@server1 \
        'cd /home/francois/myfolder; tar xvf -'
francois@server1's password: ******
myfile1
myfile2
```

In this next example, we're not going to untar the files on the receiving end, but instead **write the results to tgz files:**

```
$ ssh francois@server1 'tar czf - myfile*' | cat > myfiles.tgz
$ tar cvzf - myfile* | ssh francois@server1 'cat > myfiles.tgz'
```

The first example takes all files beginning with `myfile` from the francois user's home directory on server1, `tars` and compresses those files, and directs those compressed files to the `myfiles.tgz` file on the local system. The second example does the reverse by taking all files beginning with `myfile` in the local directory and sending them to a `myfiles.tgz` file on the remote system.

The examples just shown are good for copying files over the network. Besides providing compression they also enable you to use any `tar` features you choose, such as incremental backup features.

Backing Up Files with rsync

A more feature-rich command for doing backups is rsync. What makes rsync so unique is the rsync algorithm, which compares the local and remote files one small block at a time using checksums, and only transfers the blocks that are different. This algorithm is so efficient that it has been reused in many backup products.

The rsync command can work either on top of a remote shell (ssh), or by running an rsyncd daemon on the server end. The following example uses rsync over ssh to mirror a directory:

```
$ rsync -avz --delete chris@server1:/home/chris/pics/ chrispics/
```

The command just shown is intended to mirror the remote directory structure (/home/chris/pics/) on the local system. The -a says to run in archive mode (recursively copying all files from the remote directory), the -z option compresses the files, and -v makes the output verbose. The --delete tells rsync to delete any files on the local system that no longer exist on the remote system.

For ongoing backups, you can have rsync do seven-day incremental backups. Here's an example:

```
# mkdir /var/backups
# rsync --delete --backup                                 \
    --backup-dir=/var/backups/backup-`date +%A` \
    -avz chris@server1:/home/chris/Personal/     \
    /var/backups/current-backup/
```

When the command just shown runs, all the files from /home/chris/Personal on the remote system server1 are copied to the local directory /var/backups/current-backup. All files modified today are copied to a directory named after today's day of the week, such as /var/backups/backup-Monday. Over a week, seven directories will be created that reflect changes over each of the past seven days.

Another trick for rotated backups is to use hard links instead of multiple copies of the files. This two-step process consists of rotating the files, then running rsync:

```
# rm -rf /var/backups/backup-old/
# mv /var/backups/backup-current/ /var/backups/backup-old/
# rsync --delete --link-dest=/var/backups/backup-old -avz \
    chris@server1:/home/chris/Personal/ /var/backups/backup-current/
```

In the previous procedure, the existing backup-current directory replaces the backup-old directory, deleting the two-week-old full backup with last-week's full backup. When the new full backup is run with rsync using the --link-dest option, if any of the files being backed up from the remote Personal directory on server1 existed during the previous backup (now in backup-old), a hard link is created between the file in the backup-current directory and backup-old directory.

You can save a lot of space by having hard links between files in your backup-old and backup-current directory. For example, if you had a file named file1.txt in both directories, you could check that both were the same physical file by listing the files' inodes as follows:

```
$ ls -i /var/backups/backup*/file1.txt
260761   /var/backups/backup-current/file1.txt
260761   /var/backups/backup-old/file1.txt
```

Backing Up with unison

Although the rsync command is good to back up one machine to another, it assumes that the machine being backed up is the only one where the data is being modified. What if you have two machines that both modify the same file and you want to sync those files? Unison is a tool that will let you do that.

It's common for people to want to work with the same documents on their laptop and desktop systems. Those machines might even run different operating systems. Because unison is a cross-platform application, it can let you **sync files** that are on both Linux and Windows systems. To use unison in Fedora, you must install the unison package (type the yum install unison command).

With unison, you can define two *roots* representing the two paths to synchronize. Those roots can be local or remote over ssh. For example:

```
$ unison /home/francois ssh://francois@server1//home/fcaen
$ unison /home/francois /mnt/backups/francois-homedir
```

Unison contains both graphical and command-line tools for doing unison backups. It will try to run the graphical version by default. This may fail if you don't have a desktop running or if you're launching unison from within screen. To **force unison to run in command line mode,** add the -ui text option as follows:

```
$ unison /home/francois ssh://francois@server1//home/fcaen -ui text
Contacting server...
francois@server1's password:
Looking for changes
   Waiting for changes from server
Reconciling changes
local          server1
newfile ---->            memo.txt   [f] y
Propagating updates
   ...
```

The unison utility will then compare the two roots and for each change that occurred since last time, ask you what you want to do. In the example above, there's a new file called memo.txt on the local system. You are asked if you want to proceed with the update (in this case, copy memo.txt from the local machine to server1). Type y to do the updates.

If you trust unison, add -auto to make it take default actions without prompting you:

```
$ unison /home/francois ssh://francois@server1//home/fcaen -auto
```

There is no man page for unison. However, you can view unison options using the -help option. You can also display and page through the unison manual using the -doc all option as shown here:

```
$ unison -help                    See unison options
$ unison -doc all | less          Display unison manual
```

If you find yourself synchronizing two roots frequently, you can create a profile, which is a series of presets. In graphical mode, the default screen makes you create profiles. Profiles are stored in .prf text files in the ~/.unison/ directory. They can be as simple as the following:

```
root = /home/francois
root = ssh://francois@server1//home/fcaen
```

If this is stored in a profile called fc-home.prf, you can invoke it simply with the following command line:

```
$ unison fc-home
```

Backing Up to Removable Media

The capacity of CDs and DVDs, and the low costs of those media, has made them attractive options as computer backup media. Using tools that commonly come with Linux systems, you can gather files to back up into CD or DVD images and burn those images to the appropriate media.

Command line tools such as mkisofs (for creating CD images) and cdrecord (for burning images to CD or DVD) once provided the most popular interfaces for making backups to CD or DVD. Now there are many graphical front-ends to those tools you could also consider using. For example, GUI tools for mastering and burning CDs/DVDs include K3b (the KDE CD and DVD Kreator) and Nautilus (GNOME's file manager that offers a CD-burning feature). Other GUI tools for burning CDs include gcombust, X-CD-Roast, and graveman.

The commands for creating file system images to back up to CD or DVD, as well as to burn those images, are described in this section.

Creating Backup Images with mkisofs

Most data CDs and DVDs can be accessed on both Windows and Linux systems because they are created using the ISO9660 standard for formatting the information on those discs. Because most modern operating systems need to save more information about files and directories than the basic ISO9660 standard includes, extensions to that standard were added to contain that information.

Using the mkisofs command, you can back up the file and directory structure from any point in your Linux file system and produce an ISO9660 image. That image can include the following kinds of extensions:

❑ **System Use Sharing Protocol** (SUSP) are records identified in the Rock Ridge Interchange Protocol. SUSP records can include Unix-style attributes, such as ownership, long file names, and special files (such as character devices and symbolic links).

❑ **Joliet** directory records store longer file names in a form that makes them usable to Windows systems.

❑ **Hierarchical File System** (HFS) extensions allow the ISO image to appear as an HFS file system, which is the native file system for Macintosh computers. Likewise, Data and Resource forks can be added in different ways to be read by Macs.

When you set out to create your ISO image, consider where you will ultimately need to access the files you back up using mkisofs (Linux, Windows, or Macs). Once the image is created, it can be used in different ways, the most obvious of which is to burn the image to a CD or DVD.

Besides being useful in producing all or portions of a Linux file system to use on a portable medium, mkisofs is also useful for creating live CDs/DVDs. It does this by adding boot information to the image that can launch a Linux kernel or other operating system, bypassing the computer's hard drive.

> **NOTE** *Although you can still use the* mkisofs *command in Fedora,* mkisofs *is now a pointer to* genisoimage. *The* genisoimage *command was derived from* mkisofs, *which was part of the* cdrtools *package (see* http://cdrecord .berlios.de). *Development of* genisoimage *is part of the cdrkit project* (www.cdrkit.org).

Because most Linux users store their personal files in their home directories, a common way to use mkisofs to back up files is to back up everything under the /home directory. Here are some examples of using mkisofs to **create an ISO image from all files and directories under the /home directory:**

```
# cd /tmp
# mkisofs -o home.iso /home              Create basic ISO9660 image
# mkisofs -o home2.iso -J -R /home       Add Joliet Rock Ridge extensions
# mkisofs -o home3.iso -J -R -hfs /home  Also add HFS extensions
```

In each of the three examples above, all files and directories beneath the /home directory are added to the ISO image (home.iso). The first example has no extensions, so all file names are converted to DOS-style naming (8.3 characters). The second example uses Joliet and Rock Ridge extensions, so file names and permissions should appear as they did on the original Linux system when you open the ISO on a Linux or Windows system. The last example also makes the files on the image readable from a Mac file system.

You can **have multiple sources added to the image.** Here are some examples:

```
# mkisofs -o home.iso -R -J music/ docs/ \   Multiple directories/files
        chris.pdf /var/spool/mail
# mkisofs -o home.iso -J -R              \   Graft files on to the image
    -graft-points Pictures/=/var/pics/  \
    /home/chris
```

The first example above shows various files and directories being combined and placed on the root of the ISO image. The second example grafts the contents of the /var/pics directory into the /home/chris/Pictures directory. As a result, on the CD image the /Pictures directory will contain all content from the /var/pics directory.

Adding information into the header of the ISO image can help you identify the contents of that image later. This is especially useful if the image is being saved or distributed online, without a physical disc you can write on. Here are some examples:

```
# mkisofs -o /tmp/home.iso -R -J           \   Add header info to ISO
    -p www.handsonhistory.com             \
    -publisher "Swan Bay Folk Art Center"  \
    -V "WebBackup"                         \
    -A "mkisofs"                           \
    -volset "1 of 4 backups, July 30, 2007" \
    /home/chris
```

In the example above, -p indicates the preparer ID, which could include a phone number, mailing address, or web site for contacting the preparer of the ISO image. With the option -publisher, you can indicate a 128-character description of the preparer (possibly the company or organization name). The -V indicates the volume ID. Volume ID is important because in many Linux systems, this volume ID is used to mount the CD when it is inserted. For example, in the command line shown above, the CD would be mounted on /media/WebBackup in Fedora and other Linux systems. The -A option can be used to indicate the application used to create the ISO image. The -volset option can contain a string of information about a set of ISO images.

When you have created your ISO image, and before you burn it to disc, you **can check the image** and make sure you can access the files it contains. Here are ways to check it out:

```
# volname home.iso              Display volume name
WebBackup
# isoinfo -d -i home.iso        Display header information
CD-ROM is in ISO 9660 format
System id: LINUX
```

```
Volume id: WebBackup
Volume set id: All Website material on November 2, 2007
Publisher id: Swan Bay Folk Art Center
Data preparer id: www.handsonhistory.com
Application id: mkisofs
Copyright File id:
Abstract File id:
Bibliographic File id:
Volume set size is: 1
Volume set sequence number is: 1
Logical block size is: 2048
Volume size is: 23805
Joliet with UCS level 3 found
Rock Ridge signatures version 1 found
```

You can see a lot of the information entered on the `mkisofs` command line when the image was created. If this had been an image that was going to be published, we might also have indicated the locations on the CD of a copyright file (`-copyright`), abstract file (`-abstract`), and bibliographic file (`-biblio`). Provided that the header is okay, you can next try accessing files on the ISO image by mounting it:

```
# mkdir /mnt/myimage                        Create a mount point
# mount -o loop home.iso /mnt/myimage       Mount the ISO in loopback
# ls -l /mnt/myimage                        Check the ISO contents
# umount /mnt/myimage                       Unmount the image when done
```

Besides checking that you can access the files and directories on the ISO, make sure that the date/time stamps, ownership, and permissions are set as you would like. That information might be useful if you need to restore the information at a later date.

Burning Backup Images with cdrecord

The `cdrecord` command is the most popular Linux command line tool for burning CD and DVD images. After you have created an ISO image (as described earlier) or obtained one otherwise (such as downloading an install CD or live CD from the Internet), `cdrecord` makes it easy to put that image on a disc.

> **NOTE** *As of Fedora 7, `cdrecord` was replaced with the `wodim` command. The `wodim` command was created from the `cdrecord` code base and still supports most of the same options. If you run `cdrecord`, you will actually be running `wodim` in this Fedora release. If you have problems with that utility, contact the CDRkit project (`http://cdrkit.org`).*

There is no difference in making a CD or DVD ISO image, aside from the fact that a DVD image can obviously be bigger than a CD image. Check the media you have for their capacities. A CD can typically hold 650MB, 700MB, or 800MB, whereas mini CDs can hold 50MB, 180MB, 185MB, or 193MB. Single-layer DVDs hold 4.7GB, while double-layer DVDs can hold 8.4GB.

NOTE *Keep in mind, however, that CD/DVD manufacturers list their capacities based on 1000 KB per 1 MB, instead of 1024 KB. Type* du --si home.iso *to list the size of your ISO, instead of* du -sh *as you would normally, to check if your ISO will fit on the media you have.*

Before you begin burning your image to CD or DVD, check that your drive supports CD/DVD burning and determine the address of the drive. Use the --scanbus option to cdrecord to do that:

```
# cdrecord --scanbus          Shows a drive that cannot do burning
scsibus0:
        0,0,0  0) 'SAMSUNG ' 'DVD-ROM SD-616E ' 'F503' Removable CD-ROM
        0,0,0  1) *
        0,0,0  2) *
               . . .
# cdrecord --scanbus          Shows a drive that can burn CDs or DVDs
scsibus0:
        0,0,0  0) 'LITE-ON ' 'DVDRW SOHW-1633S' 'BS0C' Removable CD-ROM
        0,0,0  1) *
        0,0,0  2) *
               . . .
```

In the two examples shown, the first indicates a CD/DVD drive that only supports reading and cannot burn CDs (DVD-ROM and CD-ROM). The second example shows a drive that can burn CDs or DVDs (DVDRW). Insert the medium you want to record on. Assuming your drive can burn the media you have, here are some simple cdrecord commands for burning a CD or DVD images:

```
# cdrecord -dummy home.iso         Test burn without actually burning
# cdrecord -v home.iso             Burn CD (default settings) in verbose
# cdrecord -v speed=24 home.iso    Set specific speed
# cdrecord -pad home.iso           Can't read track so add 15 zeroed sectors
# cdrecord -eject home.iso         Eject CD/DVD when burn is done
# cdrecord /dev/cdrw home.iso      Identify drive by device name (may differ)
# cdrecord dev=0,2,0 home.iso      Identify drive by SCSI name
```

The cdrecord command can also burn multi-session CDs/DVDs. Here is an example:

```
# cdrecord -multi home.iso     Start a multi-burn session
# cdrecord -msinfo             Check the session offset for next burn
Using /dev/cdrom of unknown capabilities
0,93041
# mkisofs -J -R -o new.iso \   Create a second ISO to burn
  -C 0,93041 /home/chris/more  Indicate start point and new data for ISO
# cdrecord new.iso             Burn new data to existing CD
```

You can use multiple -multi burns until the CD is filled up. For the final burn, don't use -multi, so that the CD will be closed.

Making and Burning DVDs with growisofs

Using the `growisofs` command, you can **combine the two steps of gathering files into an ISO image (mkisofs) and burning that image to DVD (cdrecord)**. Besides saving a step, the `growisofs` command also offers the advantage of keeping a session open by default until you close it, so you don't need to do anything special for multi-burn sessions.

Here is an example of some `growisofs` commands for a **multi-burn session**:

```
# growisofs -Z /dev/dvd -R -J /home/chris      Master and burn to DVD
# growisofs -Z /dev/dvd -R -J /home/francois   Add to burn
# growisofs -M /dev/dvd=/dev/zero              Close burn
```

If you want to add options when creating the ISO image, you can simply add `mkisofs` options to the command line. (For example, see how the `-R` and `-J` options are added in the above examples.)

If you want to **burn a DVD image using growisofs**, you can use the **-dvd-compat** option. Here's an example:

```
# growisofs -dvd-compat -Z /dev/dvd=image.iso Burn an ISO image to DVD
```

The `-dvd-compat` option can improve compatibility with different DVD drives over some multi-session DVD burning procedures.

Summary

Linux and its predecessor Unix systems handled data backups by combining commands that each handled a discrete set of features. Backups of your critical data can still be done in this way. In fact, many of the tools you can use will perform more securely and efficiently than ever before.

The tape archiver utility (`tar` command) has expanded well beyond its original job of making magnetic tape backups of data files. Because nearly every Linux and UNIX system includes `tar`, it has become a standard utility for packaging software and backing up data to compressed archives. Those archives can then be transported and stored in a variety of ways.

To move backed up data to other machines over a network, you can use remote execution features of OpenSSH tools (such as `ssh`). You can also use an excellent utility called `rsync`. With `rsync`, you can save resources by only backing up files (or parts of files) that have changed.

Inexpensive CDs and DVDs have made those media popular for doing personal and small-office backups. The `mkisofs` command can create file systems of backed up data in ISO9660 format that can be restored on a variety of systems (Linux, Windows, or Mac). Once `mkisofs` command has created an ISO image, the image can be burned to CD or DVD using the `cdrecord` or `growisofs` command.

9

Checking and Managing Running Processes

When an executable program starts up, it runs as a process that is under the management of your Linux system's process table. Linux provides all the tools you need to view and change the processes running on your system.

The ps and top commands are great for viewing information on your running processes. There are literally dozens of options to ps and top to help you view process information exactly the way you want to. The pgrep command can further help find the process you want.

There are commands such as nice and renice for raising and lowering processor priority for a process. You can move processes to run in the background (bg command) or back to the foreground (fg command).

Sending signals to a process is a way of changing its behavior or killing it altogether. Using the kill and killall commands, you can send signals to processes by PID or name, respectively. You can also send other signals to processes to do such things as reread configuration files or continue with a stopped process.

To run commands at scheduled times or so they are not tied to your shell session, you can use the at and batch commands. To run commands repetitively at set times, there are the cron and anacron facilities. Or you can drop scripts (or symbolic links to scripts) into /etc/cron.hourly (or cron.daily, cron.weekly, or cron.monthly).

Listing Active Processes

To see which processes are currently running on a system, most people use the ps and top commands. The ps command gives you a snapshot (in a simple list) of processes running at the moment. The top command offers a screen-oriented, constantly updated listing of running commands, sorted as you choose (by CPU use, memory use, UID, and so on).

Viewing Active Processes with ps

Every Linux system (as well as every system derived from Unix, such as BSD, Mac OS X, and others) includes the ps command. Over the years, however, many slightly different versions of ps have appeared, offering slightly different options. Because ps dates back to the first Unix systems, it also supports nonstandard ways of entering some options (for example, allowing you to drop the dash before an option in some cases).

The different uses of ps shown in this chapter will work on Fedora, RHEL, CentOS, and most other Linux systems. Here are some examples you can run to **show processes running for the current user** (Table 9-1 contains column descriptions of ps output):

```
$ ps                      List processes of current user at current shell
  PID TTY          TIME CMD
2552 pts/0     00:00:00 bash
3438 pts/0     00:00:00 ps
$ ps -u chris             Show all chris' running processes (simple output)
 PID   TTY  TIME COMMAND
2678  tty1 0:00 startx
2689  tty1 0:00 xinit
2710  tty1 0:06 gnome-session
  ...
$ ps -u chris u           Show all chris' running processes (with CPU/MEM)
USER     PID %CPU %MEM    VSZ    RSS TTY    STAT START TIME COMMAND
chris   2678  0.0  0.0   4328    852 tty1   S+   Aug14 0:00 /bin/sh startx
chris   2689  0.0  0.1   2408    488 tty1   S+   Aug14 0:00 xinit
chris   2710  0.0  1.1  22016   5496 tty1   S    Aug14 0:06 gnome-session
  ...
$ ps -fu chris            Show all chris' running processes (with PPID)
UID        PID  PPID  C STIME TTY          TIME CMD
chris     2678  2645  0 Aug14 tty1     00:00:00 /bin/sh /usr/X11R6/bin/startx
chris     2689  2678  0 Aug14 tty1     00:00:00 xinit /etc/X11/xinit/xinitrc
chris     2710  2689  0 Aug14 tty1     00:00:09 /usr/bin/gnome-session
  ...
$ ps -Fu chris            Show all chris' running processes (with SZ and PSR)
UID      PID  PPID  C    SZ   RSS PSR STIME TTY          TIME CMD
chris   2678  2645  0  1082   852   0 Aug14 tty1     00:00:00 /bin/sh startx
chris   2689  2678  0   602   488   0 Aug14 tty1     00:00:00 xinit
chris   2710  2689  0  5504  5440   0 Aug14 tty1     00:00:09 gnome-session
  ...
```

These examples illustrate some of the processes from a user running a GNOME desktop session. The first example above shows ps alone being run from a Terminal window, so you only see the processes for the current shell running in that window. Other examples let you display different information for each process (see later examples for ways of producing custom output). See Table 9-1 for descriptions of columns displayed by ps.

Here are ps examples showing output for **every process currently running on the system**:

```
$ ps -e                 Show every running process
  PID TTY          TIME CMD
    1 ?        00:00:01 init
    2 ?        00:00:00 migration/0
    3 ?        00:00:00 ksoftirqd/0
 . . .
$ ps -el                Show every running process, long listing
F S   UID   PID  PPID  C PRI  NI ADDR SZ WCHAN  TTY          TIME CMD
4 S     0     1     0  0  75   0 -   534 -      ?        00:00:01 init
1 S     0     2     1  0 -40   - -     0 -      ?        00:00:00 migration/0
1 S     0     3     1  0  94  19 -     0 -      ?        00:00:00 ksoftirqd/0
 . . .
$ ps -ef                Show every running process, full-format listing
UID        PID  PPID  C STIME TTY          TIME CMD
root         1     0  0 Aug05 ?        00:00:01 init [5]
root         2     1  0 Aug05 ?        00:00:00 [migration/0]
root         3     1  0 Aug05 ?        00:00:00 [ksoftirqd/0]
 . . .
$ ps -eF                Show every running process, extra full-format listing
UID        PID  PPID  C    SZ   RSS PSR STIME TTY          TIME CMD
root         1     0  0   534   556   0 Aug05 ?        00:00:01 init [5]
root         2     1  0     0     0   0 Aug05 ?        00:00:00 [migration/0]
root         3     1  0     0     0   0 Aug05 ?        00:00:00 [ksoftirqd/0]
 . . .
$ ps ax         Show every running process, short BSD style
  PID TTY      STAT   TIME COMMAND
    1 ?        Ss     0:01 init [5]
    2 ?        S      0:00 [migration/0]
    3 ?        SN     0:00 [ksoftirqd/0]
 . . .
$ ps aux        Show every running process, long BSD style
USER    PID %CPU %MEM    VSZ   RSS TTY      STAT START   TIME COMMAND
root      1  0.0  0.0   2136   556 ?        Ss   Aug05   0:01 init [5]
root      2  0.0  0.0      0     0 ?        S    Aug05   0:00 [migration/0]
root      3  0.0  0.0      0     0 ?        SN   Aug05   0:00 [ksoftirqd/0]
 . . .
$ ps auwx       Show every running process, long BSD style, wide format
$ ps auwwx      Show every running process, long BSD style, unlimited width
```

Some processes start up other processes. For example, a web server (httpd daemon) will spin off multiple httpd daemons to wait for requests to your web server. You can **view the hierarchy of processes (in a tree view)** using various options with ps:

```
$ ps -ejH               Show process hierarchy with process/session IDs
  PID  PGID   SID TTY          TIME CMD
    1     1     1 ?        00:00:01 init
    2     1     1 ?        00:00:00  migration/0
```

```
2043   2043   2043 ?          00:00:00     sshd
2549   2549   2549 ?          00:00:00       sshd
2551   2549   2549 ?          00:00:00         sshd
2552   2552   2552 pts/0      00:00:00            bash
7760   7760   7760 ?          00:00:00     httpd
7762   7760   7760 ?          00:00:00       httpd
7763   7760   7760 ?          00:00:00       httpd
```

$ ps axjf   *Show process hierarchy in BSD-style output*

```
 PPID   PID   PGID    SID TTY    TPGID STAT   UID     TIME COMMAND
    0     1      1      1 ?          -1 Ss       0    0:01 init [5]
    1     2      1      1 ?          -1 S        0    0:00 [migration/0]
    1  2043   2043   2043 ?          -1 Ss       0    0:00 /usr/sbin/sshd
 2043  2549   2549   2549 ?          -1 Ss       0    0:00 \_ sshd: chris [priv]
 2549  2551   2549   2549 ?          -1 S      500    0:00 |   \_ sshd: chris@pts
 2551  2552   2552   2552 pts/0    8398 Ss     500    0:00 |       \_ -bash
    1  7760   7760   7760 ?          -1 Ss       0    0:00 /usr/sbin/httpd
 7760  7762   7760   7760 ?          -1 S       48    0:00 \_ /usr/sbin/httpd
 7760  7763   7760   7760 ?          -1 S       48    0:00 \_ /usr/sbin/httpd
```

$ ps -ef --forest   *Show process hierarchy in forest format*

```
UID          PID  PPID  C STIME TTY          TIME CMD
root           1     0  0 Aug05 ?        00:00:01 init [5]
root           2     1  0 Aug05 ?        00:00:00 [migration/0]
root           3     1  0 Aug05 ?        00:00:00 [ksoftirqd/0]
root        2043     1  0 Aug05 ?        00:00:00 /usr/sbin/sshd
root        2549  2043  0 Aug16 ?        00:00:00  \_ sshd: chris [priv]
chris       2551  2549  0 Aug16 ?        00:00:00  |   \_ sshd: chris@pts/0
chris       2552  2551  0 Aug16 pts/0    00:00:00  |       \_ -bash
root        7760     1  0 18:27 ?        00:00:00 /usr/sbin/httpd
apache      7762  7760  0 18:27 ?        00:00:00  \_ /usr/sbin/httpd
apache      7763  7760  0 18:27 ?        00:00:00  \_ /usr/sbin/httpd
```

$ pstree   *Show processes alphabetically in tree format*

```
init-+-Xorg
     |-at-spi-registry
     |-atd
     |-auditd-+-audispd
     |         `-{auditd}
 ...
     |-sshd-+-sshd---sshd---bash---pstree
     |      |-sshd---sshd---bash---su---bash
     |      `-sshd---sshd---bash---su---bash---su---bash---vim
 ...
```

The "tree" examples just shown illustrate different ways of displaying the hierarchy of processes. The output was snipped to compare several of the same processes with different output. Note that the PPID (Parent Process ID) is the ID of the process that started each child process shown. The sshd processes show a running Secure Shell Daemon with a user logging in over the network, resulting in a bash shell (and eventually a vim editor) starting. The httpd daemon represents the Apache web server, with the parent started by the root user and child processes started as the apache user. The last example shows the pstree command, which is specifically used for displaying tree views of processes.

If you prefer personalized views of ps output, you can select exactly which columns of data to display with ps using the -o option. You can then use the --sort option to sort the output by any of those data. Table 9-1 shows available column output and the options to add to -o to have each column print with ps.

Table 9-1: Selecting and Viewing ps Column Output

Option	Column Head	Description
%cpu	%CPU	CPU utilization of process's lifetime in *00.0* format
%mem	%MEM	Percentage of process's machine's physical memory use (resident set size)
args	COMMAND	Command with all arguments
bsdstart	START	Start time of command started: *HH:MM* or *Mon Day*
bsdtime	TIME	Total (user and system) CPU time
comm	COMMAND	Command name only (no arguments shown)
cp	CP	CPU utilization in tenth-of-a-percentage
cputime	TIME	Total CPU time in [*DD-*]*HH:MM:SS* format
egid	EGID	Effective group ID of the process (as integer)
egroup	EGROUP	Effective group ID of the process (as name)
etime	ELAPSED	Time since process was started, in [[*DD-*]*HH:*]*MM:SS* format
euid	EUID	Effective user ID of the process (as integer)
euser	EUSER	Effective user ID of the process (as name)
fgid	FGID	File system access group ID (as number)
fgroup	FGROUP	File system access group ID (as name)
fname	COMMAND	First eight characters of command name
fuid	FUID	File system access user ID (as number)
fuser	FUSER	File system access user ID (as name)

Continued

Table 9-1: Selecting and Viewing ps Column Output (*continued*)

Option	Column Head	Description
lstart	STARTED	Date and time the command started
nice	NI	Nice value, from 19 (nicest) to –20 (CPU hog)
pgid	PGID	Process group ID of process
pid	PID	Process ID number of process
ppid	PPID	Parent process ID of process
psr	PSR	Processor process is assigned to (first CPU is 0)
rgid	RGID	Real group ID (as number)
rgroup	RGROUP	Real group (as name)
rss	RSS	Non-swapped physical memory (resident set size) in KB
rtprio	RTPRIO	Real-time priority
ruid	RUID	Real user ID (as number)
ruser	RUSER	Real user (as name)
s	S	One-character state display (**D**:sleep, no interrupt; **R**:running; **S**:sleep, can interrupt; **T**:stopped; **W**:paging; **X**:dead; **Z**:zombie)
sess	SESS	Session ID of session leader
sgi_p	P	Processor that process is currently running on
size	SZ	Rough amount of swap space needed if process were to swap out
start	STARTED	Time command started: *HH:MM:SS* or *Month Day*
start_time	START	Time command started: *HH:MM* or *MonthDay*
stat	STAT	Multi-character state: One-character "s" state plus other state characters (<:High priority; **N**:Low priority; **L**:Has pages locked in memory; **s**:Is session leader; **l**:Multi-threaded; +:in foreground process group)
sz	SZ	Size of process's core image (physical pages)

Table 9-1: Selecting and Viewing ps Column Output (*continued*)

Option	Column Head	Description
tname	TTY	Controlling tty (terminal)
user	USER	Effective user ID of process (as name)
vsize	VSZ	Process's virtual memory (1024-byte units)

Note that some values that are meant to print user names may still print numbers (UIDs) instead, if the name is too long to fit in the given space.

Using a comma-separated list of column options, you can produce your custom output. Here are some examples of custom views of running processes:

```
$ ps -eo ppid,user,%mem,size,vsize,comm --sort=-size      Sort by mem use
  PPID USER     %MEM    SZ    VSZ COMMAND
     1 root     27.0 68176  84264 yum-updatesd
$ ps -eo ppid,user,bsdstart,bsdtime,%cpu,args --sort=-%cpu  Sort by CPU use
  PPID USER      START    TIME %CPU COMMAND
     1 root      Jul 30  44:20 27.1 /usr/bin/python /usr/sbin/yum-updatesd
$ ps -eo ppid,user,nice,cputime,args --sort=-nice     Sort by low priority
  PPID USER      NI    TIME COMMAND
     1 root      19 00:44:26 /usr/bin/python /usr/sbin/yum-updatesd
$ ps -eo ppid,user,stat,tname,sess,cputime,args --sort=user    Sort by user
  PPID USER     STAT TTY   SESS    TIME COMMAND
     1 avahi    Ss   ?     2221 00:00:07 avahi-daemon: running [example.net]
```

Here are a few other extraneous examples of the ps command:

```
$ ps -C httpd                          Display running httpd processes
  PID TTY          TIME CMD
 1493 ?        00:00:00 httpd
 1495 ?        00:00:00 httpd
$ ps -p 5413 -o pid,ppid,bsdtime,args       Display info for PID 5413
  PID  PPID   TIME COMMAND
 5413     1   0:08 gpm -m /dev/input/mice -t exps2
$ ps -U chris,francois -o pid,ruser,tty,stat,args See info for 2 users
  PID RUSER    TT       STAT COMMAND
 1010 chris    pts/0    Ss   -bash
 5951 francois pts/1    Ss+  /bin/bash
```

Watching Active Processes with top

If you want to see the processes running on your system on an ongoing basis, you can use the top command. The top command runs a screen-oriented view of your running processes that is updated continuously. If you start the top command with no options, it displays your system's uptime, tasks, CPU usage, and memory usage, followed by a list of your running processes, sorted by CPU usage. Here's an example:

```
$ top
top - 01:39:43 up 4 days,  1:53,  6 users,  load average: 1.25, 1.08, 1.11
Tasks: 119 total,  1 running, 117 sleeping,  0 stopped,  1 zombie
Cpu(s): 46.8% us,  3.3% sy,  0.0% ni, 49.5% id,  0.0% wa,  0.3% hi,  0.0% si
Mem:    482992k total,   472688k used,    10304k free,   24312k buffers
Swap: 5863716k total,   534512k used,  5329204k free,   68072k cached

  PID USER      PR  NI  VIRT  RES  SHR S %CPU %MEM    TIME+  COMMAND
 2690 root      15   0  344m  76m 7116 S 32.2 16.2  2349:08 X
 2778 chris     15   0 16212 7992 4836 S  1.7  1.7  4:30.61 metacity
22279 chris     15   0  227m 109m  23m S  1.0 23.3 34:34.00 firefox-bin
```

Here are examples of other options you can use to **start top to continuously display running processes:**

```
$ top -d 5           Change update delay to 5 seconds (from default 3)
$ top -u francois    Only see processes of effective user name francois
$ top -p 190,2690    Only display processes 190 and 2690
$ top -n 10          Refresh the screen 10 times before quitting
$ top -b             Run in non-interactive non-screen-oriented mode
```

The last example (`top -b`) formats the output of `top` in a way that is suitable for output to a file, as opposed to redrawing the same screen for interactive viewing. This can be used to create a log of processes, for example when hunting down that runaway processes that eats up all your resources in the middle of the night. Here's how to **run top and log the output** for 10 hours:

```
$ top -b -n 12000 > myprocesslog
```

When `top` is running, you can **update and sort the process list in different ways.** To **immediately update the process list**, press Space or Enter. Press Shift+n to **sort by PID.** Press Shift+p to **sort by CPU usage.** Press Shift+m to **sort by memory usage.** Press Shift+t to **sort by CPU time consumed.** You can also change the column to sort by using the Shift+< (**sort column to left**) or Shift+> (**sort column to right**) characters. Or, press f and **select the letter of the column you want to sort by** when the list of columns appears.

There are several ways to **change the behavior of top as it's running.** Press d and type a number representing seconds to **change the delay between refreshes.** Press u and enter a user name to **only display processes for the selected user.** To **view only a select number of processes,** type **n** and type the number you want to see. Press = at any point to **return to the original top display.**

You can **act on any of the running processes** in different ways. To **signal (kill) a running process,** type **k** followed by the PID of the process you want to send the signal to. Then type **9** to end it or a different signal number to send that signal to the process. To **give a process higher or lower run priority,** type **n** and then add a negative number (to increase priority) or a positive number (to reduce priority).

If you want to **find more information about how to use top**, type **?** during a `top` session. The man page also has a lot of information about how to use `top`:

```
$ man top          View the top man page
```

When you are done using top, type **q** to exit.

Finding and Controlling Processes

Changing a running process first means finding the process you want to change, then modifying the processing priority or sending the process a signal to change its behavior. If you are looking for a particular process, you might find it tough to locate it in a large list of processes output by ps or top. The pgrep command offers ways of searching through your active processes for the ones you are looking for. The renice command lets you change the processing priority of running processes. The kill, pkill, and killall commands let you send signals to running processes (including signals to end those processes).

Using pgrep to Find Processes

In its most basic form, you can use pgrep to search for a command name (or part of one) and produce the process ID of any process that includes that name. For example:

```
$ pgrep init          Show PID for any process including 'init' string
1
2689
```

Because we know there is only one init command running, we next use the -l option to see each process's command name (to learn why two processes showed up):

```
$ pgrep -l init          Show PID and name for any process including 'init' string
1 init
2689 xinit
```

You can also **search for processes that are associated with a particular user:**

```
$ pgrep -lu chris     List all processes owned by user chris
2551 sshd
2552 bash
2803 vim
```

Probably the most useful way to use pgrep is to have it **find the process IDs of the running processes and pipe those PIDs to another command** to produce the output. Here are some examples (look for other commands if metacity or firefox aren't running):

```
$ ps -p `pgrep metacity`     Search for metacity and run ps (short)
  PID TTY          TIME CMD
```

```
 2778 ?        00:05:00 metacity
$ ps -fp $(pgrep xinit)         Search for xinit and run ps (full)
UID       PID  PPID  C STIME TTY      TIME CMD
chris    2689  2678  0 Aug14 tty1 00:00:00 xinit /etc/X11/xinit/xinitrc
# renice -5 $(pgrep firefox)    Search for firefox, improve its priority
20522: old priority 0, new priority -5
20557: old priority 0, new priority -5
```

Any command that can take a process ID as input can be combined with pgrep in these ways. As the previous example of pgrep illustrates, you can use commands such as renice to change how a process behaves while it is running.

Using fuser to Find Processes

Another way to locate a particular process is by what the process is accessing. The fuser command can be used to find which processes have a file or a socket open at the moment. After the processes are found, fuser can be used to send signals to those processes.

The fuser command is most useful for finding out if files are being held open by processes on mounted file systems (such as local hard disks or Samba shares). Finding those processes allows you to close them properly (or just kill them if you must) so the file system can be unmounted cleanly.

Here are some examples of the fuser command for **listing processes that have files open on a selected file system:**

```
# fuser -mauv /boot        Verbose output of processes with /boot open
                    USER        PID ACCESS COMMAND
/boot/grub/:        root       3853 ..c.. (root)bash
                    root      19760 ..c.. (root)bash
                    root      28171 F.c.. (root)vi
                    root      29252 ..c.. (root)man
                    root      29255 ..c.. (root)sh
                    root      29396 F.c.. (root)vi
```

The example just shown displays the process ID for running processes associated with /boot. They may have a file open, a shell open, or be a child process of a shell with the current directory in /boot. Specifically in this example, there are two bash shells open in the /boot file system, two vi commands with files open in /boot, and a man command running in /boot. The -a shows all processes, -u indicates which user owns each process, and -v produces verbose output.

Here are other examples using fuser to **show processes with files open:**

```
# fuser /boot              Show parent PIDs for processes opening /boot
/boot:       19760c 29396c
# fuser -m /boot           Show all PIDs for processes opening /boot
/boot:       3853c 19760c 28171c 29396c 29252c 29255c
```

```
# fuser -u /boot          Show PIDs/user for this shell open in /boot
/boot:      19760c(root) 29396c(root) 29252c(root) 29255c(root)
```

After you know which processes have files open, you can close those processes manually or kill them. Close processes manually if at all possible, because simply killing processes can leave files in an unclean state! Here are examples of using fuser to kill or send other signals to all processes with files open to a file system:

```
# fuser -k /boot      Kill all processes with /boot files open (SIGKILL)
# fuser -l            List supported signals
HUP INT QUIT ILL TRAP ABRT IOT BUS FPE KILL USR1 SEGV USR2 PIPE ALRM TERM
STKFLT CHLD CONT STOP TSTP TTIN TTOU URG XCPU XFSZ VTALRM PROF WINCH IO
PWR SYS UNUSED
# fuser -k -HUP /boot Send HUP signal to all processes with /boot open
```

Changing Running Processes

Even after a process is running, you can change its behavior in different ways. With the renice command, shown earlier, you can adjust a running process's priority in your system's scheduler. With the nice command, you can determine the default priority and also set a higher or lower priority at the time you launch a process.

Another way you can change how a running process behaves is to send a signal to that process. The kill and killall commands can be used to send signals to running processes. Likewise, the pkill command can send a signal to a process.

Adjusting Processor Priority with nice

Every running process has a *nice* value that can be used to tell the Linux process scheduler what priority should be given to that process. Positive values of niceness actually give your process a lower priority. The concept came about during the days of large, multi-user Unix systems where you could be "nice" by running a non-urgent process at a lower priority so other users had a shot at the CPU.

Niceness doesn't enforce scheduling priority, but is merely a suggestion to the scheduler. To see your current nice value, you can type the nice command with no options:

```
$ nice          Run nice to determine current niceness
0
```

The default nice value is 0. You can use the nice command to run a process at a higher or lower priority than the default. The priority number can range from –20 (most favorable scheduling priority) to 19 (least favorable scheduling priority). Although the root user can raise or lower any user's nice value, a regular user can only lower the priorities of a process (setting a higher nice value).

> **WARNING!** *Proceed with caution when assigning negative nice values to processes. This can possibly crash your machine if critical system processes lose their high priority.*

Here are a few examples of starting a command with nice to **change a command's nice value**:

```
$ nice -n 12 nroff -man a.roff | less   Format man pages at low priority
# nice -n -10 gimp                       Launch gimp at higher priority
```

When a process is already running, you can **change the process's nice value using the renice command**. Here are some examples of the renice command:

```
$ renice +2 -u francois              Renice francois' processes +2
$ renice +5 4737                     Renice PID 4737 by +5
# renice -3 `pgrep -u chris spamd`   Renice chris' spamd processes -3
9688: old priority -1, new priority -3
20279: old priority -1, new priority -3
20282: old priority -1, new priority -3
```

The backticks are used in the previous command line to indicate that the output of the pgrep command (presumably PIDs of spamd daemons run by chris) is fed to the renice command.

The niceness settings for your processes are displayed by default when you run top. You can also see niceness settings using -o nice when you produce custom output from the ps command.

Running Processes in the Background and Foreground

When you run a process from a shell, it is run in the foreground by default. That means that you can't type another command until the first one is done. By adding an ampersand (&) to the end of a command line, you can run that command line in the background. Using the fg, bg, and jobs commands, along with various control codes, you can move commands between background and foreground.

In the following sequence of commands, we start the GIMP image program from a Terminal window. After that is a series of control keys and commands to **stop and start the process and move it between foreground and background**:

```
$ gimp                       Run gimp in the foreground
<Ctrl+z>                     Stop process and place in background
[1]+  Stopped        gimp
$ bg 1                       Start process running again in background
$ fg 1                       Continue running process in foreground
gimp
<Ctrl+c>                     Kill process
```

Note that processes placed in the background are given a job ID number (in this case, 1). By placing a percentage sign in front of the number (for example, %1) you can identify a particular background process to the bg and fg commands or simply type the number with the command (as in `fg 1`). With one or more background jobs running at the current shell, you can use the jobs command to manage your background jobs:

```
$ jobs                  Display background jobs for current shell
[1]    Running          gimp &
[2]    Running          xmms &
[3]-   Running          gedit &
[4]+   Stopped          gtali
$ jobs -1               Display PID with each job's information
[1]   31676 Running         gimp &
[2]   31677 Running         xmms &
[3]- 31683 Running          gedit &
[4]+ 31688 Stopped          gtali
$ jobs -1 %2            Display information only for job %2
[2]   31677 Running         xmms &
```

The processes running in the `jobs` examples might have been done while you were logged in (using `ssh`) to a remote system, but want to run remote GUI applications on your local desktop. By running those processes in the background, you can have multiple applications running at once, while still having those applications associated with your current shell. Once a process is running, you can disconnect the process from the current shell using the disown command:

```
$ disown %3             Disconnect job %3 from current shell
$ disown -a             Disconnect all jobs from current shell
$ disown -h             Protect all jobs from HUP sent to current shell
```

After you have disowned a process, you can close the shell without also killing the process.

> **NOTE** With `fg`, bg, or `disown`, *if you don't indicate which process to act on, the current job is used. The current job has a plus sign (+) next to it.*

The `fg` and `bg` commands manipulate running processes by moving those processes to the foreground or background. Another way to manipulate running commands is to send signals directly to those processes. A common way to send signals to running processes is with the `kill` and `killall` commands.

Killing and Signaling Processes

You can stop or change running processes by sending signals to those processes. Commands such as `kill` and `killall` can send signals you select to running processes, which as their names imply, is often a signal to kill the process.

Signals are represented by numbers (9, 15, and so on) and strings (`SIGKILL`, `SIGTERM`, and so on). Table 9-2 shows standard signals you can send to processes in Linux.

Table 9-2: Standard Signals to Send to Processes

Signal Number	Signal Name	Description
1	SIGHUP	Hang up from terminal or controlling process died
2	SIGINT	Keyboard interrupt
3	SIGQUIT	Keyboard quit
4	SIGILL	Illegal instruction
6	SIGABRT	Abort sent from abort function
8	SIGFPE	Floating point exception
9	SIGKILL	Kill signal
11	SIGSEGV	Invalid memory reference
13	SIGPIPE	Pipe broken (no process reading from pipe)
14	SIGALRM	Timer signal from alarm system call
15	SIGTERM	Termination signal
30,10,16	SIGUSR1	User-defined signal 1
31,12,17	SIGUSR2	User-defined signal 2
20,17,18	SIGCHLD	Child terminated or stopped
19,18,25	SIGCONT	Continue if process is stopped
17,19,23	SIGSTOP	Stop the process
18,20.24	SIGTSTP	Stop typed at terminal
21,21,26	SIGTTIN	Terminal input for background process
22,22,27	SIGTTOU	Terminal output for background process

The kill command can send signals to processes by process ID or job number while the killall command can signal processes by command name. Here are some examples:

```
$ kill 28665              Send SIGTERM to process with PID 28665
$ kill -9 4895            Send SIGKILL to process with PID 4895
$ kill -SIGCONT 5254      Continue a stopped process (pid 5254)
$ kill %3                 Kill the process represented by job %3
$ killall spamd           Kill all spamd daemons currently running
$ killall -SIGHUP sendmail Have sendmail processes reread config files
```

The SIGKILL (9) signal, used generously by trigger-happy novice administrators, should be reserved as a last resort. It does not allow the targeted process to exit cleanly but forces it to end abruptly. This can potentially result in loss or corruption of data handled by that process. The SIGHUP signal was originally used on Unix systems to indicate that a terminal was being disconnected from a mainframe (such as from a hang-up of a dial-in modem). However, daemon processes, such as sendmail and httpd, were implemented to catch SIGHUP signals as an indication that those processes should reread configuration files.

Running Processes Away from the Current Shell

If you want a process to continue to run, even if you disconnect from the current shell session, there are several ways to go about doing that. You can use the nohup command to run a process in a way that it is impervious to a hang-up signal:

```
$ nohup updatedb &            Run updatedb with no ability to interrupt
# nohup nice -9 gcc hello.c &  Run gcc uninterrupted and higher priority
```

Using nohup is different than running the command with an ampersand alone because with nohup the command will keep running, even if you exit the shell that launched the command.

The nohup command was commonly used in the days of slow processors and dial-up connections (so you didn't have to stay logged in to an expensive connection while a long compile completed). Also, today using tools such as screen (described in Chapter 14) you can keep a shell session active, even after you disconnect your network connection to that shell.

Scheduling Processes to Run

Commands associated with the cron facility can be used to set a command to run at a specific time (including now) so that it is not connected to the current shell. The at command runs a command at the time you set:

```
$ at now +1 min            Start command running in one minute
at> updatedb
at> <Ctrl+d> <EOT>
job 5 at Mon Aug 20 20:37:00 2007
$ at teatime               Start command at 4pm today
$ at now +5 days           Start a command in five days
$ at 06/25/08              Start a command at current time on June 25, 2008
```

Another way to run a command that's not connected with the current shell is with the batch command. With batch, you can set a command to start as soon as the processor is ready (load average below .8):

```
$ batch              Start command running immediately
at> find /mnt/isos | grep jpg$ > /tmp/mypics
at> <Ctrl+d> <EOT>
```

Note that after the at or batch commands you see a secondary at> prompt. Type the command you want to run at that prompt and press Enter. After that, you can continue to enter commands. When you are done, press Ctrl+d on a line by itself to queue the commands you entered to run.

After the commands are entered, you can **check the queue of at jobs that are set** to run by typing the atq command:

```
$ atq
11          Wed Sep  5 21:10:00 2007 a francois
10          Fri Aug 24 21:10:00 2007 a francois
8           Thu Aug 23 20:53:00 2007 a francois
```

Regular users can only see their own at jobs that are queued. The root user can see everyone's queued at jobs. If you want to **delete an at job from the queue**, use the atrm command:

```
$ atrm 11                    Delete at job number 11
```

The at and batch commands are for queuing up a command to run as a one-shot deal. You can use the cron facility to **set up commands to run repeatedly**. These commands are scripted into cron jobs which are scheduled in crontab files. There is one system crontab file (/etc/crontab). Also, each user can create a personal crontab file that can launch commands at times that the user chooses. To **create a personal crontab file**, type the following.

```
$ crontab -e                 Create a personal crontab file
```

The crontab -e command opens your crontab file (or creates a new one) using the vi text editor. Here are examples of several entries you could add to a crontab file:

```
15 8 * * Mon,Tue,Wed,Thu,Fri mail chris < /var/project/stats.txt
* * 1 1,4,7,10 * find / | grep .doc$ > /var/sales/documents.txt
```

The first crontab example shown sends a mail message to the user named chris by directing the contents of /var/project/stats.txt into that message. That mail command is run Monday through Friday at 8:15 a.m. In the second example, on the first day of January, April, July, and October, the find command runs to look for every .doc file on the system and sends the resulting list of files to /var/sales/documents.txt.

The last part of each crontab entry is the command that is run. The first five fields represent the time and date the command is run. The fields from left to right are: minute (0 to 59), hour (0 to 23), day of the month (0 to 31), month (0 to 12 or Jan, Feb, Mar, Apr, May, Jun, Jul, Aug, Sep, Oct, Nov, or Dec), and day of the week (0 to 7 or Sun, Mon, Tue, Wed, Thu, Fri, or Sat). An asterisk (*) in a field means to match any value for that field.

Here are some **other options with the crontab command**:

```
# crontab -eu chris          Edit another user's crontab (root only)
$ crontab -l                 List contents of your crontab file
15 8 * * Mon,Tue,Wed,Thu,Fri mail chris < /var/project/stats.txt
* * 1 1,4,7,10 * find / | grep .doc$ > /var/sales/documents.txt
$ crontab -r                 Delete your crontab file
```

The traditional way to configure system cron jobs was to add them to the system crontab. Although this is still an option, Fedora provides an easier way to create hourly, daily, weekly, and monthly cron jobs, by **associating the command you want to run with a cron directory**. Simply create a script that you want to run. Then copy the script to the `/etc/cron.hourly`, `/etc/cron.daily`, `/etc/cron.weekly`, or `/etc/cron.monthly` directory. The command will then run in the time frame indicated by the directory (hourly, daily, weekly, or monthly).

An alternative to the cron facility is the anacron facility. With anacron, as with cron, you can configure commands to run periodically. However, anacron is most appropriate for machines that are not on all the time. If a command is not run because the computer was off during the scheduled time, the next time the computer is on, the anacron facility makes sure that the commands that were missed during the downtime are run after the system resumes.

Summary

Watching and working with the processes that run on your Linux system are important activities to make sure that your system is operating efficiently. Using commands such as ps and top, you can view the processes running on your system. You can also use pgrep to search for and list particular processes.

With commands such as nice and renice, you can adjust the recommended priorities at which selected processes run. When a process is running, you can change how it is running or kill the process by sending it a signal from the kill or killall command.

After launching a command from the current shell, you can set that command's process to run in the background (bg) or foreground (fg). You can also stop and restart the process using different control codes.

To schedule a command to run at a later time, you can use the at or batch command. To set up a command to run repeatedly at set intervals, you can use the cron or anacron facilities.

10

Managing the System

Without careful management, the demands on your Linux system can sometimes exceed the resources you have available. Being able to monitor your system's activities (memory, CPU, and device usage) over time can help you make sure that your machine has enough resources to do what you need it to. Likewise, managing other aspects of your system, such as the device drivers it uses and how the boot process works, can help avoid performance problems and system failures.

This chapter is divided into several sections that relate to ways of managing your Fedora or other Linux system. The first section can help you monitor the resources (processing power, devices, and memory) on your Linux system. The next section describes how to check and set your system clock. Descriptions of the boot process and subsequent run levels follow. The last sections describe how to work with the kernel and related device drivers, as well as how to view information about your computer's hardware components.

Monitoring Resources

Fedora, RHEL, CentOS, and other Linux systems do a wonderful job of keeping track of what they do. If you care to look, you can find lots of information about how your CPU, hard disks, virtual memory, and other computer resources are being used.

You can go to where the Linux kernel stores real-time information about your system by directly viewing the contents of files in the /proc file system (see Appendix C). An alternative, however, is to use commands to view information about how your computer's virtual memory, processor, storage devices, and network interfaces are being used on your system.

There are commands that can monitor several different aspects of your system's resources. Because this book is not just a man page, however, we have divided the following sections by topic (monitoring memory, CPU, and storage devices) rather than by the commands that do them (top, vmstat, and iostat).

NOTE *Many of the applications described in this section are installed by default in Fedora, in packages such as the procps package. To use* iostat *or* sar, *however, you need to install the sysstat package.*

Monitoring Memory Use

Few things will kill system performance faster than running out of memory. Commands such as free and top let you see basic information about how your RAM and swap are being used. The vmstat command gives detailed information about memory use and can run continuously. The slabtop command can show how much memory the kernel (slab cache) is consuming.

The free command provides the quickest way to **see how much memory is being used** on your system. It shows the total amount of RAM (Mem:) and swap space (Swap:), along with the amount currently being used. Here are examples of the free command:

```
$ free                List memory usage in kilobytes (-k default)
              total        used         free     shared     buffers        cached
Mem:        742476      725108        17368          0      153388        342544
-/+ buffers/cache:      229176       513300
Swap:      1020116          72      1020044
$ free -m             List memory usage in megabytes
              total        used         free     shared     buffers        cached
Mem:           725         706           18          0         148           333
-/+ buffers/cache:         223          501
Swap:          996           0          996
$ free -b             List memory usage in blocks
              total        used         free     shared     buffers        cached
Mem:     760295424   742510592     17784832          0   157114368    350765056
-/+ buffers/cache: 234631168   525664256
Swap: 1044598784       73728 1044525056
$ free -mt            List memory usage with totals displayed (Swap + Mem)
              total        used         free     shared     buffers        cached
Mem:           725         708           16          0         149           334
-/+ buffers/cache:         223          501
Swap:          996           0          996
Total:        1721         708         1013
$ free -g             List memory usage in gigabytes
$ free -s 5           Continuously display memory usage every 5 seconds
```

To avoid wasting RAM and speed up applications, Linux uses as much otherwise-unused RAM as possible for the disc cache. For that reason, the first line of output from free that often shows little free RAM can be misleading. We recommend you pay closer attention to the second line of output, which shows the amount of RAM actually available for applications. That amount is 501MB in this example:

```
-/+ buffers/cache:        223        501
```

One way to guess how much memory you need on a system is to go to another computer running Fedora, then open every application you think you may be running at once. Run free with the total option (free -t) to see how much memory is being used. Then make sure that your new system has at least that much total memory (with most or all of it preferably being available in RAM).

The top command provides a means of watching the currently running processes, with those processes sorted by CPU usage or memory (see Chapter 9 for a description of top for watching running processes). However, you can also use top to **watch your memory usage in a screen-oriented way**. Here is an example:

```
$ top
top - 14:14:59 up 3 days, 18:26,  1 user,  load average: 0.11, 0.04, 0.01
Tasks: 114 total,   3 running, 111 sleeping,   0 stopped,   0 zombie
Cpu(s): 0.0%us, 0.0%sy, 0.0%ni,100.0%id, 0.0%wa,  0.0%hi,  0.0%si,  0.0%st
Mem:    742476k total,    727232k used,     15244k free,    153708k buffers
Swap:  1020116k total,        72k used,   1020044k free,    343924k cached
  PID USER      PR  NI  VIRT  RES  SHR S %CPU %MEM    TIME+  COMMAND
 2347 root      34  19 89552  77m 5636 S  0.0 10.7  6:05.75 yum-updatesd
 2797 chris     18   0 80612  27m  18m S  0.0  3.8  0:01.29 nautilus
 2814 chris     15   0 44420  22m  20m S  0.0  3.1  0:00.17 nm-applet
```

To exit top, press q. Like the output for free, top shows the total memory usage for RAM (Mem:) and swap space (Swap:). However, because top is screen oriented and provides ongoing monitoring, you can watch memory usage change every three seconds (by default). With top running, press Shift+m, and running processes will be displayed in memory-use order (so you can watch which processes are consuming the most memory). The most useful column to analyze a process' memory usage is RES, which shows the process' actual physical RAM usage, also known as *resident size*. The %MEM column is based on this resident size.

For a more detailed view of your virtual memory statistics, use the vmstat command. With vmstat you can **view memory use over a given time period**, such as since the previous reboot or using a sample period. The following example shows vmstat redisplaying statistics every three seconds:

```
$ vmstat 3
procs -----------memory---------- --swap-- ----io---- --system-- -----cpu-----
 r  b   swpd   free   buff  cache   si   so    bi    bo   in   cs us sy id wa st
 1  0  97740  32488   3196 148360    0    0     0     1   26 3876 85 15  0  0  0
 1  1  98388   7428   3204 151472    0  216     0   333   30 3200 82 18  0  0  0
 1  0 113316   8148   2980 146968    0 4980     4  5121   79 3846 77 23  0  0  0
 2  0 132648   7472   2904 148488    0 6455     3  6455   90 3644 83 17  0  0  0
 2  0 147892   8088   2732 144208    0 5085     9  5220   79 3468 84 16  0  0  0
 1  0 157948   7680   2308 134812    0 3272    12  3296   69 3174 77 23  0  0  0
 3  0 158348   7944   1100 123888   21  144    25   275   26 3178 86 14  0  1  0
```

```
2  0 166116   7320   568 120280  11 2401   20 2403   51 3175 84 16  0  0  0
3  0 181048   7708   648 119452  53 4852  796 4984  123 1783 86 13  0  1  0
```

To exit vmstat, press Ctrl+c. The vmstat example shows a 30-second time period where more than 100 applications are started. Notice that when the free space goes from 32488 kilobytes to 7428 kilobytes (RAM is filling up), data begins being moved to the swap area (see the 216 under the so column). Because the swap area resides on the hard disk, you can see that the block written to disk device (bo) increases as the swap out increases. You can see the amount of swap space being used increasing under the swpd column.

The CPU is also straining in the example, with no idle time showing (id 0). Notice also that when some of the applications need to be swapped back in (see the last three lines of output), the processor has to wait on two occasions for input/output to complete (wa 1).

Here are some other options for using vmstat:

```
$ vmstat -S m           Display output in 1000k megabytes
$ vmstat -S M           Display output in 1024k megabytes
$ vmstat -S k           Display output in 1000-byte kilobytes
$ vmstat -S K           Display output in 1024-byte kilobytes
$ vmstat -n 2 10        Output every two seconds, repeat 10 times
$ vmstat -s | less      Display event counters and memory statistics
$ vmstat -S M -s | less Display statistics in megabytes
      725 M total memory
      717 M used memory
      486 M active memory
      175 M inactive memory
        7 M free memory
        1 M buffer memory
      120 M swap cache
      996 M total swap
      802 M used swap
      193 M free swap
          . . .
```

The previous example shows various memory statistics (-s) output in megabytes (-S M), which we find more convenient to get a general view of memory usage. The other examples show how to display vmstat output in megabytes and kilobytes (in both marketing and technical terms). After that, the -n 2 10 option tells vmstat to repeat every set number of seconds (2) for a limited number of times (10).

With commands such as ps and top, you can see how much memory each application is consuming on your system. The kernel itself, however, has its own memory cache to keep track of its resources, called the *kernel slab*. You can use the vmstat command to display kernel slab memory cache statistics (from /proc/slabinfo) as follows:

```
$ vmstat -m | less      Page through kernel slab memory cache
Cache            Num   Total  Size  Pages
nf_nat:help        2      13   308     13
```

```
nf_nat:base          0      0    276    14
bridge_fdb_cache     0      0     64    59
   ...
ext3_inode_cache   1236   2928    488     8
ext3_xattr           29    156     48    78
   ...
```

The slab memory cache information shows each cache name, the number of objects active for that cache type, the total number of objects available for that cache type, the size of the cache (in bytes), and the number of pages for each cache. You can **display kernel slab memory cache information in a screen-oriented view** (similar to the top command) using slabtop:

```
$ slabtop
Active / Total Objects (% used)   : 49127 / 70942 (69.2%)
Active / Total Slabs (% used)     : 3094 / 3094 (100.0%)
Active / Total Caches (% used)    : 101 / 145 (69.7%)
Active / Total Size (% used)      : 8830.29K / 12013.73K (73.5%)
Minimum / Average / Maximum Object : 0.01K / 0.17K / 128.00K

 OBJS ACTIVE  USE OBJ SIZE   SLABS OBJ/SLAB CACHE SIZE NAME
11600   4303  37%   0.13K    400     29      1600K dentry_cache
 2928   1246  42%   0.48K    366      8      1464K ext3_inode_cache
 4355   2535  58%   0.28K    335     13      1340K radix_tree_node
  219    219 100%   4.00K    219      1       876K size-4096
 4128   3485  84%   0.16K    172     24       688K filp
```

The slabtop output updates every three seconds. By default, slab caches are sorted by the number of objects (first column) in each cache. By pressing c you can sort by cache size instead (as shown in the previous example).

Monitoring CPU Usage

An overburdened CPU is another obvious place to look for performance problems on your system. The vmstat command, shown earlier, can produce basic statistics relating to CPU usage (user activity, system activity, idle time, I/O wait time, and time stolen from a virtual machine). The iostat command (from the sysstat package), however, can generate more detailed reports of CPU utilization.

Here are two examples of using iostat to **display a CPU utilization report:**

```
$ iostat -c 3       CPU stats every 3 seconds (starting apps)
Linux 2.6.21-1.3194.fc7 (davinci)      08/10/2007
avg-cpu:  %user   %nice %system %iowait  %steal   %idle
          0.50    0.00    0.00    0.00    0.00   99.50
avg-cpu:  %user   %nice %system %iowait  %steal   %idle
         28.71    0.00    5.45   18.32    0.00   47.52
avg-cpu:  %user   %nice %system %iowait  %steal   %idle
         98.99    0.00    1.01    0.00    0.00    0.00
avg-cpu:  %user   %nice %system %iowait  %steal   %idle
         99.50    0.00    0.50    0.00    0.00    0.00
```

```
$ iostat -c 3          CPU stats every 3 seconds (copying files)
Linux 2.6.21-1.3194.fc7 (davinci)          08/10/2007
avg-cpu:  %user   %nice %system %iowait  %steal   %idle
          0.50    0.00    0.00    0.00    0.00    0.00
avg-cpu:  %user   %nice %system %iowait  %steal   %idle
          0.50    0.00   24.88   74.63    0.00    0.00
avg-cpu:  %user   %nice %system %iowait  %steal   %idle
          0.50    0.00   10.00   89.50    0.00    0.00
avg-cpu:  %user   %nice %system %iowait  %steal   %idle
          0.50    0.00   17.41   82.09    0.00    0.00
avg-cpu:  %user   %nice %system %iowait  %steal   %idle
          0.00    0.00   14.65   85.35    0.00    0.00
```

The first `iostat` example above starts with a quiet system, then several applications started up. You can see that most of the processing to start the applications is being done in user space. The second `iostat` example shows a case where several large files are copied from one hard disk to another. The result is a high percentage of time being spent at the system level, also known as kernel space (in this case, reading from and writing to disk partitions). Notice that the file copies also result in a higher amount of time waiting for I/O requests to complete (%iowait).

Here are examples using `iostat` to **print CPU utilization reports with timestamps:**

```
$ iostat -c -t            Print time stamp with CPU report
Linux 2.6.21-1.3194.fc7 (davinci)          08/10/2007

Time: 9:28:03 AM
avg-cpu:  %user   %nice %system %iowait  %steal   %idle
          0.50    0.00    0.00    0.00    0.00   99.50
$ iostat -c -t 2 10       Repeat every 2 seconds for 10 times
```

The `dstat` command (dstat package) is available as an alternative to `iostat` for **viewing information about your CPU usage** (as well as other performance-related items). One advantage of `dstat` over other tools is that it more precisely shows the units of measurement it is displaying (such as kilobytes or megabytes) and also uses colors to differentiate the data. Here is an example of `dstat` for displaying CPU information:

```
$ dstat -t -c 3          View CPU usage continuously with time stamps
-----time----- ----total-cpu-usage----
  date/time    |usr sys idl wai hiq siq
11-08 11:44:03| 14    1  85    0    0    0
11-08 11:44:06|  0    0 100    0    0    0
11-08 11:44:09|  0    0 100    0    0    0
11-08 11:44:12|  0    5  80   14    0    0
11-08 11:44:15|  0    0  95    4    0    0
11-08 11:44:18|  0   37   0   62    0    0
11-08 11:44:21|  1   45   0   53    0    1
11-08 11:44:24|  1   42   0   55    0    2
11-08 11:44:27|  0   16   0   83    0    1
```

Notice in this example that the output includes a date/time stamp (-t) for the CPU report (-c) that is produced every three seconds (3). This report runs continuously until you stop it (Ctrl+c).

If you want to find out specifically which processes are consuming the most process-ing time, you can use the top command. Type top, then press Shift+p to sort by CPU usage (this is the default sorting order):

```
$ top                  Display running processes and sort by CPU usage
Tasks: 120 total,   3 running, 116 sleeping,   0 stopped,   1 zombie
Cpu(s): 86.8% us, 6.0% sy, 0.0% ni, 3.3% id, 4.0% wa,  0.0% hi,  0.0% si
Mem:    482992k total,   476884k used,     6108k free,    1220k buffers
Swap: 5863716k total, 1166252k used,  4697464k free,    52984k cached

  PID USER      PR  NI  VIRT  RES  SHR S %CPU %MEM   TIME+  COMMAND
 9648 chris     16   0  309m 123m  16m R 72.6 26.1 287:55.22 firefox-bin
  552 root      15   0  762m  65m 5732 S 15.6 14.0  4388:27 X
```

The full output would show many more processes, all sorted by current CPU usage (%CPU column). In this example, the Firefox web browser (72.6%) and the X display server (15.6%) are consuming most of the CPU. If you decided you wanted to kill the Firefox process, you could type k followed by the process ID of Firefox (9648) and the number 9 signal (if for some reason you couldn't just close the Firefox window normally).

If you want **information about the processor itself**, you can view information directly from the /proc/cpuinfo file. Here is an example:

```
$ cat /proc/cpuinfo       View CPU information from /proc
processor       : 0
vendor_id       : AuthenticAMD
cpu family      : 6
model           : 4
model name      : AMD Athlon(tm) processor
stepping        : 4
cpu MHz         : 1340.080
cache size      : 256 KB
  . . .
flags           : fpu vme de pse tsc msr pae mce cx8 apic mtrr pge mca cmov pat
pse36 mmx fxsr syscall mmxext 3dnowext 3dnow up
bogomips        : 2680.91
clflush size    : 32
```

An interesting thing to note about your CPU are the flags that represent features that it supports. Some features in Fedora require that particular CPU extensions associated with those flags be on for the Fedora feature to work. For example, to use the Xen vir-tualization para-virtualized guests, the pae flag must be set. To run fully virtualized guests, the CPU must have either the vmx flag (for Intel processors) or svm flag (for AMD processors) extension support.

171

Similar information about your processor(s) is collected by the system at the very beginning of the boot process, and can be obtained by looking at the beginning of your /var/log/dmesg file.

Monitoring Storage Devices

Basic information about storage space available to your Linux file systems can be seen using commands such as du and df (as described in Chapter 7). If you want details about how your storage devices are performing, however, commands such as vmstat and iostat can be useful.

Some of the same kind of output from the iostat command shown earlier can be used to **tell if bottlenecks occur while doing disk reads and writes.** Here's an example:

```
$ iostat 3      Check disk reads and writes per disk
Linux 2.6.21-1.3194.fc7 (davinci)       08/11/2007

avg-cpu:  %user   %nice %system %iowait  %steal   %idle
          13.15    0.60    0.59    0.16    0.00   85.49
Device:            tps   Blk_read/s   Blk_wrtn/s   Blk_read   Blk_wrtn
sda               1.09        32.08        58.94   16086324   29554312
sdb               0.29         5.27        11.23    2644482    5631348

avg-cpu:  %user   %nice %system %iowait  %steal   %idle
           1.00    0.00   42.14   45.15    0.00   11.71
Device:            tps   Blk_read/s   Blk_wrtn/s   Blk_read   Blk_wrtn
sda             411.37     66515.05         2.68     198880          8
sdb              68.23         2.68     14696.99          8      43944

avg-cpu:  %user   %nice %system %iowait  %steal   %idle
           0.67    0.00   41.00   58.33    0.00    0.00
Device:            tps   Blk_read/s   Blk_wrtn/s   Blk_read   Blk_wrtn
sda             239.67     52530.67       106.67     157592        320
sdb             236.00         0.00     55077.33          0     165232
```

The first part of the output of iostat shows averages of CPU usage since the last reboot. The next part reflects processing that occurs when a large amount of data is copied from the first disk (sda) to the second disk (sdb). High iowait values indicate that disk input/output is the bottleneck on the system. In other words, faster disk writing would improve performance more than a faster CPU.

The vmstat command can also list statistics about your disks. Here's an example of using vmstat to **list information about disk reads and writes:**

```
$ vmstat -d          Display disk read, write, and input/output statistics
disk- -----------reads------------ -----------writes-------- ----IO---
      total merged  sectors    ms   total  merged sectors ms   cur  sec
      ...
sda 332773  74844 19022380 2524211 245477 3473801 29758560 37140075   0 1372
sdb  79963 253716  2646922 2158000  76044  977122  8428140 12489809   0  506
```

The Linux system in this example has two hard disks (sda and sdb). You can see the total number of sectors successfully read and written from those hard disks. You can also see how many seconds were spent on input/output (IO) for those disks. You can also see if there are any I/O operations in progress. You can also list read/write information for selected disk partitions. Here is an example:

```
$ vmstat -p sda1        Display read/write stats for a disk partition
sda1        reads        read sectors  writes    requested writes
            174060       12993689      2778      22224
```

Unfortunately the preceding command does not work with softraid md partitions, lvm partitions, and some hardware RAID driver-specific devices.

If you want to find out **what files and directories are currently open on your storage devices**, you can use the lsof command. This command can be particularly useful if you are trying to unmount a file system that keeps telling you it is busy. You can check what open file is preventing the unmount and decide if you want to kill the process holding that file open and force an unmount of the file system. Here is an example of lsof:

```
# lsof | less      List processes holding files and directories open
COMMAND     PID   USER   FD     TYPE DEVICE   SIZE     NODE NAME
init          1   root   cwd    DIR    8,5    4096        2 /
init          1   root   rtd    DIR    8,5    4096        2 /
init          1   root   txt    REG    8,5    38620 2049530 /sbin/init
    ...
bash      23857  chris   cwd    DIR    8,1    4096  2719746 /mnt/sda1/dx
```

The first files shown as being open are those held open by the init process (the first running process on the system). Files held open by system processes (such as udevd) and daemons (such as sshd and syslogd) follow init. Eventually, you will see files held open by individual users (which are probably the ones you are interested in if you are unable to unmount a disk partition).

When you are looking at the lsof output, you want to see the name of the file or directory that is open (NAME), the command that has it open (COMMAND), and the process ID of that running command (PID). As is often the case when a file system you want to unmount is being held open, the /mnt/sda1 file system is being held open by a bash shell in the preceding example (/mnt/sda1/dx is the bash shell's current working directory). In fact, instead of piping lsof output to less or grep, here are a few other ways you can find what you are looking for from lsof output:

```
# lsof -c bash           List files open by bash shells
# lsof -d cwd            List directories open as current working directory
# lsof -u chris          List files and directories open by user chris
# lsof /mnt/sda1         List anything open on /mnt/sda1 file system
# lsof +d /mnt/sda1/dx   List anything open under /mnt/sda1/dx directory
```

Mastering Time

Keeping correct time on your Linux system is critical to the system's proper functioning. Your computer running Linux keeps time in two different ways: a system clock (which Linux uses to keep track of time) and a hardware clock (that sets the system time when Linux boots up).

The system time is what is used to set timestamps for file creation, process runtimes, and anything else where date and time are used. System time can be viewed and set manually (with the `date` command) or automatically (with the `ntpd` service).

The hardware clock is part of the motherboard's CMOS and runs on a battery attached to the motherboard when the system is powered off. You set the hardware clock with the `hwclock` command.

There are many other tools that can be used to work with time in Linux systems. For example, there are tools for checking time in different ways, such as using `clockdiff` (to measure clock difference between computers) and `uptime` (to see how long your system has been up).

Changing Time/Date with Graphical Tools

Graphical tools in Fedora, RHEL, and other Linux systems for changing the date, time, and time zone used on your system include the Date/Time Properties window (`system-config-date` command). That window can also be used to enable the Network Time Protocol (NTP), to automatically synchronize your Linux system's date and time with a selected time server over the network.

The Date/Time Properties window modifies the `/etc/sysconfig/clock` file. During Fedora startup, the `/etc/sysconfig/clock` file is read to set your time zone and whether your system is using UTC time.

Your Linux system's time zone is set based on the contents of the `/etc/localtime` file. You can set a new time zone immediately by copying the file representing your time zone from a subdirectory of `/usr/share/zoneinfo`. For example, to change the current time zone to that of America/Chicago, you could do the following:

```
# cp /usr/share/zoneinfo/America/Chicago /etc/localtime
```

This can also be accomplished by creating a symlink:

```
# ln -s /usr/share/zoneinfo/America/Chicago /etc/localtime
```

To change the time zone permanently, set the ZONE value in `/etc/sysconfig/clock` to the time zone you want. For example, ZONE="America/Chicago".

Displaying and Setting Your System Clock

The `date` command is the primary command-based interface for viewing and changing date and time settings, if you are not having that done automatically with NTP. Here are examples of `date` commands for **displaying dates and times** in different ways:

```
$ date                        Display current date, time and time zone
Sun Aug 12 01:26:50 CDT 2007
$ date '+%A %B %d %G'         Display day, month, day of month, year
Sunday August 12 2007
$ date '+The date today is %F.' Add words to the date output
The date today is 2007-08-12
$ date --date='4 weeks'       Display date four weeks from today
Sun Sep  9 10:51:18 CDT 2007
$ date --date='8 months 3 days' Display date 8 months 3 days from today
Tue Apr 15 10:59:44 CDT 2008
$ date --date='4 Jul' +%A     Display day on which July 4 falls
Wednesday
```

Although our primary interest in this section is time, since we are on the subject of dates as well, the `cal` command is a quick way to **display dates by month**. Here are examples:

```
$ cal                 Show current month calendar (today is highlighted)
     August 2007
Su Mo Tu We Th Fr Sa
          1  2  3  4
 5  6  7  8  9 10 11
12 13 14 15 16 17 18
19 20 21 22 23 24 25
26 27 28 29 30 31
$ cal 2007            Show whole year's calendar
                    2007
      January              February                March
Su Mo Tu We Th Fr Sa   Su Mo Tu We Th Fr Sa   Su Mo Tu We Th Fr Sa
    1  2  3  4  5  6             1  2  3                   1  2  3
 7  8  9 10 11 12 13    4  5  6  7  8  9 10    4  5  6  7  8  9 10
14 15 16 17 18 19 20   11 12 13 14 15 16 17   11 12 13 14 15 16 17
21 22 23 24 25 26 27   18 19 20 21 22 23 24   18 19 20 21 22 23 24
28 29 30 31            25 26 27 28            25 26 27 28 29 30 31

   . . .
$ cal -j              Show Julian calendar (numbered from January 1)
August 2007
Sun Mon Tue Wed Thu Fri Sat
            213 214 215 216
217 218 219 220 221 222 223
224 225 226 227 228 229 230
231 232 233 234 235 236 237
238 239 240 241 242 243
```

The date command can also be used to change the system date and time. For example:

```
# date 081215212008          Set date/time to Aug. 12, 2:21PM, 2008
Tue Aug 12 11:42:00 CDT 2008
# date --set='+7 minutes'     Set time to 7 minutes later
Sun Aug 12 11:49:33 CDT 2008
# date --set='-1 month'       Set date/time to one month earlier
Sun Jul 12 11:50:20 CDT 2008
```

The next time you boot Fedora, the system time will be reset based on the value of your hardware clock (or your NTP server, if NTP service is enabled). And the next time you shut down, the hardware clock will be reset to the system time, in order to preserve that time while the machine is powered off. To change the hardware clock, you can use the hwclock command.

Displaying and Setting Your Hardware Clock

Anyone can use the hwclock command to view hardware clock settings; however, you must have root privileges to change those settings. To use hwclock to view the current time from your computer's hardware clock, type the following:

```
# hwclock -r          Display current hardware clock settings
Sun 12 Aug 2007 03:45:40 PM CDT   -0.447403 seconds
```

Even if your hardware clock is set to UTC time, hwclock displays local time by default. If your system time strays from your hardware clock (for example, if you tried some of the date commands shown previously), you can reset your system clock from your hardware clock as follows:

```
# hwclock --hctosys    Reset system clock from hardware clock
```

Likewise if your hardware clock is set incorrectly (for example, if you replaced the CMOS battery on your motherboard), you can set the hardware clock from your system clock as follows:

```
# hwclock --systohc    Reset system clock from hardware clock
```

Over time your hardware clock can drift. Because the clock tends to drift the same amount each day, hwclock can keep track of this drift time (which it does in the /etc/adjtime file). You can adjust the hardware clock time based on the adjtime file as follows:

```
# hwclock --adjust     Adjust hardware clock time for drift
```

To set the hardware clock to a specific time, you can use the --set option. Here is an example:

```
# hwclock --set --date="3/18/08 18:22:00"     Set clock to new date/time
```

In this example, the hardware clock is set to March 18, 2008 at 6:22 p.m. This update does not immediately affect the system clock.

Using Network Time Protocol to Set Date/Time

When you install Fedora, RHEL, or CentOS, you are given the opportunity to set your system date and time. An option at that time is to use preconfigured Network Time Protocol (NTP) servers to automatically get the current date and time when your system reboots. If you choose that option, the installer will set up the ntpd daemon and use it to keep your time synchronized.

If you didn't configure NTP to set the time for your system when you first installed your Linux system, you can do so later by **turning on the ntpd service**. Here is how:

```
# yum install ntpd          Install ntpd package if necessary.
# service ntpd start        Start NTP service immediately
# chkconfig ntpd on         Set NTP service to start at each reboot
```

The ntpd service uses information in the /etc/sysconfig/ntpd file. For example, by default the date/time from the NTP server is not used to reset the hardware clock. To have the hardware clock updated, set SYNC_HWCLOCK to yes (SYNC_HWCLOCK=yes) in the /etc/sysconfig/ntpd file.

Whether you install ntpd manually or let the anaconda installer do it automagically, the resulting setup turns your machine into a time server, listening on UDP port 123. Unless you have very specific needs (and your own GPS or atomic clock), running ntpd on your machine can be both a waste of resources and a security risk. For that reason, some system administrators prefer using ntpdate (often in a daily cronjob) to set their system time via NTP:

```
# ntpdate pool.ntp.org
15 Aug 00:37:12 ntpdate[9706]:
adjust time server 66.92.68.11 offset 0.009204 sec
```

If you try running ntpdate while ntpd is running, you will get the following error:

```
# ntpdate pool.ntp.org
15 Aug 00:37:00 ntpdate[9695]: the NTP socket is in use, exiting
```

Note that the ntpdate command has been marked as deprecated and will disappear in the future. It has been replaced by the following options of ntpd:

```
# ntpd -qg
```

The -q option tells ntpd to exit after setting the clock (as opposed to keep running as a daemon). The -g option prevents ntpd from panicking if the system clock is off by more than 1000 seconds.

Trying Other Date/Time Commands

There are a few extraneous commands you can use to work with time settings on your system. The `clockdiff` command can be used to check the difference between the date/time set on your system and that on another system. For example:

```
# clockdiff pool.ntp.org     Compare clocks on local/remote host
.............................................
host=pool.ntp.org rtt=63(0)ms/60ms delta=4ms/5ms
     Sun Aug 12 16:35:25 2007
```

A matter of pride among Linux enthusiasts is how long they can keep their Linux systems running without having to reboot. Linux systems have been known to run for years without having to reboot. The time that a Linux system has been running since the previous reboot is referred to as *uptime*. You can check your system's uptime as follows:

```
$ uptime              Check how long your system has been running
  6:53pm  up 196 days, 14:25,  3 users,  load average: 1.66, 0.88, 0.35
```

The output of `uptime` shows the current time, how many days and hours the system has been up, and how many users are currently logged in. After that, `uptime` shows the system load over the past 1-, 5-, and 15-minute time periods.

Managing the Boot Process

When a computer first starts up, the basic input/output system (BIOS) looks to its boot order settings to determine where to find the operating system to boot. Typically, if a bootable medium has not been inserted into a removable drive (CD, DVD, floppy disk, and so on), the BIOS looks to the master boot record (MBR) on the first bootable hard disk. At this point, for most Linux systems, control of the boot process is handed to the *boot loader*.

For Fedora, RHEL, CentOS, and, in fact, most Linux systems these days, the Grand Unified Boot Loader (GRUB) is the boot loader that is used by default. GRUB is a replacement for LILO, which was the most popular Linux boot loader during the 1990s. GRUB can be set up to boot not only your Linux system, but also to boot any other operating systems installed on your hard disks (Windows, BSD, or others). GRUB can also include boot options with each bootable operating system to refine the boot process, such as to turn on or off support for a particular type of hardware.

Once a Linux system is selected to boot from the boot loader, the boot loader loads the kernel. The following dilemma then occurs: the kernel needs to mount the root file system on the hard drive. This requires the appropriate storage drivers (block device kernel modules). And those drivers are located on the hard drive itself! To break that vicious cycle, a small initial ramdisk (initrd) containing the block device modules is mounted by the boot loader. This allows the Linux kernel to read the root file system. After that, the `init` process takes over and begins starting the system services, based on the *run level* that is set for the system.

The following sections describe commands for modifying the boot loader, startup scripts, and run levels associated with your Linux system.

Using the GRUB Boot Loader

Assuming GRUB was set up when you first installed Fedora, the settings for your boot loader are stored in the /boot/grub/grub.conf file. (You may find some references to /etc/grub.conf, but that is just a symlink to the same file.) Any changes you make to that file are picked up automatically when you reboot Fedora. Here's an example of the contents of the /boot/grub/grub.conf file:

```
default=0
timeout=5
splashimage=(hd0,0)/boot/grub/splash.xpm.gz
hiddenmenu

title Fedora (2.6.21-1.3194.fc7)
    root (hd0,0)
    kernel /boot/vmlinuz-2.6.21-1.3194.fc7 ro root=LABEL=/1 rhgb quiet
     initrd /boot/initrd-2.6.21-1.3194.fc7.img
```

This example shows only one bootable operating system (Fedora). The default=0 line says that the first title entry is booted by default. The timeout=5 line says that GRUB pauses five seconds at the splash screen before booting. The image on that splash screen is a compressed xpm file (splash.xpm.gz) from the /boot/grub directory on the first partition of the first hard disk (hd0,0). The hiddenmenu line indicates that you won't see the list of bootable titles when the boot splash screen appears (press a key during the timeout period to see the menu).

The actual boot entry (title Fedora) points to the first partition on the first hard disk (hd0,0), which contains the kernel and initial RAM disk (initrd) to be booted. To change how that kernel boots, you can add options to the end of the kernel line. Or you can add entirely new title entries to boot different kernels or operating systems.

Some available boot options are described in Table 2-1 in Chapter 2. Options you might want to add to the end of the kernel line include 3 (to boot into runlevel 3, text mode) or ide=nodma (to turn off DMA if your system is having hard disk errors).

In normal circumstances, you don't need to run any commands to have changes to grub.conf picked up by your boot loader. When you reboot, the grub.conf file is read directly from the hard disk. However, if your MBR becomes corrupted for some reason and your system won't boot, you may need to reload the GRUB boot loader.

To reinstall GRUB on your hard disk's MBR, boot a Fedora live CD or install CD in rescue mode and follow the instructions to change root (chroot) to the hard disk partition containing your Fedora system. Then, assuming that you're booting from your computer's first SATA hard disk, type the following to **reload the boot loader to the MBR**:

```
# grub-install /dev/sda
```

179

The boot loader should now be installed on your hard disk's MBR. If your `grub.conf` file is correct, your system should be able to reboot from hard disk now.

Repairing the initial ramdisk (initrd)

The initrd file is located in `/boot` with a name like `initrd-2.6.20-1.2316.fc5.img`. If your initrd becomes corrupted, or if you need to add new block device drivers to it, run the `mkinitrd` command. First, make sure you make a copy of your existing initrd file. Then run the following command:

```
# mkinitrd -v -f /boot/initrd-2.6.20-1.2320.fc5.img 2.6.20-1.2320.fc5
```

Replace the kernel version in the example above (2.6.20-1.2320.fc5) with your own kernel version. Alternatively, to use the currently running kernel version, you can use:

```
# mkinitrd -v -f /boot/initrd-`uname -r`.img `uname -r`
```

Unfortunately, you will often realize that you need to rebuild your initrd file after it is too late, as you witness a kernel panic during the root file system mount stage of boot. When that occurs, boot into rescue mode as described in the previous section and run `mkinitrd` after `chroot`ing to the proper hard disk partition.

Controlling Startup and Run Levels

After the kernel has started up, it hands control of the system to the `init` process. The `init` process becomes the first running process on the system (`PID 1`), directing the startup of other processes based on the contents of the `/etc/inittab` file, the default run level, and the `init` scripts set to run at that run level.

The default run level is typically set to 5 for desktop systems and 3 for server systems (based on the value of `initdefault` in the `/etc/inittab` file). As noted earlier, that value can be overridden by adding a different run level number (S, 1, 2, 3, 4, or 5) to the end of the kernel boot line from the boot screen.

Most Linux administrators leave the basic startup features alone and focus on which services are turned on or off at the selected run level. The mechanism for starting run level scripts in Fedora, RHEL, and similar systems is based on the System V Init facility (sysvinit and initscripts packages), used originally in AT&T UNIX System V systems.

This section contains commands for working with `init` scripts and changing run levels. As root, you can use the `runlevel` command to **see the current run level:**

```
# runlevel            Display current and previous run levels
N 3
```

Because the system in this example booted directly to run level 3, there is no previous run level (N). To **change the current run level**, you can use the `init` command:

```
# init 5          Change the current run level to 5 (X Desktop)
```

In this example, the current run level changes from the previous level (in this case, 3) to run level 5 (which starts the X Window graphical user interface). You can also use the q option to the `init` command to **reexamine the /etc/inittab file and start or stop processes based on changes made to that file**:

```
# init q          Start or stop changed processes in inittab file
```

Note that running `init q` does not start or stop System V services. It is used mostly when tinkering with the `gettys` defined in `inittab`.

To manage services, you can use the `chkconfig` and `service` commands. For example, to **start the Samba service immediately**, you could type this:

```
# service smb start      Start Samba service immediately
Starting SMB services:           [  OK  ]
```

The `service` command starts the `init` script named (`smb` in this example) from the `/etc/init.d` directory. Most of those scripts support start and stop options, whereas some support other features as well. Here's how to use `service` to **start and stop services**:

```
# service smb            Show usage statement (with no options)
Usage: /etc/init.d/smb {start|stop|restart|reload|status|condrestart}
# service smb restart    Restart Samba service (first off, then on)
Shutting down SMB services:      [  OK  ]
Shutting down NMB services:      [  OK  ]
Starting SMB services:           [  OK  ]
Starting NMB services:           [  OK  ]
# service smb condrestart    Restart Samba service (if already running)
Shutting down SMB services:      [  OK  ]
Shutting down NMB services:      [  OK  ]
Starting SMB services:           [  OK  ]
Starting NMB services:           [  OK  ]
# service smb reload     Reload settings in smb.conf file
Reloading smb.conf file:         [  OK  ]
# service smb status     Check if the Samba service is running (smbd)
smbd (pid 25917 25915) is running...
# service smb stop       Stop Samba service
Shutting down SMB services:      [  OK  ]
Shutting down NMB services:      [  OK  ]
```

Any of the `init` scripts contained in `/etc/init.d` can be started in this way, but not all scripts support all the features just shown. Most `init` scripts, however, will show their usage statement with no option (as shown in the first example above).

Although the `service` command starts the run level script service immediately, to have a service start automatically at boot time or during a run level change, you can use the `chkconfig` command. With `chkconfig`, you can list services, turn them on, or turn them off on a per–run level basis. Here are examples:

```
# chkconfig smb on              Turn on the Samba service
# chkconfig --list smb          List runlevels service is on or off
smb      0:off    1:off    2:on    3:on    4:on    5:on    6:off
# chkconfig --list              List all services, indicating on or off
# chkconfig --level 2 smb off   Turn off Samba service for run level 2
```

When an `init` script is added to `/etc/init.d`, `chkconfig` needs to be made aware of its existence. This is done automatically when the new `init` script is part of an rpm, and needs to be done manually if you add your own `init` scripts. To do so, run the following:

```
# chkconfig --add mydaemon      Add /etc/init.d/mydaemon to chkconfig
```

Although you can use the `init` command to change to any run level, including `init 0` (shut down) and `init 6` (reboot), there are also specific commands for stopping Linux. The advantages of commands such as `halt`, `reboot`, `poweroff`, and `shutdown` are that they include options to let you stop some features before shutdown occurs. For example:

WARNING! *Don't try the following commands if you don't intend to actually turn off your system, especially on a remote system.*

```
# reboot                Reboot the computer
# halt -n               Don't run sync to sync hard drives before shutdown
# halt -h               Put hard drives in standby mode before halting
# shutdown 10           Shutdown in ten minutes after warning the users
# shutdown -r 10        Reboot in ten minutes after warning the users
# shutdown 10 'Bye!'    Send custom message to users before shutdown
```

Besides the `reboot` and `init 6` commands, you can also use the old PC keystrokes Ctrl+Alt+Del to reboot your computer. If you'd like to disable that feature, for example on a public-access PC, simply comment out the following line from `/etc/inittab`:

```
ca::ctrlaltdel:/sbin/shutdown -t3 -r now
```

Straight to the Kernel

In general, when the kernel starts up on your Linux system, you shouldn't have to do too much with it. However, there are tools for checking the kernel that is in use and for seeing information about how the kernel started up. Also, if something goes wrong or if there is some extra support you need to add to the kernel, there are tools to do those things.

To find out **what kernel is currently running on your system**, type the following:

```
$ uname -r          Display name of kernel release
2.6.21-1.3194.fc7
$ uname -a          Display all available kernel info
Linux server.domain.com 2.6.20-1.2320.fc5 #1 SMP Tue Jun 12 18:50:49 EDT
2007 x86_64 x86_64 x86_64 GNU/Linux
```

When the kernel starts, messages about what occurs are placed in the kernel ring buffer. You can **display the contents of the kernel ring buffer** using the `dmesg` command:

```
$ dmesg |less
Linux version 2.6.21-1.3194.fc7 (kojibuilder@xenbuilder4.fedora.phx.redhat.com)
(gcc version 4.1.2 20070502 (Red Hat 4.1.2-12)) #1 SMP Wed May 23 22:35:01 EDT
2007
BIOS-provided physical RAM map:
sanitize start
sanitize end
   . . .
CPU: L2 Cache: 256K (64 bytes/line)
CPU: After all inits, caps: 0183f3ff c1c7fbff 00000000 00000420 00000000
00000000 00000000
Intel machine check architecture supported.
Intel machine check reporting enabled on CPU#0.
```

If that buffer fills up, it may no longer contain the beginning of the recorded information. In that case, you can use `less /var/log/dmesg`.

Other information of interest about kernel processing can be found in the `/var/log` files — in particular, the `messages` file. You can page through those files as follows:

```
# cat /var/log/messages* | less      Page through /var/log/messages
Aug  5 21:55:46 davinci syslogd 1.4.2: restart.
Aug  6 22:12:03 davinci kernel: eth0: link up, 100Mbps, lpa 0x45E1
Aug  6 22:13:06 davinci kernel: eth0: link down
Aug  6 22:13:07 davinci kernel: eth0: link up, 100Mbps, lpa 0x45E1
Aug 10 10:53:46 davinci init: Switching to runlevel: 3
```

In the best circumstances, all the hardware connected to your computer should be detected and configured with the proper Linux drivers. In some cases, however, either the wrong driver is detected or the necessary driver may not be available on your system. For those cases, Linux offers ways of listing loadable kernel modules and adding new ones to your system.

The `lsmod` command lets you **view the names of the loaded modules**, their size, and what other modules are using them. Here is an example:

```
# lsmod
Module               Size   Used by
  . . .
parport_pc           29797  1
parport              38025  2 lp,parport_pc
```

```
snd_ens1371          28769  1
gameport             19017  1 snd_ens1371
snd_rawmidi          26561  1 snd_ens1371
snd_ac97_codec       96357  1 snd_ens1371
ac97_bus              6465  1 snd_ac97_codec
snd_timer            24773  2 snd_seq,snd_pcm
soundcore            11553  2 snd
e100                 37193  0
```

If you want to find out more information about a particular module, you can use the `modinfo` command. Here's an example:

```
# modinfo snd_ens1371
filename:       /lib/modules/2.6.21-1.3194.fc7/kernel/sound/pci/
                  snd-ens1371.ko
description:    Ensoniq/Creative AudioPCI ES1371+
license:        GPL
author:         Jaroslav Kysela <perex@suse.cz>, Thomas Sailer
                  <sailer@ife.ee.ethz.ch>
srcversion:     411FDA312BD30C6B2A8F6E7
alias:          pci:v00001102d00008938sv*sd*bc*sc*i*
alias:          pci:v00001274d00005880sv*sd*bc*sc*i*
alias:          pci:v00001274d00001371sv*sd*bc*sc*i*
depends:        snd-pcm,snd,snd-rawmidi,gameport,snd-ac97-codec
vermagic:       2.6.21-1.3194.fc7 SMP mod_unload 686 4KSTACKS
parm:   index:Index value for Ensoniq AudioPCI soundcard. (array of int)
parm:   id:ID string for Ensoniq AudioPCI soundcard. (array of charp)
parm:   enable:Enable Ensoniq AudioPCI soundcard. (array of bool)
parm:   joystick_port:Joystick port address. (array of int)
```

If you decide you need to add or remove a loadable module to get some hardware item on your system working properly, you can use the `modprobe` command. You can also use `modprobe` to list all available modules and remove modules. Here are examples:

```
# modprobe -1 | grep c-qcam    List all modules, then look for c-qcam
/lib/modules/2.6.21-1.3228.fc7/kernel/drivers/media/video/c-qcam.ko
# modprobe c-qcam              Load module for Color QuickCam
# modprobe -r c-qcam           Remove module for Color QuickCam
```

> **NOTE** *You may hear about the command* insmod. insmod *is to* modprobe *what* rpm *is to* yum: modprobe *can intelligently load module dependencies. For that reason, we recommend you use only* modprobe.

You can control kernel parameters with the system running using the `sysctl` command. You can also add parameters permanently to the `/etc/sysctl.conf` file, so they can load as a group or at each reboot. Here are some examples:

```
# sysctl -a | less          List all kernel parameters
kernel.panic = 0
kernel.exec-shield = 1
  ...
```

```
# sysctl kernel.hostname        List value of particular parameter
# sysctl -p                     Load parms from /etc/sysctl.conf
# sysctl -w kernel.hostname=joe Set value of kernel.hostname
```

As noted earlier, if you want to change any of your kernel parameters permanently, you should add them to the `/etc/sysctl.conf` file. Parameter settings in that file are in the form *parameter = value*.

Poking at the Hardware

If you just generally want to find out more about your computer's hardware, there are a few commands you can try. The `lspci` command lists information about PCI devices on your computer:

```
# lspci                         List PCI hardware items
00:00.0 Host bridge: VIA Technologies, Inc. VT8375 [KM266/KL266] Host Bridge
00:01.0 PCI bridge: VIA Technologies, Inc. VT8633 [Apollo Pro266 AGP]
00:10.0 USB Controller: VIA Technologies, Inc. VT82xxxxx UHCI USB 1.1
00:11.0 ISA bridge: VIA Technologies, Inc. VT8235 ISA Bridge
00:12.0 Ethernet controller: VIA Technologies, Inc. VT6102 [Rhine-II]
01:00.0 VGA compatible controller: S3 Inc. VT8375 [ProSavage8 KM266/KL266]
...
# lspci -v                      List PCI hardware items with more details
# lspci -vv                     List PCI hardware items with even more details
```

Using the `dmidecode` command, you can display information about your computer's hardware components, including information about what features are supported in the BIOS. Here is an example:

```
# dmidecode | less              List hardware components
# dmidecode 2.7
SMBIOS 2.3 present.
32 structures occupying 919 bytes.
Table at 0x000F0100.

Handle 0x0000, DMI type 0, 20 bytes.
BIOS Information
 Vendor: Award Software International, Inc.
 Version: F2
 Release Date: 10/06/2003
  ...
Processor Information
 Socket Designation: Socket A
 Type: Central Processor
 Family: Athlon
 Manufacturer: AMD
 ID: 44 06 00 00 FF FB 83 01
 Signature: Family 6, Model 4, Stepping 4
 Flags:
```

```
FPU (Floating-point unit on-chip)
VME (Virtual mode extension)
DE (Debugging extension)
```

You can use the `hdparm` command to **view and change information relating to your hard disk.**

> **WARNING!** *Although it's safe to view information about features of your hard disks, it can potentially damage your hard disk to change some of those settings.*

Here are some examples of printing information about your hard disks:

```
# hdparm /dev/sda          Display hard disk settings (SATA or SCSI drive)
/dev/sda:
 IO_support     = 0 (default 16-bit)
 readonly       = 0 (off)
 readahead      = 256 (on)
 geometry       = 30401/255/63, sectors = 488395055, start = 0
# hdparm /dev/hda          Display hard disk settings (IDE drive)
# hdparm -I /dev/sda       Display detailed drive information
/dev/sda:
ATA device, with non-removable media
        Model Number:       FUJITSU MPG3409AT  E
        Serial Number:      VH06T190RV9W
        Firmware Revision:  82C5
 ...
```

Summary

Fedora, RHEL, CentOS, and other Linux systems make it easy for you to watch and modify many aspects of your running system to make sure it is operating at peak performance. Commands such as `free`, `top`, `vmstat`, `slabtop`, `iostat`, and `dstat` let you see how your system is using its memory, CPU, and storage devices. Using commands such as `date`, `hwclock`, and `cal`, as well as services such as NTP, you can watch and manage your system's date and time settings.

To manage the features that are set and services that come up when you boot your system, you can modify features associated with your GRUB boot loader and system run levels. You can start, stop, list, add, and remove individual system services using commands such as `service` and `chkconfig`. Commands such as `reboot`, `halt`, and `shutdown` let you safely stop or reboot your computer.

When it comes to managing your computer's hardware, commands such as `lsmod`, `modinfo`, and `modprobe` let you work with loadable modules. You can view information about your hardware with such commands as `lspci`, `dmidecode`, and `hdparm`.

11

Managing Network Connections

Connecting to a network from Linux is often as easy as attaching your computer's network interface card to your ISP's hardware (such as a DSL or cable modem) and rebooting. However, if your network interface doesn't come up or requires some manual intervention, there are many commands available for configuring network interfaces, checking network connections, and setting up special routing.

This chapter covers many useful commands for configuring and working with your network interface cards (NICs), such as ethtool, mii-tool, and ifconfig. In particular, it covers ways of configuring wired Ethernet, wireless Ethernet, and modem network hardware. With your hardware connected and network interfaces in place, the chapter describes commands such as netstat, dig, ip, and ping for getting information about your network.

Configuring Networks from the GUI

When you first install Fedora, RHEL, or CentOS, the anaconda installer lets you configure any wired Ethernet cards attached to your computer, with the use of a DHCP server detected on your network. Alternatively, you can set a static IP address, along with your hostname and IP addresses for your gateway machine and name servers. After installation, there are also graphical tools for configuring your network interfaces.

IN THIS CHAPTER

Using ethtool and mii-tool to work with network interface cards

Getting network statistics with netstat

Starting network devices with service, chkconfig, ifup, and ifdown

Viewing Ethernet information with ifconfig and ip

Managing wireless cards with iwconfig

Configuring modems with wvdialconf, stty, and minicom

Checking DNS name resolution with dig, host, and hostname

Checking connectivity with ping and arp

Tracing connections with traceroute, route, and ip

Watching the network with netstat, tcpdump, and nmap

The Network Configuration window (select System ➾ Administration ➾ Network from the GNOME desktop) offers a GUI for configuring your network interface, network hardware, DNS servers, host list, and even IPsec virtual private networks. You can configure both dynamic (DHCP, bootp) and static IP addresses. You can even set up static network routes.

In some cases, however, your network interfaces may not be working. Likewise, there may be ways you want to work with your network interfaces that are not supported from the GUI. For those cases, the following sections describe how to work with your network interfaces from the command line.

Managing Network Interface Cards

If the network hardware on your computer didn't immediately come up and let you connect to the Internet, there are some steps you should go through to troubleshoot the problem:

❑ Check that your network interface card (NIC) is properly installed and that the cable is connected to your network (ISP's CPE, switch, and so on).

❑ After the cable is connected, make sure you have a link with no speed or duplex mismatches.

❑ If all else fails, consider replacing your NIC with known-good spare to isolate a hardware failure.

To check your link from Linux, and to set speed and duplex, there are two commands you can use: the older mii-tool (net-tools package) and the newer ethtool (ethtool rpm). Use ethtool unless you have a very old NIC and NIC driver that are not compatible with the ethtool command.

To **view the syntax of the ethtool command**, type the following:

```
# ethtool 2>&1 | less          View options to the ethtool command
```

The ethtool command outputs its built-in help to stderr. To be able to page through that help with less, we redirect stderr to stdout.

To **display settings for a specific Ethernet card**, add the interface name to the command. For example, to view card information for eth0, type:

```
# ethtool eth0                  See settings for NIC at eth0
Settings for eth0:
        Supported ports: [ TP MII ]
        Supported link modes:   10baseT/Half 10baseT/Full
                                100baseT/Half 100baseT/Full
        Supports auto-negotiation: Yes
```

```
Advertised link modes:  10baseT/Half 10baseT/Full
                        100baseT/Half 100baseT/Full
Advertised auto-negotiation: Yes
Speed: 100Mb/s
Duplex: Full
Port: MII
PHYAD: 1
Transceiver: internal
Auto-negotiation: on
Supports Wake-on: g
Wake-on: g
Current message level: 0x00000007 (7)
Link detected: yes
```

To find out about the driver being used for a particular network card, use the -i option:

```
# ethtool -i eth0      Display driver information for NIC
driver: e1000
version: 7.3.15-k2-NAPI
firmware-version: 0.5-7
bus-info: 0000:04:00.0
```

Use the -S option to **display detailed statistics for a NIC:**

```
# ethtool -S eth0      Show statistics for NIC at eth0
NIC statistics:
     rx_packets: 1326384
     tx_packets: 773046
     rx_bytes: 1109944723
     tx_bytes: 432773480
     rx_errors: 5
     tx_errors: 2
     rx_dropped: 0
     tx_dropped: 0
     multicast: 0
     collisions: 0
     rx_length_errors: 0
     rx_over_errors: 0
     rx_crc_errors: 5
     rx_frame_errors: 0
     rx_fifo_errors: 0
     rx_missed_errors: 0
     tx_aborted_errors: 0
     tx_carrier_errors: 2
  . . .
```

The ethtool command can be used to **change NIC settings** as well as display them. To turn off auto-negotiation and hard-set the NIC to 100 Mpbs, full duplex, type this:

```
# ethtool -s eth0 speed 100 duplex full autoneg off   Change NIC settings
```

To turn off auto-negotiation and hard-set the speed to 10 Mpbs, half-duplex, type this:

```
# ethtool -s eth0 speed 10 duplex half autoneg off    Change NIC settings
```

The changes just made to your NIC settings are good for the current session. When you reboot, however, those setting will be lost. To **make these settings stick at the next reboot or network restart**, add the options you want to the ETHTOOL_OPTS line in the /etc/ sysconfig/network-scripts/ifcfg-eth0 file. For example:

```
ETHTOOL_OPTS="speed 10 duplex half autoneg off"
```

As mentioned earlier, ethtool may not work on some older NICs. So **if you have an older NIC, try using mii-tool** as follows:

```
# mii-tool        Show negotiated speed and link status of old NIC
eth0: negotiated 100baseTx-FD flow-control, link ok
```

This example was taken from the same machine as the examples above, with the NIC auto-negotiating at 1000 Mbps, full-duplex. The mii-tool command is mis-reading the speed setting. This is why we recommend using mii-tool only as a last resort if ethtool doesn't work with your old NIC.

To **display mii-tool output with more verbosity,** use the -v option:

```
# mii-tool -v       Show verbose output of settings for old NIC
eth0: negotiated 100baseTx-FD flow-control, link ok
  product info: vendor 00:50:43, model 12 rev 2
  basic mode:   autonegotiation enabled
  basic status: autonegotiation complete, link ok
  capabilities: 100baseTx-FD 100baseTx-HD 10baseT-FD 10baseT-HD
  advertising:  100baseTx-FD 100baseTx-HD 10baseT-FD 10baseT-HD flow-control
  link partner: 100baseTx-FD 100baseTx-HD 10baseT-FD 10baseT-HD flow-control
```

In the example just shown, you can see that each mode (100baseTx and 10baseT) supports both half-duplex (HD) and full duplex (FD). To **disable auto-negotiation and force a particular setting,** use the -F option as follows:

```
# mii-tool -F 10baseT-FD eth0    Force speed/duplex to 10baseT-FD
```

If you change your mind and later want to **re-enable auto-negotiation,** use the -r option:

```
# mii-tool -r eth0       Re-enable auto-negotiation for an old NIC
restarting autonegotiation...
```

mii-tool does not provide a capability to save settings like ethtool does, so you have to run it after every reboot. This can be done by adding it at the end of /etc/ rc.local.

The netstat command provides another way to **get network interface statistics:**

```
$ netstat -i          Get network interface statistics for eth0
Kernel Interface table
Iface MTU Met RX-OK RX-ERR RX-DRP RX-OVR TX-OK TX-ERR TX-DRP TX-OVR Flg
eth0 1500 0 1757208    6     0      0 996834    4     0      0 BMRU
```

Use the -c option to get netstat to **refresh network interface statistics every second:**

```
$ netstat -ic          Refresh network statistics every second
```

You can **get cleaner (screen-oriented) refreshed output** from netstat by combining it with the watch command as follows:

```
$ watch netstat -i     Refresh network statistics (screen oriented)
Every 2.0s: netstat -i                  Wed Aug 22 01:55:48 2007

Kernel Interface table
Iface MTU Met RX-OK RX-ERR RX-DRP RX-OVR TX-OK TX-ERR TX-DRP TX-OVR Flg
eth0 1500 0 1757208    6     0      0 996834    4     0      0 BMRU
```

As the output indicates, the netstat statistics are updated every 2.0 seconds.

Managing Network Connections

Starting and stopping the network interfaces for your wired Ethernet connections to your LAN or the Internet is usually handled automatically at the time you boot and shut down your Fedora system. However, you can use the service command to start and stop your network interfaces any time you want or chkconfig to change whether or not your network starts automatically.

The ifconfig and ip commands can also be used to configure, activate, and deactivate interfaces. However, on Fedora and other Red Hat derivatives, service and chkconfig commands provide simpler tools to start and stop network interfaces. Therefore, in most cases, you should only use ifconfig and ip commands to gather information about your Ethernet interfaces and NICs (as shown later in this section).

Starting and Stopping Ethernet Connections

The reason that your wired Ethernet interfaces just come up in many cases when you boot Fedora is that the network service is set to be on when the system enters the common boot run levels (run level 3 and 5). There is a set of underlying configuration files and scripts that make that happen and a few simple commands that let you control it.

For Fedora, RHEL, and CentOS, control scripts and configuration files are located in the /etc/sysconfig/network-scripts/ directory. NICs are configured by editing /etc/sysconfig/network-scripts/ifcfg-*interface*, where *interface* is your NIC's network interface. For example, for the first Ethernet interface, the configuration file is named ifcfg-eth0.

To **get more information on network-scripts files**, type the following and search for the network-scripts section:

```
$ less /usr/share/doc/initscripts-*/sysconfig.txt
```

The script that starts the configured network-scripts files is /etc/init.d/network. As with other Linux services, you can start and stop the network service using the service command and set it to start automatically with the chkconfig command.

To **take all NICs offline then bring them back online**, allowing any change to the network scripts to take effect, type the following:

```
# service network restart        Shutdown and bring up network interfaces
Shutting down interface eth0:                        [ OK ]
Shutting down loopback interface:                    [ OK ]
Bringing up loopback interface:                      [ OK ]
Bringing up interface eth0:                          [ OK ]
```

Use the start and stop options to **start and stop your network interfaces**, respectively:

```
# service network stop        Shutdown network interfaces
# service network start       Bring up network interfaces
```

To **check the status of your network interfaces**, type the following:

```
# service network status        Check network interface status
Configured devices:
lo eth0
Currently active devices:
lo eth0
```

The service command starts your network interfaces for the current session, but doesn't configure them to start the next time your system boots. To **configure your network connections to start when Linux boots**, use the chkconfig command as follows:

```
# chkconfig network on         Turn on network service to start at boot
# chkconfig --list network     View runlevels where network is off or on
network      0:off    1:off    2:on    3:on    4:on    5:on    6:off
```

If you have multiple network interfaces, you may want to just **bring one interface up or down**. To do that, use the ifup and ifdown commands:

```
# ifdown eth0        Take the eth0 network interface offline
# ifup eth0          Bring the eth0 network interface online
```

Once your network interfaces are up, there are tools you can use to view information about those interfaces and associated NICs.

Viewing Ethernet Connection Information

To view the media access control (MAC) address for your NIC and IP address for your TCP/IP connections, you can use the `ifconfig` command. The following command line shows the address information and status of your eth0 Ethernet interface:

```
# ifconfig eth0
eth0      Link encap:Ethernet  HWaddr 00:D0:B7:79:A5:35
          inet addr:10.0.0.155  Bcast:10.0.0.255  Mask:255.255.255.0
          inet6 addr: fe80::2d0:b7ff:fe79:a535/64 Scope:Link
          UP BROADCAST RUNNING MULTICAST  MTU:1500  Metric:1
          RX packets:1413382 errors:6 dropped:0 overruns:0 frame:6
          TX packets:834839 errors:4 dropped:0 overruns:0 carrier:4
          collisions:0 txqueuelen:1000
          RX bytes:1141608691 (1.0 GiB)  TX bytes:470961026 (449.1 MiB)
```

In this example, the eth0 interface is the first Ethernet interface on the computer. The MAC address (HWaddr) of the NIC is 00:D0:B7:79:A5:35. You can see the eth0 IP address (10.0.0.155), broadcast address (10.0.0.255), and subnet mask (255.255.255.0). Other information includes the number of packets received and transmitted, as well as problems (errors, dropped packets, and overruns) that occurred on the interface.

To get information on both active and inactive NICs, use the `-a` option:

```
# ifconfig -a
```

Instead of using `ifconfig` (and several other commands described in this chapter), you can use the newer `ip` command. The `ip` command was made to show information about your network interfaces, as well as changing settings for network devices, routing, and IP tunnels. Here the `ip` command is used to show information about the eth0 interface:

```
# ip addr show eth0
1: eth0: <BROADCAST,MULTICAST,UP,LOWER_UP> mtu 1500 qdisc pfifo_fast qlen 1000
    link/ether 00:d0:b7:79:a5:35 brd ff:ff:ff:ff:ff:ff
    inet 10.0.0.155/24 brd 10.0.0.255 scope global eth0
    inet6 fe80::2d0:b7ff:fe79:a535/64 scope link
       valid_lft forever preferred_lft forever
```

The `ip` command allows for shorthand syntax. If you're familiar with the Cisco IOS command line interface, the `ip` command works the same way. For example, instead of typing `ip addr show`, you could type the following to see information on all interfaces:

```
# ip a
```

The `ip` command can operate on multiple network components, known as *objects*. One of these objects is `addr`, which allows `ip` to configure network addresses. We will cover other objects of the `ip` command below.

To **see how the ip command is used,** use the `help` option. Along with the `help` option, you can identify an `ip` object to get information on using that object:

```
$ ip help            View ip usage statement
Usage: ip [ OPTIONS ] OBJECT { COMMAND | help }
       ip [ -force ] [-batch filename
where  OBJECT := { link | addr | route | rule | neigh | ntable | tunnel|
                   maddr | mroute | monitor | xfrm }
       OPTIONS := { -V[ersion] | -s[tatistics] | -r[esolve] |
                    -f[amily] { inet | inet6 | ipx | dnet | link } |
                    -o[neline] | -t[imestamp] }
$ ip addr help       View help for the addr object
$ ip route help      View help for the route object
$ ip tunnel help     View help for the tunnel object
```

Understanding subnetwork masks can be confusing if you're not used to them. You may find `ipcalc` useful to **calculate a host computer's netmask from its CIDR IP address:**

```
$ ipcalc -bmn 192.168.1.100/27
NETMASK=255.255.255.224
BROADCAST=192.168.1.127
NETWORK=192.168.1.96
```

In the example just shown, the netmask (which indicates which part of an IP address represents the network and which represents the host) is 255.255.255.224. That was derived from the /27 value at the end of the IP address 192.168.1.100.

Using Wireless Connections

Setting up wireless connections in Fedora has been tricky in the past, primarily due to the fact that open source drivers have not been available for the vast majority of wireless LAN cards on the market. The Fedora Project helped greatly to solve this problem starting with Fedora 7 by including firmware for wireless LAN cards that could be freely distributed (although not available as open source). So now many wireless cards can be detected and configured automatically in Fedora.

Wireless configuration is an area where we would suggest you use the GUI tools (in particular, the Network Configuration window described earlier in this chapter, or Network Manager) to do basic configuration. You may need to add wireless tools packages to get this to work, such as wireless-tools and bcm43xx-fwcutter packages, which are available with Fedora. Likewise, you may need firmware that is available in the following packages: ipw2100-firmware, ipw2200-firmware, zd1211-firmware, and iwlwifi-firmware packages.

If you are not able to configure your wireless LAN card using the Network Configuration window, you might be able to get your wireless card working using drivers and tools available from Atheros (www.atheros.com), the MadWifi (www.madwifi.org) project, or the Ndiswrapper project (ndiswrapper.sourceforge.net). RPM packages of software from those projects are available from the rpm.livna.org repository, described in Chapter 2.

If you need help determining exactly what wireless card you have, type the following:

```
# lspci | grep -i wireless          Search for wireless PCI cards
01:09.0 Network controller: Broadcom Corporation BCM4306 802.11b/g
    Wireless LAN Controller (rev 03)
```

Assuming that your wireless card is up and running, there are some useful commands in the wireless-tools package you can use to view and change settings for your wireless cards. In particular, the iwconfig command can help you work with your wireless LAN interfaces. The following scans your network interfaces for supported wireless cards and lists their current settings:

```
# iwconfig
eth0      no wireless extensions.
eth1      IEEE 802.11-DS  ESSID:""  Nickname:"HERMES I"
          Mode:Managed  Frequency:2.457 GHz  Access Point: Not-Associated
          Bit Rate:11 Mb/s   Tx-Power=15 dBm   Sensitivity:1/3
          Retry limit:4   RTS thr:off   Fragment thr:off
          Encryption key:off
          Power Management:off
```

Wireless interfaces may be named wlanX or ethX, depending on the hardware and driver used. You may be able to obtain more information after setting the link up on the wireless interface:

```
# ip link set eth1 up
# iwconfig eth1

eth1      IEEE 802.11-DS  ESSID:""  Nickname:"HERMES I"
          Mode:Managed  Frequency:2.457 GHz  Access Point: None
          Bit Rate:11 Mb/s   Tx-Power=15 dBm   Sensitivity:1/3
          Retry limit:4   RTS thr:off   Fragment thr:off
          Encryption key:off
          Power Management:off
          Link Quality=0/92  Signal level=134/153  Noise level=134/153
          Rx invalid nwid:0  Rx invalid crypt:0  Rx invalid frag:0
          Tx excessive retries:0  Invalid misc:0   Missed beacon:0
```

The settings just shown can be modified in a lot of ways. Here are some ways to use iwconfig to modify your wireless interface settings. In the following examples, we operate on a wireless interface named wlan0. These operations may or may not be supported, depending on which wireless card and driver you are using.

```
# iwconfig wlan0 essid "MyWireless"    Set essid to MyWireless
# iwconfig wlan0 channel 3             Set the channel to 3
# iwconfig wlan0 mode Ad-Hoc           Change from Managed to Ad-Hoc mode
# iwconfig wlan0 ap any                Use any access point available
# iwconfig wlan0 sens -50              Set sensitivity to -50
# iwconfig wlan0 retry 20              Set MAC retransmissions to 20
# iwconfig wlan0 key 1234-5555-66      Set encryption key to 1234-5555-66
```

The essid is sometimes called the Network Name or Domain ID. Use it as the common name to identify your wireless network. Setting the channel lets your wireless LAN operate on that specific channel.

With Ad-Hoc mode, the network is composed of only interconnected clients with no central access point. In Managed/Infrastructure mode, by setting ap to a specific MAC address, you can force the card to connect to the access point at that address, or you can set ap to any and allow connections to any access point.

If you have performance problems, try adjusting the sensitivity (sens) to either a negative value (which represents dBm) or positive value (which is either a percentage or a sensitivity value set by the vendor). If you get retransmission failures, you can increase the retry value so your card can send more packets before failing.

Use the key option to set an encryption key. You can enter hexadecimal digits (XXXX-XXXX-XXXX-XXXX or XXXXXXXX). By adding an s: in front of the key, you can enter an ASCII string as the key (as in s:My927pwd).

Using Dial-up Modems

Although high-speed DSL, cable modem, and wireless LAN hardware have become widely available, there may still be times when a phone line and a modem are your only way to get on the Internet. Linux offers both graphical and command line tools for configuring and communicating with modems.

As with other network connections in Fedora, dial-up modem connections can be configured using the Network Configuration window. Most external serial modems will work with Linux without any special configuration. Most hardware PCI modems will also work. However, many software modems (also sometimes called Winmodems) often will not work in Linux (although some can be configured with special drivers, and are therefore referred to as Linmodems).

Instead of describing the contortions you must go through to get some Winmodems working in Linux, we recommend that you purchase either a modem that connects to an external serial port or a hardware modem. If you want to try configuring your Winmodem yourself, refer to the Linmodems site (www.linmodems.org).

If you are not able to get your modem working from the Network Configuration window, you can try several commands. First try the wvdialconf command to try to scan any modems connected to your serial ports and create a configuration file:

```
# wvdialconf /etc/wvdial.conf    Scan serial ports, create config file
Scanning your serial ports for a modem.

ttyS0: ATQ0 V1 E1 -- OK
ttyS0: ATQ0 V1 E1 Z -- OK
  . . .
```

In this example, a modem was found on the COM1 port (serial port /dev/ttyS0). Further output should show which speeds are available and various features that are supported. The configuration information that results is, in this case, written to the file /etc/wvdial.conf. Here's an example of what that file might look like:

```
[Dialer Defaults]
Modem = /dev/ttyS0
Baud = 115200
Init1 = ATZ
Init2 = ATQ0 V1 E1 S0=0 &C1 &D2 S11=55 +FCLASS=0
;Phone =
;Username =
;Password =
```

Open wvdial.conf in a text editor and remove the comment characters (;) from in front of the Phone, Username, and Password entries. Then add the phone number you need to dial to reach your ISP's bank of dial-in modems. Next add the user name and password you need to log in to that modem connection.

To use the dial-up entry you just configured, you can use the wvdial command:

```
# wvdial                     Dial out and connect to your ISP
--> WvDial: Internet dialer version 1.54.0
--> Initializing modem.
--> Sending: ATZ
ATZ
OK
--> Modem initialized.
  . . .
```

After the connection is established between the two modems, a Point-to-Point Protocol (ppp) connection is created between the two points. After that, you should be able to start communicating over the Internet.

If you find that you are not able to communicate with your modem, there are some ways of querying your computer's serial ports to find out what is going wrong. The first thing to check at the low level is that your /dev/ttyS? device talks to the hardware serial port.

By default, the Linux system knows of four serial ports: COM1 (/dev/ttyS0), COM2 (/dev/ttyS1), COM3 (/dev/ttyS2), and COM4 (/dev/ttyS3). To see a listing of those serial ports use the setserial command with the -g option, as follows:

```
# setserial -g /dev/ttyS0 /dev/ttyS1 /dev/ttyS2 /dev/ttyS3 See port info
/dev/ttyS0, UART: 16550A, Port: 0x03f8, IRQ: 4
/dev/ttyS1, UART: unknown, Port: 0x02f8, IRQ: 3
/dev/ttyS2, UART: unknown, Port: 0x03e8, IRQ: 4
/dev/ttyS3, UART: unknown, Port: 0x02e8, IRQ: 3
```

To see more detailed information on your serial ports, use the -a option:

```
# setserial -a /dev/ttyS0          View serial port details
/dev/ttyS0, Line 0, UART: 16550A, Port: 0x03f8, IRQ: 4
        Baud_base: 115200, close_delay: 50, divisor: 0
        closing_wait: 3000
        Flags: spd_normal skip_test
# setserial -ga /dev/ttyS0 /dev/ttyS1   Check multiple port details
```

The setserial command can also be used to re-map physical serial ports to logical /dev/ttyS? devices. Unless you're running kernel 2.2 with a jumper-configured ISA serial card, you won't need this. Modern Linux systems running on modern hardware make COM1 and COM2 serial ports work right out of the box, so we won't cover these options.

The stty command is another command you can use to work with serial ports. To view the current settings for the COM1 port (ttyS0), type the following:

```
# stty -F /dev/ttyS0 -a          View tty settings for serial port
speed 9600 baud; rows 0; columns 0; line = 0;
intr = ^C; quit = ^\; erase = ^?; kill = ^U; eof = ^D; eol = <undef>; eol2 =
<undef>; swtch = <undef>; start = ^Q; stop = ^S;
susp = ^Z; rprnt = ^R; werase = ^W; lnext = ^V; flush = ^O; min = 1; time = 0;
-parenb -parodd cs8 hupcl -cstopb cread clocal -crtscts
-ignbrk -brkint -ignpar -parmrk -inpck -istrip -inlcr -igncr icrnl ixon -ixoff -
iuclc -ixany -imaxbel -iutf8
opost -olcuc -ocrnl onlcr -onocr -onlret -ofill -ofdel nl0 cr0 tab0 bs0 vt0 ff0
isig icanon iexten echo echoe echok -echonl -noflsh -xcase -tostop -echoprt
echoctl echoke
```

The dialer will typically change these settings as needed, although you can use the stty command to change these settings as well. Refer to the stty man page (man stty) for descriptions of any of the tty settings.

You can **talk directly to the modem or other serial devices** using the minicom command. In fact, it can be useful to troubleshoot dialing by issuing AT commands to the modem using minicom. The first time you run minicom, use -s to **enter setup mode**:

```
# minicom -s          Create your modem settings
+-----[configuration]-----+
| Filenames and paths     |
| File transfer protocols  |
| Serial port setup       |
| Modem and dialing       |
| Screen and keyboard     |
| Save setup as dfl       |
| Save setup as..         |
| Exit                    |
| Exit from Minicom       |
+-------------------------+
```

Let's forget about modems for a moment and assume you want to use COM1 to connect to a Cisco device at 9600 baud. Use the arrow keys to navigate to Serial port setup and press Enter to select it. Press a to edit the serial device and change that device to /dev/ttyS0. Next, press e for port settings and when the Comm Parameters screen appears, press e for 9600 baud. To toggle off hardware flow control, press f. Press Enter to return to the configuration screen.

To change modem parameters, select modem and dialing. Then clear the init, reset, connect, and hangup strings (which are not appropriate for the Cisco device configured here). When that's done, select save setup as dfl (default) from the configuration screen and choose Exit (not Exit from Minicom).

You're now in the minicom terminal. To learn more about how to use minicom, press Ctrl+a, then z for help. When you are done, press Ctrl+a, then x to exit from minicom.

> **WARNING!** *Do not run minicom inside* screen *with the default key bindings! Otherwise, Ctrl+a gets intercepted by* screen*! If you do so by mistake, go to another* screen *window and type:* killall minicom.

Checking Name Resolution

Because IP addresses are numbers, and people prefer to address things by name, TCP/IP networks (such as the Internet) rely on DNS to resolve hostnames into IP addresses. Fedora provides several tools for looking up information related to DNS name resolution.

When you first installed Fedora, you either identified Domain Name System (DNS) servers to do name resolution or had them assigned automatically from a DHCP server. That information is then stored in the /etc/resolv.conf file, looking something like the following:

```
nameserver 11.22.33.44
nameserver 22.33.44.55
```

The numbers shown above are replaced by real IP addresses of computers that serve as DNS name servers. When you can connect to working DNS servers, you can use commands to query those servers and look up host computers.

You can use the dig command (which should be used instead of the deprecated nslookup command) to look up information from a DNS server. The host command can be used to look up address information for a hostname or domain name.

To search your DNS servers for a particular host name (www.turbosphere.com in the following examples), use the dig command as follows:

```
$ dig www.turbosphere.com     Search DNS servers set in /etc/resolv.conf
```

199

Instead of using your assigned name server, you can **query a specific name server.** The following example queries the DNS server at 4.2.2.1:

```
$ dig www.turbosphere.com @4.2.2.1
```

Using dig, you can also **query for a specific record type:**

```
$ dig turbosphere.com mx    Queries for the mail exchanger
$ dig turbosphere.com ns    Queries for the authoritative name servers
```

Use the +trace option to **trace a recursive query** from the top-level DNS servers down to the authoritative servers:

```
$ dig +trace www.turbosphere.com    Recursively trace DNS servers
```

If you just want to **see the IP address of a host computer,** use the +short option:

```
$ dig +short www.turbosphere.com    Display only name/IP address pair
turbosphere.com.
66.113.99.70
```

You can use dig **to do a reverse lookup to find DNS information based on an IP address:**

```
$ dig -x 66.113.99.70              Get DNS information based on IP address
```

You can use host **to do a reverse DNS lookup** as well:

```
$ host 66.113.99.70
70.99.133.66.in-addr.arpa domain name pointer boost.turbosphere.com.
```

To **get hostname information for the local machine,** use the hostname and dnsdomainname commands:

```
$ hostname                  View the local computer's full DNS host name
boost.turbosphere.com
$ hostname -s               View the local computer's short host name
boost
$ hostname -d               View the local computer's domain name
turbosphere.com
$ dnsdomainname             Another way to view the local domain name
turbosphere.com
```

You can also use hostname to **set the local hostname temporarily** (until the next reboot). Here's an example:

```
# hostname server1.example.com    Set local hostname
```

Changing the hostname of a running machine may adversely affect some running daemons. Instead, we recommend you **set the local hostname so it is set each time the system**

starts up. Edit the `HOSTNAME=` line in the `/etc/sysconfig/network` file. Here is an example:

```
HOSTNAME=server1.example.com
```

Troubleshooting Network Problems

Troubleshooting networks is generally done from the bottom layer up. As discussed in the beginning of this chapter, the first step is to make sure that the physical network layer components (cables, NICs, and so on) are connected and working. Next, check that the links between physical nodes are working. After that, there are lots of tools for checking the connectivity to a particular host.

Checking Connectivity to a Host

When you know you have a link and no duplex mismatch, the next step is to `ping` your default gateway. You should have configured the default gateway (gw) either in the `/etc/sysconfig/network` file or in the individual network card's `/etc/sysconfig/network-script/ifcfg-eth?` script. To **check your default gateway in the actual routing table,** use the `ip` command as follows:

```
# ip route
10.0.0.0/24 dev eth0  proto kernel  scope link  src 10.0.0.155
169.254.0.0/16 dev eth0  scope link
default via 10.0.0.1 dev eth0
```

The gateway for the default route is 10.0.0.1. To **make sure there is IP connectivity to that gateway,** use the `ping` command as follows:

```
$ ping 10.0.0.1
PING 10.0.0.1 (10.0.0.1) 56(84) bytes of data.
64 bytes from 10.0.0.1: icmp_seq=1 ttl=64 time=0.382 ms
64 bytes from 10.0.0.1: icmp_seq=2 ttl=64 time=0.313 ms
64 bytes from 10.0.0.1: icmp_seq=3 ttl=64 time=0.360 ms
64 bytes from 10.0.0.1: icmp_seq=4 ttl=64 time=1.43 ms

--- 10.0.0.1 ping statistics ---
4 packets transmitted, 4 received, 0% packet loss, time 2999ms
rtt min/avg/max/mdev = 0.313/0.621/1.432/0.469 ms
```

By default, `ping` continues until you press Ctrl+c. Other `ping` options include the following:

```
$ ping -a 10.0.0.1        Add an audible ping as ping progresses
$ ping -c 4 10.0.0.1      Ping 4 times and exit (default in Windows)
$ ping -q -c 5 10.0.0.1   Show summary of pings (works best with -c)
# ping -f 10.0.0.1        Send a flood of pings (must be root)
```

```
$ ping -i 3 10.0.0.1      Send packets in 3-second intervals
# ping -I eth0 10.0.0.1   Set source to eth0 (use if multiple NICs)
PING 10.0.0.1 (10.0.0.1) from 10.0.0.155 eth0: 56(84) bytes of data.
# ping -I 10.0.0.155 10.0.0.1    Set source to 10.0.0.155
PING 10.0.0.1 (10.0.0.1) from 10.0.0.155 : 56(84) bytes of data.
$ ping -s 1500 10.0.0.1   Set packet size to 1500 bytes
PING 10.0.0.1 (10.0.0.1) 1500(1528) bytes of data.
```

Use the ping flood option with caution. By default, ping sends small packets (56 bytes). Large packets (such as the 1500-byte setting just shown) are good to make faulty NICs or connections stand out.

Checking Address Resolution Protocol (ARP)

If you're not able to ping your gateway, you may have an issue at the Ethernet MAC layer. The Address Resolution Protocol (ARP) can be used to find information at the MAC layer. To view and configure ARP entries, use the arp or ip neighbor command. This example shows arp listing computers in the ARP cache by hostname:

```
# arp -v           List ARP cache entries by name
Address         HWtype  HWaddress          Flags Mask    Iface
ritchie         ether   00:10:5A:AB:F6:A7  C              eth0
einstein        ether   00:0B:6A:02:EC:98  C              eth0
Entries: 1  Skipped: 0  Found: 1
```

In this example, you can see the names of other computers that the local computer's ARP cache knows about and the associated hardware type and hardware address (MAC address) of each computer's NIC. You can **disable name resolution to see those computers' IP addresses** instead:

```
# arp -vn          List ARP cache entries by IP address
Address         HWtype  HWaddress          Flags Mask    Iface
10.0.0.1        ether   00:10:5A:AB:F6:A7  C              eth0
10.0.0.50       ether   00:0B:6A:02:EC:98  C              eth0
Entries: 1  Skipped: 0  Found: 1
```

To **delete an entry from the ARP cache,** use the -d option:

```
# arp -d 10.0.0.50          Delete address 10.0.0.50 from ARP cache
```

Instead of just letting ARP dynamically learn about other systems, you can **add static ARP entries to the cache** using the -s option:

```
# arp -s 10.0.0.51 00:0B:6A:02:EC:95    Add IP and MAC addresses to ARP
```

To do the same actions with the `ip` command that you just did with the `arp` command, use the `neighbor` object (notice that `neighbor`, `nei`, and `n` objects can be used interchangeably):

```
# ip neighbor
10.0.0.1 dev eth0 lladdr 00:10:5a:ab:f6:a7 DELAY
10.0.0.50 dev eth0 lladdr 00:0b:6a:02:ec:98 REACHABLE
# ip nei del 10.0.0.50 dev eth0
# ip n add 10.0.0.51 lladdr 00:0B:6A:02:EC:95 dev eth0
```

To **query a subnet to see if an IP is already in use**, and to find the MAC address of the device using it, use the `arping` command. The `arping` command is used by `ifup` to avoid IP conflicts when bringing an Ethernet NIC up. Here are examples:

```
# arping 10.0.0.50              Query subnet to see if 10.0.0.50 is in use
ARPING 10.0.0.50 from 10.0.0.195 eth0
Unicast reply from 10.0.0.50 [00:0B:6A:02:EC:98]  0.694ms
Unicast reply from 10.0.0.50 [00:0B:6A:02:EC:98]  0.683ms
# arping -I eth0 10.0.0.50    Specify interface to query from
```

Like the `ping` command, the `arping` command continuously queries for the address until the command is ended by typing Ctrl+c. Typically, you just want to know if the target is alive, so you can run one of the following commands:

```
# arping -f 10.0.0.50      Query 10.0.0.50 and stop at the first reply
# arping -c 2 10.0.0.51    Query 10.0.0.50 and stop after 2 counts
```

Tracing Routes to Hosts

After you make sure that you can ping your gateway and even reach machines that are outside of your network, you may still have issues reaching a specific host or network. If that's true, you can **use traceroute to find the bottleneck or point of failure**:

```
$ traceroute boost.turbosphere.com   Follow the route taken to a host
traceroute to boost.turbosphere.com (66.113.99.70),30 hops max,40 byte packets
 1  10.0.0.1 (10.0.0.1)  0.281 ms  0.289 ms  0.237 ms
 2  t1-03.hbci.com (64.211.114.1)  6.213 ms  6.189 ms  6.083 ms
 3  172.17.2.153 (172.17.2.153)  14.070 ms  14.025 ms  13.974 ms
 4  so-0-3-2.ar2.MIN1.gblx.net (208.48.1.117)  19.076 ms  19.053 ms 19.004 ms
 5  so1-0-0-2488M.ar4.SEA1.gblx.net(67.17.71.210)94.697 ms 94.668 ms 94.612ms
 6  64.215.31.114 (64.215.31.114)  99.643 ms  101.647 ms  101.577 ms
 7  dr02-v109.tac.opticfusion.net(209.147.112.50)262.301ms 233.316ms 233.153 ms
 8  dr01-v100.tac.opticfusion.net (66.113.96.1) 99.313 ms 99.401 ms 99.353 ms
 9  boost.turbosphere.com (66.113.99.70)  99.251 ms  96.215 ms  100.220 ms
```

As you can see, the longest hop is between 4 (Global Crossing probably in Minneapolis) and 5 (GC in Seattle). That gap is not really a bottleneck; it just reflects the distance between those hops. Sometimes, the last hops look like this:

```
28  * * *
29  * * *
30  * * *
```

The lines of asterisks (*) at the end of the trace can be caused by firewalls that block traffic to the target. However, if you see several asterisks before the destination, those can indicate heavy congestion or equipment failures and point to a bottleneck.

By default, traceroute uses UDP packets, which provide a more realistic performance picture than ICMP. That's because some Internet hops will give lower priority to ICMP traffic. If you'd still like to trace using ICMP packets, try one of these two commands:

```
# traceroute -I boost.turbosphere.com   Use ICMP packets to trace a route
# tracert boost.turbosphere.com         Use ICMP packets to trace a route
```

To trace a route to a remote host using TCP packets, use the -T option to traceroute:

```
# traceroute -T boost.turbosphere.com   Use TCP packets to trace a route
```

By default, traceroute connects to port 80. You can set a different port using the -p option:

```
# traceroute -T -p 25 boost.turbosphere.com   Connect to port 25 in trace
```

You can view IP addresses instead of hostnames by disabling name resolution of hops:

```
$ traceroute -n boost.turbosphere.com   Disable name resolution in trace
```

An alternative to traceroute is the tracepath command, which also uses UDP to perform the trace:

```
$ tracepath boost.turbosphere.com       Use UDP to trace the route
```

To view and manipulate the kernel's routing table, the route command used to be the tool of choice. This is slowly being replaced by the ip route command. For the most part, the Fedora network scripts rely on ip route. But it doesn't hurt to be familiar with both commands, because route is still quite commonly used.

You can use the old route command to display your local routing table. Here are two examples of the route command, with and without DNS name resolution:

```
# route                  Display local routing table information
Kernel IP routing table
```

```
Destination   Gateway    Genmask         Flags Metric Ref    Use Iface
10.0.0.0      *          255.255.255.0   U     0      0        0 eth0
default       ritchie    0.0.0.0         UG    0      0        0 eth0
# route -n         Display routing table without DNS lookup
Kernel IP routing table
Destination   Gateway    Genmask         Flags Metric Ref    Use Iface
10.0.0.0      *          255.255.255.0   U     0      0        0 eth0
0.0.0.0       10.0.0.1   0.0.0.0         UG    0      0        0 eth0
```

You can **add a default gateway** using the gw option:

```
# route add default gw 10.0.0.2     Add 10.0.0.2 as default gateway
```

You can **add a new route to your network** by specifying either the interface (eth0) or IP address of the gateway (such as gw 10.0.0.100):

```
# route add -net 192.168.0.0 netmask 255.255.255.0 eth0
# route add -net 192.168.0.0 netmask 255.255.255.0 gw 10.0.0.100
```

You can **delete a route** using the del option:

```
# route del -net 192.168.0.0 netmask 255.255.255.0   Delete a route
```

Using the newer ip command, you can do the same activities just shown with the route command. Here are three different ways to show the same basic routing information:

```
# ip route show          Display basic routing information
10.0.0.0/24 dev eth0  proto kernel  scope link  src 10.0.0.195
169.254.0.0/16 dev eth0  scope link
default via 10.0.0.1 dev eth0
# ip route               Display basic routing (example #2)
# ip r                   Display basic routing (example #3)
```

Here are some examples for **adding and deleting routes with ip:**

```
# ip r add 192.168.0.0/24 via 10.0.0.100 dev eth0 Add route to interface
# ip r add 192.168.0.0/24 via 10.0.0.100          Add route no interface
# ip r del 192.168.0.0/24                          Delete route
```

To **make a new route permanent,** create a /etc/sysconfig/network-scripts/ file named route-ethX (for example, route-eth0) and place the information about the new route in that file. For example, to add the route added with the ip command above, add the following lines to /etc/sysconfig/network-scripts/route-eth0:

```
ADDRESS0=192.168.0.0
NETMASK0=255.255.255.0
GATEWAY0=10.0.0.100
```

Displaying netstat Connections and Statistics

The tools above cover network troubleshooting mostly at the network layer (layer 3). To display information about packets sent between transport-layer protocols (TCP and UDP) and ICMP, you can use the netstat command:

```
$ netstat -s | less      Show summary of TCP, ICMP, UDP activities
```

You can see a list of all TCP connections, including which process is handling the connection:

```
# netstat -tanp          View active TCP connections
Active Internet connections (servers and established)
Proto Recv-Q Send-Q Local Address  Foreign Address  State  PID/Program name
tcp       0      0 127.0.0.1:631   0.0.0.0:*        LISTEN 2039/cupsd
tcp       0      0 127.0.0.1:25    0.0.0.0:*        LISTEN 2088/sendmail
   ...
```

You can also view active UDP connections as follows:

```
# netstat -uanp          View active UDP connections
Active Internet connections (servers and established)
Proto Recv-Q Send-Q Local Address    Foreign Address State PID/Program name
udp       0      0 0.0.0.0:631       0.0.0.0:*             2039/cupsd
udp       0      0 192.168.122.1:123 0.0.0.0:*             2067/ntpd
   ...
```

To narrow your output from netstat to daemons bound to a TCP port, look for the word listen. For example:

```
# netstat -tanp | grep -i listen    View daemons listening to a port
```

The command just shown is a great way to resolve port usage conflicts between daemons.

Other Useful Network Tools

If you'd like to see header information about packets as they are sent and received by your system, use tcpdump. The tcpdump command has a lot of advanced features, most of which revolve around filtering and finding a needle in a haystack of packets. If you run tcpdump on a remote machine, your screen will be flooded with all the ssh traffic between your client and the remote machine. To get started without having to learn too much about how tcpdump filtering works, run the following command:

```
# tcpdump | grep -v ssh    Find packets except those associated with ssh
```

If you'd like to **dig deeper into packet-level traffic,** use `wireshark` (formerly known as `ethereal`). Make sure you have the wireshark-gnome package installed so you can use the X version of `wireshark`. You can run `wireshark` with X over ssh on a remote machine. Wireshark is a very powerful packet sniffer that rivals the best commercial tools.

To **explore networks and remote machines and see what services they offer,** use `nmap`. The nmap command is the most common port scanner. It was even featured in the movie *The Matrix Reloaded*! Make sure that you are explicitly authorized to scan the systems or networks you are scanning. The nmap command is part of the nmap package and can be run as a user, but several scan types require root privileges.

Here's how to **do a basic host scan** with `nmap`:

```
# nmap 10.0.0.1        Scan ports on computer at 10.0.0.1
```

To **get maximum verbosity** from `nmap`, use the `-vv` option:

```
# nmap -vv 10.0.0.1    Show maximum verbosity from nmap output
```

To use `nmap` to **scan an entire network,** use the network address as an argument. In the following example, we add the `-sP` option to tell `nmap` to perform a simple ping sweep:

```
# nmap -vv -sP 10.0.0.0/24   Scan hosts on an entire network
```

You can be very specific about the information that `nmap` gathers for you. In the following example, the `-P0` option tells `nmap` not to use `ping` (this is good for scanning machines that don't respond to `ping`). The `-O` option displays OS fingerprinting for the machine you are scanning. The `-p 100-200` option tells `nmap` to scan only ports 100 through 200:

```
# nmap -vv -P0 -O -p 100-200 10.0.0.1   No ping, OS fingerprint, ports 100-200
```

The `nmap` command has a lot more options for advanced usage. Refer to the `nmap` man page (`man nmap`) for further information.

Summary

Nearly every aspect of the network connections from your Fedora system can be configured, checked, and monitored using command line tools. You can view and change settings of your NICs using `ethtool` and `mii-tool` commands. You can view network statistics with `netstat`.

To start and stop your network, commands such as `service`, `chkconfig`, `ifup`, and `ifdown` are easy to manage. When a connection is established, you can see statistics about that connection using `ifconfig` and `ip` commands.

Besides using wired Ethernet cards, other network hardware such as wireless LAN cards and dial-up modems are supported in Linux. Use commands such as `iwconfig` to work with wireless interfaces, and `wvdialconf` and `minicom` to configure modems.

To check DNS name resolution, use the `dig`, `host`, and `hostname` commands. Commands for checking connectivity and routes to a host include `ping`, `arp`, `traceroute`, and `ip`.

12

Accessing Network Resources

In the time it takes to fire up a graphical FTP client, you could already have downloaded a few dozen files from a remote server using command line tools. Even when a GUI is available, commands for transferring files, web browsing, sharing directories, and reading mail can be quick and efficient to use. When no GUI is available, they can be lifesavers.

This chapter covers commands for accessing resources (files, e-mail, shared directories, and online chats) over the network.

IN THIS CHAPTER

Web browsing with elinks

Wget, curl, lftp, and scp for file transfers

Sharing directories with NFS, Samba, and SSHFS

IRC chats with irssi

Mail and mutt e-mail clients

Running Commands to Browse the Web

Text-mode web browsers provide a quick way to check that a web server is working or to get information from a web server when a useable GUI isn't available. The once-popular lynx text-based browser was supplanted in most Linux systems by the links browser, which was later replaced by elinks. (Typing links now runs elinks.)

The elinks browser runs in a terminal window. Aside from not displaying images in the terminal, elinks can handle most basic HTML content and features: tables, frames, tabbed browsing, cookies, history, mime types, and simple cascading style sheets (CSS). You can even use your mouse to follow links and select menu items.

Because `elinks` supports multiple colors, as long as the terminal you are using supports multiple colors, it's easy to spot links and headings in the text. (Colors may not work within a `screen` session.) Here are some examples of `elinks` command lines:

```
$ elinks                            Prompts for file name or URL
$ elinks www.handsonhistory.com     Opens file name or URL you request
```

If you have a mouse available, click near the top of the terminal window to see the menu. Select the menu name or item you want. Select a link to go to that link. Table 12-1 shows `elinks` keyboard navigation keys.

Table 12-1: Control Keys for Using elinks

Keys	Description	Keys	Description
Esc (or F9/F8)	Toggle menu on and off (then use arrow keys or mouse to navigate menus)	=	View page information
Down arrow	Go to next link or editable field on page	Ctrl+r	Reload page
Up arrow	Go to previous link or editable field on the page	a	Bookmark current page
Right arrow or Enter	Go forward to highlighted link. Enter text in highlighted form field	t	Open new browser tab
Left arrow	Go back to previous page	>	Go to next tab
/	Search forward	<	Go to previous tab
?	Search backwards	c	Close current tab
n	Find next	d	Download current link
N	Find previous	D	View downloads
PageUp	Scroll one page up	A	Add current link to bookmarks
PageDown	Scroll one page down	s	View bookmarks
g	Go to a URL	v	View current image
q or Ctrl+c	Exit elinks	h	View global history manager

You can add global settings for `elinks` to `/etc/elinks.conf`. Per-user settings are stored in each user's `$HOME/.elinks` directory. Type `man elinkskeys` to see available settings.

Transferring Files

Commands in Linux for downloading files from remote servers (HTTP, HTTPS, FTP, or SSH) are plentiful and powerful. You might choose one command over another because of the specific options you need. For example, you may want to perform a download over an encrypted connection, resume an aborted download, or do recursive downloads. This section describes how to use wget, ftp, lftp, scp, and scftp.

Downloading Files with wget

Sometimes you need to **download a file from a remote server** using the command line. For example, you find a link to an RPM software package, but the link goes through several HTTP redirects that prevent rpm from installing straight from HTTP. Or you may want to script the automated download of a file, such as a log file, every night.

The wget command can download files from web servers (HTTP and HTTPS) and FTP servers. With a server that doesn't require authentication, a wget command can be as simple as the wget command and the location of the download file:

```
$ wget \
http://dag.wieers.com/rpm/packages/acroread/acroread-5.0.10-1.el5.rf.i386.rpm
```

If, for example, an **FTP server requires a login and password**, you can enter that information on the wget command line in the following forms:

```
$ wget ftp://user:password@ftp.example.com/path/to/file
$ wget --user=user --password=password ftp://ftp.example.com/path/to/file
```

For example:

```
$ wget ftp://chris:mykuulpwd@ftp.linuxtoys.net/home/chris/image.jpg
$ wget --user=chris --password=mykuulpwd \
ftp://ftp.linuxtoys.net/home/chris/image.jpg
```

You can **use wget to download a single web page** as follows:

```
$ wget http://www.wiley.com      Download only the Web page
```

If you open the resulting index.html, you'll have all sorts of broken links. To download all the images and other elements required to render the page properly, use the -p option:

```
$ wget -p http://www.wiley.com      Download Web page and other elements
```

But if you open the resulting index.html in your browser, chances are you will still have all the broken links even though all the images were downloaded. That's because the links need to be translated to point to your local files. So instead, do this:

```
$ wget -pk http://www.wiley.com      Download pages and use local file names
```

And if you'd like wget to keep the original file and also do the translation, type this:

```
$ wget -pkK http://www.wiley.com    Rename to local names, keep original
```

Sometimes an HTML file you download does not have a .html extension, but ends in .asp or .cgi instead. That may result in your browser not knowing how to open your local copy of the file. You can have wget append .html to those files using the -E option:

```
$ wget -E http://www.aspexamples.com    Append .html to downloaded files
```

With the wget command, you can **recursively mirror an entire web site**. While copying files and directories for the entire depth of the server's file structure, the -m option adds timestamping and keeps FTP directory listings. (Use this with caution, because it can take a lot of time and space):

```
$ wget -m http://www.linuxtoys.net
```

Using some of the options just described, the following command line results in the most **usable local copy of a web site**:

```
$ wget -mEkK http://www.linuxtoys.net
```

If you have ever had a large file download (such as a CD or DVD image file) disconnect before it completed, you may find the -c option to wget to be a lifesaver. Using -c, wget resumes where it left off, **continuing an interrupted file download**. For example:

```
$ wget http://example.com/DVD.iso    Begin downloading large file
  ...
95%[==========  ] 685,251,583 55K/s   Download killed before completion
$ wget -c http://example.com/DVD.iso  Resume download where stopped
  ...
HTTP request sent, awaiting response... 206 Partial Content
Length: 699,389,952 (667), 691,513 (66M) remaining [text/plain]
```

Because of the continue feature (-c), wget can be particularly useful for those with slow Internet connections who need to download large files. If you have ever had a several-hour download get killed just before it finished, you'll know what we mean. (Note that if you don't use -c when you mean to resume a file download, the file will be saved to a different file: the original name with a .1 appended to it.)

Transferring Files with cURL

The client for URLs application (curl command) provides similar features to wget for transferring files using web and FTP protocols. However, the curl command can also transfer files using other popular protocols, including SSH protocols (SCP and SFTP), LDAP, DICT, Telnet, and File.

Instead of supporting large, recursive downloads (as wget does), curl is designed for *single-shot file transfers*. It does, however, support more protocols (as noted) and some neat advanced features. Here are a few interesting examples of **file transfers with curl**:

```
$ curl -O ftp://kernelorg.mirrors.tds.net/pub/linux/kernel/v1.0/patch[6-8].sign
$ curl -OO ftp://kernelorg.mirrors.tds.net/pub/linux/kernel/v2.6/ \
   ChangeLog-2.6.{1,4}
$ curl -O ftp://chris:MyPasswd@ftp.example.com/home/chris/fileA \
   -Q '-DELE fileA'
$ curl -T install.log ftp://chris:MyPasswd@ftp.example.com/tmp/ \
   -Q "-RNFR install.log" -Q "-RNTO Xinstall.log"
$ curl ftp://ftp.kernel.org/%2fpub/              List /pub/ contents
```

The first two commands show how to use square brackets to indicate a range [6-8] and curly brackets for a list {1,4} of characters or numbers to match files.

The third command line illustrates how to add a user name and password (chris:MyPasswd), download a file (fileA) from the server, and then delete the file on the server once the download is done (-Q '-DELE fileA').

The fourth example uploads (-T) the file install.log to an FTP server. Then it renames the remote file to Xinstall.log. The last example tells curl to list the contents of the /pub/ directory at ftp.kernel.org.

Transfering Files with FTP Commands

Fedora comes with the standard FTP client (ftp command), that works the same way it does on most Unix and Windows systems. We recommend you use the full-featured, user-friendly lftp instead. (The lftp command replaces ncftp, which was the default FTP client delivered with older Red Hat Linux distributions, due to licensing issues.)

With these FTP clients, you open a session to the FTP server (as opposed to just grabbing a file, as you do with wget and curl). Then you navigate the server much as you would a local file system, getting and putting documents across the network connection. Here are examples of how to **connect to an FTP server with lftp**:

```
$ lftp mirrors.kernel.org              Anonymous connection
lftp mirrors.kernel.org:~>
$ lftp francois@example.com            Authenticated connection
lftp example.com:~>
$ lftp -u francois example.com         Authenticated connection
Password: ******
lftp example.com:~>
$ lftp -u francois,Mypwd example.com   Authentication with password
lftp example.com:~>
$ lftp                                 Start lftp with no connection
lftp :~> open mirrors.kernel.org       Start connection in lftp session
lftp mirrors.kernel.org:~>
```

WARNING! *The fourth example should be avoided in real life. Passwords that are entered in a command line end up stored in clear text in your ~/.bash_history. They may also be visible to other users in the output of ps auwx.*

When a connection is established to an FTP server, you can use a set of commands during the FTP session. FTP commands are similar to shell commands. Just like in a bash shell, you can press Tab to autocomplete file names. In a session, lftp also supports sending multiple jobs to the background (Ctrl+z) and returning them to foreground (wait or fg). These are useful if you want to continue traversing the FTP site while files are downloading or uploading. Background jobs run in parallel. Type jobs to see a list of running background jobs. Type help to see a list of lftp commands.

The following sample lftp session illustrates **useful commands when downloading**:

```
$ lftp mirrors.kernel.org
lftp mirrors.kernel.org:~> pwd                      Check current directory
ftp://mirrors.kernel.org
lftp mirrors.kernel.org:~> ls                       List current directory
drwxr-sr-x   8 400   400   4096 Jul 02 20:19 debian/
drwxr-xr-x   7 537   537     77 May 21 21:37 fedora/
  ...
lftp mirrors.kernel.org:~> cd fedora/releases/7/Live/i386   Change directory
lftp mirrors.kernel.org:...> get Fedora-7-Live-i686.iso     Download a file
Fedora-7-Live-i686.iso at 776398 (1%) 467.2K/s eta:26m {Receiving data]
lftp mirrors.kernel.org:...> <Ctrl+z>               Send download to background
lftp mirrors.kernel.org:...> mget /gnu/ed/*         Get all in /gnu/ed
lftp mirrors.kernel.org:...> !ls                    Run local ls
lftp mirrors.kernel.org:...> bookmark add Live      Bookmark location
lftp mirrors.kernel.org:...> quit                   Close lftp
```

This session logs in as the anonymous user at mirrors.kernel.org. After changing to the directory containing the ISO image I was looking for, I downloaded it using the get command. By typing Ctrl+z, the download could continue while I did other activities. Next, the mget command (which allows wildcards such as *) downloaded all files from the /gnu/ed directory.

Any command preceded by an exclamation mark (such as !ls) is executed by the local shell. The bookmark command saves the current location (in this case, ftp://mirrors .kernel.org/fedora/releases/7/Live) under the name Live, so next time I can run lftp Live to return to the same location. The quit command ends the session.

Here are some **useful commands during an authenticated lftp upload session**. This assumes you have the necessary file permissions on the server:

```
$ lftp chris@example.com
Password: *******
lftp example.com:~> lcd /home/chris/songs    Change to a local directory
lftp example.com:~> cd pub/uploads           Change to server directory
lftp example.com:~> mkdir songs              Create directory on server
lftp example.com:~> chmod 700 songs          Change remote directory perms
```

```
lftp example.com:~> cd songs              Change to the new directory
lftp example.com:~> put song.ogg tune.ogg Upload files to server
3039267 bytes transferred
lftp example.com:~> mput /var/songs/*     Upload matched files
lftp example.com:~> quit                  Close lftp
```

The lftp session illustrates how you can use shell command names to operate on remote directories (provided you have permission). The mkdir and chmod commands create a directory and leave permissions open only to your user account. The put command uploads one or more files to the remote server. The mput command can use wildcards to match multiple files for download. Other commands include mirror (to download a directory tree) and mirror -R (to upload a directory tree).

lftp also provides a shell script for **non-interactive download sessions**: lftpget. The syntax of lftpget is similar to that of the wget command:

```
$ lftpget ftp://mirrors.kernel.org/centos/5.0/os/x86_64/RELEASE-NOTES-en
```

Keep in mind that standard FTP clients are insecure because they do all their work in clear text. So your alternative, especially when security is a major issue, is to use SSH tools to transfer files.

Using SSH Tools to Transfer Files

Because SSH utilities are among the most important tools in a system administrator's arsenal of communications commands, some of the more complex uses of configuring and using SSH utilities are covered in Chapter 13. However, in their most basic form, SSH utilities are the tools you should use most often for basic file transfer.

In particular, the scp command will do most of what you need to get a file from one computer to another, while making that communication safe by encrypting both the password stage and data transfer stage of the process. The ssh command replaces the rcp command as the most popular tool for host-to-host file copies.

> **WARNING!** *You do not get a warning before overwriting existing files with* scp, *so be sure that the target host doesn't contain any files or directories you want that are in the path of your* scp *file copies.*

Copying Remote Files with scp

To use scp to transfer files, the SSH service (usually the sshd server daemon) must be running on the remote system. Here are some examples of **useful scp commands**:

```
$ scp myfile francois@server1:/tmp/     Copy myfile to server1
Password: ******
$ scp server1:/tmp/myfile .             Copy remote myfile to local working dir
Password: ******
```

215

Use the -p option to **preserve permissions and timestamps** on the copied files:

```
$ scp -p myfile server1:/tmp/
```

If the SSH service is configured to listen on a port other than the default port 22, use -P to **indicate that port** on the scp command line:

```
$ scp -P 12345 myfile server1:/tmp/      Connect to a particular port
```

To do **recursive copies**, from a particular point in the remote file system, use the -r option:

```
$ scp -r mydir francois@server1:/tmp/    Copies all mydir to remote /tmp
```

Although scp is most useful when you know the exact locations of the file(s) you need to copy, sometimes it's more helpful to browse and transfer files interactively.

Copying Remote Files in sftp and lftp Sessions

The sftp command lets you use an FTP-like interface to **find and copy files over SSH protocols**. Here's an example of how to start an sftp session:

```
$ sftp chris@server1
chris@server1's password: *****
sftp>
```

Use sftp in the same manner as you use regular FTP clients. Type ? for a list of commands. You can change remote directories (cd), change local directories (lcd), check current remote and local directories (pwd and lpwd), and list remote and local contents (ls and lls). Depending on the permission of the user you logged in as, you may be able to create and remove directories (mkdir and rmdir), and change permissions (chmod) and ownership/group (chown and chgrp) of files and directories.

You can also use lftp (discussed earlier in this chapter) as an sftp client. Using lftp adds some user-friendly features such as **path completion** using the Tab key:

```
$ lftp sftp://chris@server1
Password: ********
lftp chris@server1:~>
```

Using Windows File Transfer Tools

In many cases, people need to get files from Linux servers using Windows clients. If your client operating system is Windows, you can use one of the following open source tools to get files from Linux servers:

❑ **WinSCP** (http://winscp.net) — Graphical scp, sftp, and FTP client for Windows over SSH1 and SSH2 protocols.

- **FileZilla** (`http://filezilla.sourceforge.net`) — Provides graphical client FTP and SFTP services in Windows, as well as offering FTP server features.

- **PSCP** (`www.chiark.greenend.org.uk/~sgtatham/putty/`) — Command line scp client that is part of the PuTTY suite.

- **PSFTP** (`www.chiark.greenend.org.uk/~sgtatham/putty/`) — Command line sftp client that is part of the PuTTY suite.

Sharing Remote Directories

Tools described to this point in the chapter provide atomic file access, where a connection is set up and files are transferred in one shot. In times where more persistent, ongoing access to a remote directory of files is needed, services for sharing and mounting remote file systems can be most useful. Such services include Network File System (NFS), Samba, and SSHFS.

Sharing Remote Directories with NFS

Assuming a server is already running the NFS service (typing `service nfs start` as root starts it in Fedora), you can use `exportfs` and `showmount` commands to see available and mounted shared directories. Mounting a shared directory is done with special options to the standard `mount` command.

Viewing and Exporting NFS Shares

Run from the NFS server, this `exportfs` command shows all shared directories available from that server:

```
# /usr/sbin/exportfs -v
/export/myshare    client.example.com(ro,wdelay,root_squash,no_subtree_check)
/mnt/public        <world>(rw,wdelay,root_squash,no_subtree_check)
```

The two directories being shared are `/export/myshare` and `/mnt/public`. The first is only available to host computer `client.example.com`, whereas the second is available to everyone. Options for each share are shown in parentheses. The first share is available read-only (`ro`); writes to the share are delayed to improve performance when more writes are expected (`wdelay`); and requests from the root user on the client are mapped into the anonymous UID (`root_squash`). Also, a less thorough check of file system permission is done (`no_subtree_check`). The second share allows read-write mounting (`rw`).

Add and modify shared NFS directories by making changes to the `/etc/exports` file. To get changes to take effect, type any of the following as root:

```
# service nfs reload     Reload exported shared directories
# exportfs -r            Reload exported shared directories
# exportfs -rv           Verbose reload of exported shares
exporting client.example.com:/export/myshare
exporting *:/mnt/public
```

From the Linux server system, you can use the `showmount` command to see what shared directories are available from the local system. For example:

```
# /usr/sbin/showmount -e
Export list for server.example.com
/export/myshare  client.example.com
/mnt/public      *
```

From a client Linux system, you can use the `showmount` command to see what shared directories are available from a selected computer. For example:

```
# /usr/sbin/showmount -e server.example.com
/export/myshare client.example.com
/mnt/public      *
```

Mounting NFS Shares

Use the `mount` command to mount a remote NFS share on the local computer. Here is an example:

```
# mkdir /mnt/server-share
# mount server.example.com:/export/myshare /mnt/server-share
```

This example notes the NFS server (`server.example.com`) and the shared directory from that server (`/export/myshare`). The local mount point, which must exist before mounting the share, appears at the end of the command (`/mnt/server-share`).

Pass NFS-specific options to the `mount` command by adding them after the `-o` option:

```
# mount -o rw,hard,intr server.example.com:/export/myshare /mnt/server-share
```

The `rw` option mounts the remote directory with read-write permissions, assuming that permission is available. With `hard` set, someone using the share will see a `server not responding` message when a read or write operation times out. If that happens, having set the `intr` option lets you interrupt a hung request to a remote server (type Ctrl+c).

By default, NFS version 3 (nfs3) protocol is used to connect to the share. To use NFS version 4, which is designed to work over the Internet and through firewalls, indicate that protocol as the file system type on the command line as follows:

```
# mount -t nfs4 server.example.com:/ /mnt/server-share
```

> **NOTE** *Depending on which version of Fedora you are using, the implementation of NFS v4 may not be robust enough for production. It may be safer and/or more reliable to tunnel earlier versions of NFS over SSH. You can find more Information on this topic with an Internet search for "nfs ssh".*

Sharing Remote Directories with Samba

Samba is the open source implementation of the Windows file and print sharing protocol originally known as Server Message Block (SMB) and now called Common Internet File System (CIFS). There is an implementation of Samba in Linux, as well as in many other operating systems.

Graphical tools for sharing, querying, and mounting shared SMB directories from Windows include the Samba SWAT web-based administration tool. To **use the SWAT tool** in Linux, install the samba-swat package, enable the xinetd service (by typing `service xinetd start`), and turn on SWAT (`chkconfig swat on`). Open SWAT by pointing your browser at the SWAT service (`http://localhost:901`) and typing the root user name and password.

Commands for working with Samba shares can be used to query SMB servers, mount directories, and share directories.

Viewing and Accessing Samba Shares

To **scan your network for SMB hosts**, type the following:

```
$ findsmb
                              *=DMB
                              +=LMB
IP ADDR         NETBIOS NAME  WORKGROUP/OS/VERSION
---------------------------------------------------------------------
192.168.1.1     SERVER1       +[MYWORKGROUP] [Unix] [Samba 3.0.25a-3.fc7]
```

To **view a text representation of your network neighborhood** (shared directories and printers), use smbtree:

```
# smbtree
Password: ******
MYGROUP
   \\THOMPSON              Samba Server Version 3.0.25a-3.fc7
      \\THOMPSON\hp2100    HP LaserJet 2100M Printer
      \\THOMPSON\IPC$      IPC Service (Samba Server Version 3.0.25a-3.fc7)
   \\EINSTEIN              Samba Server
      \\EINSTEIN\hp5550    HP DeskJet 5550 Printer
      \\EINSTEIN\IPC$      IPC Service (Samba Server)
```

To **add an existing Linux user as a Samba user**, use the smbpasswd command:

```
# smbpasswd -a francois
New SMB password: ******
Retype new SMB password: ******
Added user francois
```

To list services offered by a server to an anonymous user, type the following:

```
$ smbclient -L server
Password: ******
Anynymous login successful
Domain=[MYGROUP] OS=[Unix] Server=Samba 3.0.25a-3.fc7
tree connect failed: NT_STSTUS_LOGON_FAILURE
```

Here's the output from `smbclient` for a specific user named francois:

```
$ smbclient -L server -U francois
Password: ******
Domain=[MYGROUP] OS=[Unix] Server=[Samba 3.0.25a-3.fc7]

     Sharename    Type    Comment
     ---------    ----    -------
     IPC$         IPC     IPC Service (Samba Server Version 3.0.25a-3.fc7)
     hp5550       Printer HP DeskJet 5550 Printer

        Server               Comment
        ---------            -------
        THOMPSON             Samba Server Version 3.0.25a-3.fc7

        Workgroup            Master
        ---------            -------
        MYGROUP              THOMPSON
```

To connect to a Samba share FTP-style, type the following:

```
$ smbclient //192.168.1.1/myshare -U francois
Password:
Domain=[MYWORKGROUP] OS=[Unix] Server=[Samba 3.0.25a-3.fc7]
smb: \>
```

As with most FTP clients, type `help` or ? to see a list of available commands. Like-wise, you can use common shell-type commands, such as `cd`, `ls`, `get`, `put`, and `quit`, to get around on the SMB host.

Mounting Samba Shares

You can mount remote Samba shares on your local file system much as you would a local file system or remote NFS file system. To mount the share:

```
# mount -t cifs -o username=francois,password=MySecret \
     //192.168.1.1/myshare /mnt/mymount/
```

> **NOTE** *The Samba file system (`smbfs`) is deprecated and should no longer be used. Instead, indicate CIFS (`-t cifs`) as the file system type when you mount a remote Samba share.*

You can **see the current connections and file locks** on a server using the smbstatus command. This will tell you if someone has mounted your shared directories or is currently using an smbclient connection to your server:

```
# smbstatus
Samba version 3.0.25a-3.fc7
PID    Username    Group    Machine
------------------------------------------
 5466  francois      francois 10.0.0.55   (10.0.0.55)


Service    pid   machine     Connected at
------------------------------------------
myshare    5644  10.0.0.55  Tue Jul  3 15:08:29 2007

No locked files
```

To see a more **brief output**, use the -b option:

```
$ smbstatus -b
```

Looking Up Samba Hosts

NetBIOS names are used to identify hosts in Samba. You can **determine the IP address of a computer** using the nmblookup command to broadcast for a particular NetBIOS name on the local subnet as follows:

```
$ nmblookup thompson
querying thompson on 192.168.1.255
192.168.1.1 server1<00>
```

To **find the IP address for a server on a specific subnet,** use the -U option:

```
$ nmblookup -U 192.168.1.255 server1
querying server1 on 192.168.1.255
192.168.1.1 server1<00>
```

Checking Samba Configuration

If you are unable to use a Samba share or if you have other problems communicating with your Samba server, you can test the Samba configuration on the server. The testparm command can be used to **check your main Samba configuration file** (smb.conf):

```
$ testparm
Load smb config files from /etc/samba/smb.conf
Processing section "[homes]"
Processing section "[printers]"
Processing section "[myshare]"
Loaded services file OK.
Server role: ROLE_STANDALONE
Press Enter to see a dump of your service definitions
```

After pressing Enter as instructed, you can see the settings from your `smb.conf` file. Here's how an entry for the `myshare` shared directory, used earlier in an example, might appear in the `smb.conf` file:

```
[myshare]
        path = /home/francois
        username = francois
        valid users = francois
        hosts allow = einstein
        available = yes
```

This entry allows the Samba user francois to access the `/home/francois` directory (represented by the `myshare` share name) from the host computer named einstein. The share is shown as being currently available.

The previous example of `testparm` showed the entries you set in the `smb.conf` file. However, it doesn't **show all the default entries you didn't set**. You can view those using the `-v` option. Pipe it to the `less` command to page through the settings:

```
$ testparm -v | less
```

If you want to **test a configuration file before it goes live**, you can tell `testparm` to use a file other than `/etc/samba/smb.conf`:

```
$ testparm /etc/samba/test-smb.conf
```

Sharing Remote Directories with SSHFS

Another magical trick you can do over the SSH protocol is mount remote file systems. Using the SSH file system (`sshfs`), you can mount any directory from an SSH server that your user account can access from your local Linux system. `sshfs` provides encryption of the mount operation as well as of all the data being transferred. Another cool aspect of `sshfs` is that it requires no setup on the server side (other than having SSH service running).

Here is a quick procedure for **mounting a directory of documents from a remote server to a local directory**. Doing this only requires that the remote server is running SSH, is accessible, and that the directory you want is accessible to your user account on the server. Here we are mounting a directory named `/var/docs` from the host at `10.0.0.50` to a mount point called `/mnt/docs` on the local system:

```
# yum install fuse-sshfs                            Install fuse-sshfs software
# mkdir /mnt/docs                                   Create mount point
# sshfs chris@10.0.0.50:/var/docs /mnt/docs   Mount remote directory
```

When you are done using the remote directory, you can **unmount** it with the `fusermount` command:

```
# fusermount -u /var/docs                           Unmount remote directory
```

Chatting with Friends in IRC

Despite the emergence of instant messaging, Internet Relay Chat (IRC) is still used by a lot of people today. Freenode.net has tons of chat rooms dedicated to supporting major open source software projects. In fact, many people stay logged into them all day and just watch the discussions of their favorite Linux projects scroll by. This is known as *lurking*.

The xchat utility is a good graphical, multi-operating system IRC client. From Fedora, select Applications ⇨ Internet ⇨ IRC. But the elite way to do IRC is to run a text-mode client in `screen` on an always-on machine, such as an old server. Another similar option is to use an IRC proxy client, also known as a *bouncer*, such as `dircproxy`.

The original IRC client was `ircII`. It allowed the addition of scripts — in some ways similar to macros found in productivity suites — that automated some of the commands and increased usability. The most popular was PhoEniX by Vassago. Then came BitchX, which started as an `ircII` script and then became a full-blown client. Today, most people use `irssi`. To **install and launch irssi** from Fedora, type:

```
# yum install irssi
$ irssi -n JayJoe199x
```

In this example, the user name (nick) is set to JayJoe199x (you should choose your own). You should see a blue status bar at the bottom of the screen indicating that you are in Window 1, the status window. IRC commands are preceded with a / character. For example, to **connect to the freenode server**, type:

```
/connect chat.freenode.net
```

If you didn't add your user name on the command line, you are connected to `chat` `.freenode.net` with the user name you are logged in under. On IRC, a chat room is called a *channel* and has a pound sign (#) in front of the name. Next, try **joining the #centos IRC channel:**

```
/join #centos
```

Your screen should look similar to Figure 12-1.

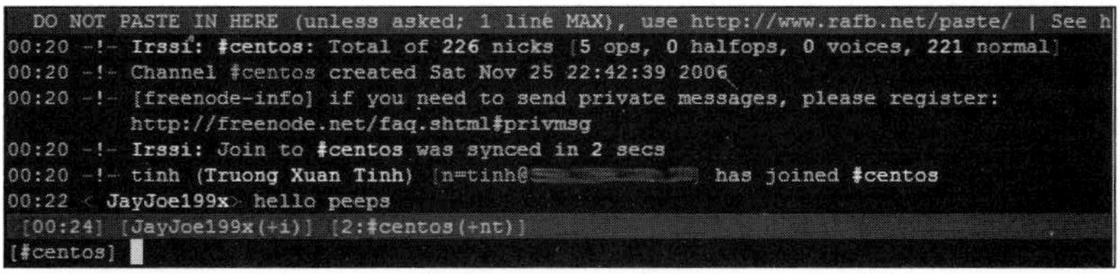

Figure 12-1: irssi connected to #centos on Freenode

You are now in the channel in Window 2, as indicated in the status bar. Switch among the irssi windows by typing Alt+1, Alt+2, and so on (or Ctrl+n and Ctrl+p). To get help at any time, type /help *command*, where *command* is the name of the command you want more information on. Help text will output in the status window, not necessarily the current window.

To add to the IRC chat, simply type a message and press Enter to send the message to those in the channel. Type /part to leave a channel. Type /quit to exit the program.

There is a lot more to irssi. You can customize it and improve your experience significantly. Refer to the irssi documentation (www.irssi.org/documentation) for more information about how to use irssi.

Using Text-Based E-mail Clients

Most Mail User Agents (MUAs) are GUI-based these days. So if you began using e-mail in the past decade or so, you probably think of Evolution, Kmail, Thunderbird, or (on Windows systems) Outlook when it comes to e-mail clients. On the first Unix and Linux systems, however, e-mail was handled by text-based applications.

If you find yourself needing to check e-mail on a remote server or other text-based environment, venerable text-based mail clients are available and still quite useful. In fact, some hard-core geeks still use text-based mail clients exclusively, touting their efficiency and scoffing at HTML-based messages.

The mail clients described in this chapter expect your messages to be stored in standard MBOX format on the local system. That means that you are either logged into the mail server or you have already downloaded the messages locally (for example, by using POP3 or similar).

> **NOTE** *Text-based mail clients can be used to read mail already downloaded by other mail clients. For example, you could open your Evolution mail Inbox file by typing* mail -f $HOME/.evolution/mail/loc/Inbox.

Managing E-mail with mail

The oldest command, and easiest to use when you just want a quick check for messages in the root user's mailbox on a remote server, is the mail command (/bin/mail). Although mail can be used interactively, it is often used for sending script-based e-mails. Here are some examples:

```
$ mail -s 'My Fedora version' chris@example.com < /etc/redhat-release
$ ps auwx | mail -s 'My Process List' chris@example.com
```

The two mail examples just shown provide quick ways to mail off some text without having to open a GUI mail application. The first example sends the contents of the

/etc/redhat-release file to the user chris@example.com. The subject (-s) is set to 'My Fedora Version'. In the second example, a list of currently running processes (ps auwx) is sent to the same user with a subject of 'My Process List'.

Used interactively, by default the mail command opens the mailbox set by your current shell's $MAIL value. For example:

```
# echo $MAIL
/var/spool/mail/root
# mail
Mail version 8.1 6/6/93.  Type ? for help.
"/var/spool/mail/root": 25 messages 25 new
>U  1 logwatch@ab.l  Fri Jun 15 20:03  44/1667  "Logwatch for ab (Linux)"
 U  2 logwatch@ab.l  Sat Jun 16 04:32  87/2526  "Logwatch for ab (Linux)"
    3 logwatch@ab.l  Sun Jun 17 04:32  92/2693  "Logwatch for ab (Linux)"
 N  4 logwatch@ab.l  Fri Jun 22 09:28  44/1667  "Logwatch for ab (Linux)"
 N  5 MAILER-DAEMON@ab  Fri Jun 22 09:28  93/3348  "Warning: could not send "
&
```

The current message has a greater-than sign (>) next to it. New messages have an N at the beginning, unread (but not new) messages have a U, and if there is no letter, the message has been read. The prompt at the bottom (&) is ready to accept commands.

At this point, you are in command mode. You can use simple commands to **move around** and **perform basic mail functions** in mail. Type ? to see a list of commands, or type the number of the message you want to see. Type v3 to open the third message in the vi editor. Type h18 to see a list of message headers that begins with message 18. To reply to message 7, type r7 (type your message, then put a dot on a line by itself to send the message). Type d4 to delete the fourth message (or d4-9 to delete messages 4 through 9). Type !bash to escape to the shell (then exit to return to mail).

Before you exit mail, know that any messages you view will be copied from your mailbox file to your $HOME/mbox file when you exit, unless you preserve them (pre*). To have all messages stay in your mailbox, exit by typing x. To save your changes to the mailbox, type q to exit.

You can open any file that is in MBOX format when you use mail. For example, if you are logged in as root user, but want to open the mailbox for the user chris, type this:

```
# mail -f /var/spool/mail/chris
```

Managing E-mail with mutt

If you want to use a command-line mail client on an ongoing basis, we recommend you use mutt instead of mail. The mail command has many limitations, such as not being able to send attachments without encoding them in advance (such as with the uuencode command), while mutt has many features for handling modern e-mail needs. The mutt command is part of the mutt package.

Like mail, mutt can also be used to pop off a message from a script. mutt also adds the capability to **send attachments**. For example:

```
$ mutt -s "My Fedora Version" -a /etc/redhat-release \
     chris@example.com < email-body.txt
$ mutt -s "My Fedora Version" -a /etc/redhat-release \
     chris@example.com < /dev/null
```

The first example just shown includes the file email-body.txt as the body of the message and attaches the file /etc/redhat-release as an attachment. The second example sends the attachment, but has a blank message body (< /dev/null).

You can **begin your mutt mail session** (assuming your default mailbox is $MAIL) by simply typing mutt:

```
$ mutt
/home/chris/Mail does not exist. Create it? ([yes]/no): y

q:Quit  d:Del  u:Undel  s:Save  m:Mail  r:Reply  g:Group  ?:Help

   1 O    Jun 16 logwatch@ab     (  69) Logwatch for ab (Linux)
   2 O    Jun 18 logwatch@ab     ( 171) Logwatch for ab (Linux)
   3 O    Jun 18 Mail Delivery S ( 219) Warning: could not send message
   4 O    Jun 19 logwatch@ab     (  33) Logwatch for ab (Linux)

--Mutt: /var/spool/mail/root [Msgs:22 New:2 Old:20 63K]--(date/date)--(all)--
```

Because mutt is screen-oriented, it is easier to use than mail. As with mail, you **use key commands to move around in mutt**. As usual, type ? to get help. Hints appear across the top bar to help you with your mail. Use the up and down arrow keys to highlight the messages you want to read. Press Enter to view the highlighted message. Use PageUp and PageDown to page through each message. Press i to return to the message headers.

Search forward for text using slash (/) or backwards using Escape slash (Esc-/). Type n to search again. Press Tab to jump to the next new or unread message. Or go to the previous one using Esc-Tab. Type s to save the current message to a file. Type d to delete a message and u to undelete it.

To send a new mail message, type m. After adding the recipient and subject, a blank message opens in vi (or whatever you have your $EDITOR set to). After exiting the message body, type a to add an attachment, if you like. Type ? to see other ways of manipulating your message, headers or attachments. Press y to send the message or q to abort the send.

When you are done, type x to exit without changing your mailbox; type q to exit and incorporate the changes you made (messages read, deleted, and so on).

Summary

Network access commands provide quick and efficient ways to get content you need over a network. The `elinks` web browser is a popular screen-oriented command for browsing the web or taking a quick look at any HTML file. Dozens of commands are available to download files over FTP, HTTP, SSH, or other protocols, including `wget`, `curl`, `lftp`, and `scp`.

For more ongoing access to remote directories of files, this chapter covers how to use NFS, Samba, and SSHFS command tools. You can do IRC chats, which are popular among open source projects, using the `irssi` command. For text-based e-mail clients, you have choices such as the `mail` and `mutt` commands.

13

Doing Remote System Administration

Most professional Linux administrators do not run a graphical interface on their Internet servers. As a result, when you need to access other computers for remote administration, you will almost surely need to work from the command line at some time. Luckily there are many feature-rich Linux commands to help you do so.

Tools associated with the Secure Shell (SSH) service not only allow remote login and file transfer, but they also offer encrypted communication to keep your remote administration work secure. With tools such as Virtual Network Computing (VNC), you can have a server's remote desktop appear on your local client computer. These and other features for doing remote systems administration are described in this chapter.

Doing Remote Login and Tunneling with SSH

Linux's big brother Unix grew up on university networks. At a time when the only users of these networks were students and professors, and with networks mostly isolated from each other, there was little need for security.

Applications and protocols that were designed in those times (the 1970s and 1980s) reflect that lack of concern for encryption and authentication. SMTP is a perfect example of that. This is also true of the first generation of Unix remote tools: `telnet`, `ftp` (file transfer protocol), `rsh` (remote shell), `rcp` (remote copy), `rexec` (remote execution), and `rlogin` (remote login). These tools send user credentials and traffic in clear text. For that reason, they are very dangerous to use on the public, untrusted Internet, and have become mostly deprecated and replaced with the Secure Shell (SSH) commands (`ssh`, `scp`, `sftp` commands and related services).

Although there are still some uses for the legacy remote commands (see the "Using Legacy Communications Tools" sidebar), most of this section describes how to use SSH commands to handle most of your needs for remote communications commands.

Using Legacy Communications Tools

Despite the fact that SSH provides better tools for remote communications, legacy communications commands, sometimes referred to as "r" commands, are still included with most major Linux distributions. Some of these tools will perform faster than equivalent SSH commands because they don't need to do encryption. So some old-school UNIX administrators may use them occasionally on private networks or still include them in old scripts. Although for the most part you should ignore these legacy remote commands, one of these commands in particular can be useful in some cases: telnet.

The telnet command is still used to communicate with some network appliances (routers, switches, UPSes, and so on) that do not have the horsepower to run an ssh daemon. Even though it poses a security risk, some appliance manufacturers include telnet support anyway.

One good way to use the telnet command, however, is for troubleshooting many Internet protocols such as POP3, SMTP, HTTP, and others. Under the hood, these plain-text protocols are simply automated telnet sessions during which a client (such as a browser or mail user agent) exchanges text with a server. The only difference is the TCP port in use. Here is an example of how you could telnet to the HTTP port (80) of a web server:

```
$ telnet www.example.com 80
Trying 208.77.188.166...
Connected to www.example.com.
Escape character is '^]'.
GET / HTTP/1.0
          Enter a second carriage return here
HTTP/1.1 200 OK
```

Similarly, you can telnet to a mail server on port 25 (SMTP) and 110 (POP3) and issue the proper commands to troubleshoot e-mail problems. For more complete descriptions of using the telnet command to troubleshoot network protocols, refer to *Linux Troubleshooting Bible* (ISBN 076456997X, Wiley Publishing, 2004), pages 505 and 508.

If you need to forcefully exit your telnet session, type the escape sequence (Ctrl+] by default). This will stop sending your keyboard input to the remote end and bring you to the telnet command prompt where can type quit or ? for more options.

Configuring SSH

Nowadays, the Swiss Army knife of remote system administration is Secure Shell (SSH). SSH commands and services replace all the old remote tools and add strong encryption, public keys, and many other features. The most common implementation of SSH in the Linux world is OpenSSH (www.openssh.com), maintained by the OpenBSD project. OpenSSH provides both client and server components. Here are a few facts about SSH:

❑ For Windows, you can use the Linux SSH tools within Cygwin (www.cygwin.com). But unless you're already using Cygwin (a Linux-like environment for Windows), we recommend PuTTY (www.chiark.greenend.org/uk/sgatatham/putty). PuTTY is a powerful open source Telnet/SSH client.

❑ Use SSH version 2 whenever possible, because it is the most secure. Some SSH-enabled network appliances may only support older, less secure versions. OpenSSH supports all versions. Some older versions of Fedora and RHEL accepted SSH v1 and v2 connections. Newer releases accept version 2 by default.

❑ In Fedora and RHEL, as root run `service start sshd` to **start the SSH service** (sshd daemon). To configure the service, edit the /etc/ssh/sshd_config file.

❑ To **configure the ssh client**, edit the /etc/ssh/ssh_config file.

If you prefer to use graphical tools to administer your remote Linux system, you can enable *X11 Tunneling* (also called *X11 Port Forwarding*). With X11 Tunneling enabled (on both the SSH client and server), you can start an X application on the server and have it displayed on the client. All communication across that connection is encrypted.

Both Fedora and RHEL come with X11 forwarding turned on (X11Forwarding yes) for the server (sshd daemon). You still need to enable it on the client side. To **enable X11 forwarding on the client for a one-time session**, connect with the following command:

```
$ ssh -X francois@myserver
```

To **enable X11 forwarding permanently for all users**, add ForwardX11 yes to /etc/ssh/ssh_config. To enable it permanently for a specific user only, add the line to that user's ~.ssh/config. After that setting has been added, the -X option is no longer required to use X11 Tunneling. Run ssh to connect to the remote system as you would normally. To test that the tunneling is working, run xclock after ssh'ing into the remote machine, and it should appear on your client desktop.

SSH Tunneling is an excellent way to securely use remote graphical tools!

Logging in Remotely with ssh

To **securely log in to a remote host**, you can use either of two different syntaxes to specify the user name:

```
$ ssh -l francois myserver
$ ssh francois@myserver
```

However, scp and sftp commands (discussed in Chapter 12) only support the *user@server* syntax, so we recommend you get used to that one. If you don't specify the user name, ssh will attempt to log in using the same user you are logged in as locally. When connected, if you need to **forcefully exit your ssh session**, type the escape sequence of a tilde followed by a period (~.).

231

Accessing SSH on a Different Port

For security purposes, a remote host may have its SSH service listening to a different port than the default port number 22. If that's the case, use the -p option to ssh to contact that service:

```
$ ssh -p 12345 francois@turbosphere.com    Connect to SSH on port 12345
```

Using SSH to Do Tunneling (X11 Port Forwarding)

With SSH tunneling configured as described earlier, the SSH service forwards X Window System clients to your local display. However, tunneling can be used with other TCP-based protocols as well.

Tunneling for X11 Clients

The following sequence of commands illustrates starting an SSH session, then starting a few X applications so they appear on the local desktop:

```
$ ssh francois@myserver              Start ssh connection to myserver
francois@myserver's password: *******
[francois@myserver ~}$ echo $DISPLAY    Show the current X display entry
localhost:10.0                       SSH sets display to localhost:10.0
[francois@myserver ~}$ xeyes&               Show moving desktop eyes
[francois@myserver ~}$ system-config-printer&  Configure remote printers
[francois@myserver ~}$ system-config-services&  Change system services
```

Tunneling for CUPS Printing Remote Administration

X11 is not the only protocol that can be tunneled over SSH. You can forward any TCP port with SSH. This is a great way to configure secure tunnels quickly and easily. No configuration is required on the server side.

For example, myserver is a print server with the CUPS printing service's web-based user interface enabled (running on port 631). That GUI is only accessible from the local machine. On my client PC, I tunnel to that service using ssh with the following options:

```
$ ssh -L 1234:localhost:631 myserver
```

This example forwards port 1234 on my client PC to localhost port 631 on the server. I can now browse to http://localhost:1234 on my client PC. This will be redirected to cupsd listening on port 631 on the server.

Tunneling to an Internet Service

Another example for using SSH tunneling is when your local machine is blocked from connecting to the Internet, but you can get to another machine (myserver) that has an Internet connection. The following example enables you to visit the Google.com web site (HTTP, TCP port 80) across an SSH connection to a computer named `myserver` that has a connection to the Internet:

```
$ ssh -L 12345:google.com:80 myserver
```

With this example, any connection to the local port 12345 is directed across an SSH tunnel to `myserver`, which in turn opens a connection to `Google.com` port 80. You can now browse to `http://localhost:12345` and use `myserver` as a relay to the Google.com web site. Since you're only using `ssh` to forward a port and not to obtain a shell on the server, you can add the `-N` option to **prevent the execution of remote commands**:

```
$ ssh -L 12345:google.com:80 -N myserver
```

Using SSH as a SOCKS Proxy

The previous example demonstrates that you can forward a port from the client to a machine other than the server. In the real world, the best way to **get your browser traffic out of your local network via an encrypted tunnel** is using SSH's built-in SOCKS proxy feature. For example:

```
$ ssh -D 12345 myserver
```

The dynamic (`-D`) option of `ssh` enables you to log in to `myserver` (as usual). As long as the connection is open, all requests directed to port 12345 are then forwarded to `myserver`. Next, set your browser of choice to use `localhost` port 12345 as a SOCKS v5 proxy and you're good to go. Do not enter anything on the fields for HTTP and other protocols. They all work over SOCKS. See the Firefox Connections Settings window in Figure 13-1.

To test your setup, try disconnecting your ssh session and browsing to any web site. Your browser should give you a proxy error.

From a Windows client, the same port forwarding can be accomplished in Putty by selecting Connection ⇨ SSH ⇨ Tunnels.

Using ssh with Public Key Authentication

Up to this point, we've only used `ssh` with the default password authentication. The `ssh` command also supports public key authentication. This offers several benefits:

❑ **Automated logins for scripts and cron jobs**: By assigning an empty passphrase, you can use `ssh` in a script to log in automatically. Although this is convenient, it is also dangerous, because anybody who gets to your key file can connect to any machine you can. Configuring for automatic login can also be done with a passphrase and a key agent. This is a compromise between convenience and security, as explained below.

❑ **A two-factor authentication**: When using a passphrase-protected key for interactive logins, authentication is done using two factors (the key and the passphrase) instead of one.

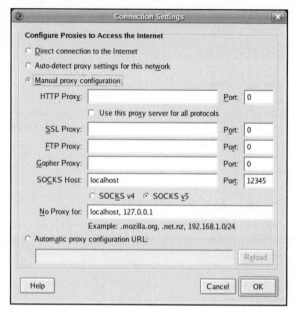

Figure 13-1: Use the Firefox Connections Settings window for proxy configuration.

Using Public Key Logins

Here's the process for **setting up key-based communications** between two Linux systems. In the following example, we use empty passphrases for no-password logins. If you prefer to protect your key with a passphrase, simply enter it when prompted during the first step (key pair creation).

On the client system, run the following `ssh-keygen` command **to generate the key pair** while logged in as the user who needs to initiate communications:

```
$ ssh-keygen
Generating public/private rsa key pair.
Enter file in which to save the key (/home/chris/.ssh/id_rsa): <Enter>
Enter passphrase (empty for no passphrase): <Enter>
Enter same passphrase again: <Enter>
Your identification has been saved in /home/chris/.ssh/id_rsa.
Your public key has been saved in /home/chris/.ssh/id_rsa.pub.
The key fingerprint is:
ac:db:a4:8e:3f:2a:90:4f:05:9f:b4:44:74:0e:d3:db chris@host.domain.com
```

Note that at each prompt, you pressed the Enter key to create the default key file name and to enter (and verify) an empty passphrase. You now have a private key that you need to keep very safe, especially since in this procedure you didn't protect it with a passphrase.

You also now have a public key (id_rsa.pub), which was created by the previous command. This public key needs to be installed on hosts you want to connect to. The content of ~/.ssh/id_rsa.pub needs to be copied (securely) to ~/.ssh/authorized_keys2 for the user you want to ssh to on the remote server. The authorized_keys2 file can contain more than one public key, if multiple users use ssh to connect to this account.

Log in to the *remote server* system as the user that you will want to ssh as with the key. If you don't already have a ~/.ssh directory, the first step is to create it as follows:

```
$ cd
$ mkdir .ssh
$ chmod 700 .ssh
```

The next step is to copy (securely) the public key file from the client and put it in an authorized keys file on the server. This can be accomplished using scp. For example, assuming a client system named myclient and a client user named chris, type the following on the server:

```
$ scp chris@myclient:/home/chris/.ssh/id_rsa.pub .   Get client id_rsa.pub
$ cat id_rsa.pub >> ~/.ssh/authorized_keys2       Add to your keys
$ chmod 600 ~/.ssh/authorized_keys2               Close permissions
$ rm id_rsa.pub                       Delete public key after copying its content
```

This procedure can also be accomplished by editing the ~/.ssh/authorized_keys2 text file on the server and copying and pasting the public key from the client. Make sure you do so securely over ssh, and make sure not to insert any line breaks in the key. The entire key should fit on a single line, even if it wraps on your screen.

Then from the client (using the client and server user accounts you just configured), you can just ssh to the server and the key will be used. If you set a passphrase, you will be asked for it as you would for a password.

Saving Private Keys to Use from a USB Flash Drive

If you'd like to **store your private key** somewhere safer than your hard drive, you can use a USB flash drive (sometimes called a thumbdrive or pen drive):

```
$ mv ~/.ssh/id_rsa /media/THUMBDRIVE1/myprivatekey
```

And then, when you want **to use the key**, insert the USB drive and type the following:

```
$ ssh -i /media/THUMBDRIVE1/myprivatekey chris@myserver
```

Using keys with passphrases is more secure than simple passwords, but also more cumbersome. To make your life easier, you can use ssh-agent to **store unlocked keys for the duration of your session**. When you add an unlocked key to your running ssh-agent, you can run ssh using the key without being prompted for the passphrase each time.

To see what the ssh-agent command does, run the command with no option. A three-line bash script appears when you run it, as follows:

```
$ ssh-agent
SSH_AUTH_SOCK=/tmp/ssh-SkEQZ18329/agent.18329; export SSH_AUTH_SOCK;
SSH_AGENT_PID=18330; export SSH_AGENT_PID;
echo Agent pid 18330;
```

The first two lines of the output just shown need to be executed by your shell. Copy and paste those lines into your shell now. You can avoid this extra step by starting ssh-agent and having the bash shell evaluate its output by typing the following:

```
$ eval `ssh-agent`
Agent pid 18408
```

You can now unlock keys and add them to your running agent. Assuming you have already run the ssh-keygen command to create a default key, let's add that default key using the ssh-add command:

```
$ ssh-add
Enter passphrase for /home/chris/.ssh/id_rsa: *******
Identity added: /home/chris/.ssh/id_rsa (/home/chris/.ssh/id_rsa)
```

Next you could add the key you stored on the USB thumbdrive:

```
$ ssh-add /media/THUMBDRIVE1/myprivatekey
```

Use the -l option to ssh-add to list the keys stored in the agent:

```
$ ssh-add -l
2048 f7:b0:7a:5a:65:3c:cd:45:b5:1c:de:f8:26:ee:8d:78 /home/chris/.ssh/id_rsa
(RSA)
2048 f7:b0:7a:5a:65:3c:cd:45:b5:1c:de:f8:26:ee:8d:78
/media/THUMBDRIVE1/myprivatekey (RSA)
```

To remove one key from the agent, for example the one from the USB thumbdrive, run ssh-add with the -d option as follows:

```
$ ssh-add -d /media/THUMBDRIVE1/myprivatekey
```

To remove all the keys stored in the agent, use the -D option:

```
$ ssh-add -D
```

Using screen: A Rich Remote Shell

The ssh command gives you only one screen. If you lose that screen, you lose all you were doing on the remote computer. That can be very bad if you were in the middle of something important, such as a 12-hour compile. And if you want to do three things at once, for example `vi httpd.conf`, `tail -f error_log`, and `service httpd reload`, you need to open three separate `ssh` sessions.

Essentially, `screen` is a terminal multiplexer. If you are a system administrator working on remote servers, `screen` is a great tool for managing a remote computer with only a command line interface available. Besides allowing multiple shells sessions, `screen` also lets you disconnect from it, and then reconnect to that same `screen` session later.

The `screen` software package is available with Fedora. To **install screen from over the Internet,** type the following from the Fedora server on which you want to use `screen`:

```
# yum install screen
```

To **use screen,** run the `ssh` command from a client system to connect to the Linux server where `screen` is installed. Then simply type the following command:

```
$ screen
```

If you ran `screen` from a Terminal window, you should see [screen 0: bash] in the title bar and a regular bash prompt in the window. To control `screen`, press the Ctrl+a key combo, followed by another keystroke. For example, Ctrl+a followed by ? (noted as Ctrl+a, ?) displays the help screen. With `screen` running, here are some commands and control keys you can use to operate `screen`.

```
$ screen -ls                              List active screens
There is a screen on:
        7089.pts-2.myserver    (Attached)  Shows screen is attached
1 Socket in /var/run/screen/S-francois.
$ Ctrl+a, a                               Change window title
Set window's title to: My Server         Type a new title
$ Ctrl+a, c                               Create a new window
$ Ctrl+a, "                               Show active window titles
Num Name                 Flags
  0 My Server                             Up/down arrows change windows
  1 bash
$ Ctrl+a, d                               Detach screen from terminal
$ screen -ls                              List active screens
There is a screen on:
        7089.pts-2.myserver    (Detached)  Shows screen is detached
1 Socket in /var/run/screen/S-francois.
```

The `screen` session just shown resulted in two windows (each running a bash shell) being created. You can create as many as you like and name them as you choose. Also, instead of detaching from the `screen` session, you could have just closed it by exiting the shell in each open window (type `exit` or Ctrl+d).

When the `screen` session is detached, you are returned to the shell that was opened when you first logged into the server. You can reconnect to that `screen` session as described in the following "Reconnecting to a screen Session" section.

Table 13-1 shows some other useful control key sequences available with screen.

Table 13-1: Control Keys for Using screen

Keys	Description
Ctrl+a, ?	Show help screen.
Ctrl+a, c	Create new window.
Ctrl+a, d	Detach screen from terminal. The screen session and its windows keep running.
Ctrl+a, "	View list of windows.
Ctrl+a, '	Prompt for number or name of window to switch to.
Ctrl+a, n	View next window.
Ctrl+a, p	View previous window.
Ctrl+a, [	Terminal's vertical scroll is disabled in screen. These keys turn on screen's scrollback mode. Press Enter twice to exit.
Ctrl+a, Shift+a	Rename current window.
Ctrl+a, w	Show the list of window names in the title bar.

Reconnecting to a screen Session

After you detach from a screen session, you can return to that screen again later (even after you log out and disconnect from the server). **To reconnect** when only one screen is running, type the following:

```
$ screen -r
```

If there are several screen sessions running, screen -r won't work. For example, this shows what happens when two detached screen sessions are running:

```
$ screen -r
There are several suitable screens on:
        7089.pts-2.myserver    (Detached)
        7263.pts-2.myserver    (Detached)
Type "screen [-d] -r [pid.]tty.host" to resume one of them.
```

As the output suggests, you could identify the `screen` session you want by its name (which, by default, is a combination of the session's process ID, tty name, and hostname). For example:

```
$ screen -r 7089.pts-2.myserver
```

Naming screen Sessions

Instead of using the default names, you can **create more descriptive names for your screen sessions** when you start `screen`. For example:

```
$ screen -S mysession
$ screen -ls
There is a screen on:
        26523.mysession (Attached)
```

Sharing screen Sessions

The `screen` command also allows the **sharing of screens**. This feature is great for tech support, because each person connected to the session can both type into and watch the current session! Creating a named screen, as in the preceding section, makes this easier. Then another person on a different computer can `ssh` to the server (using the same user name) and type the following:

```
$ screen -x mysession
```

Just as with `screen -r`, if there's only one screen running, you don't need to specify which screen you're connecting to:

```
$ screen -x
```

Using a Remote Windows Desktop

Many system administrators who become comfortable using a Linux desktop prefer to do administration of their Windows systems from Linux whenever possible. Linux provides tools such as rdesktop and tsclient, which enable you to connect to a Windows system running Windows Terminal Services.

To be able to **connect to your Windows system desktop from Linux**, you have to enable Remote Desktop from your Windows system. To do that from Windows XP (and others) right-click My Computer and select Properties. Then choose the Remote tab from the System Properties window and select the Allow users to connect remotely to this computer check box. Select which users you want to let connect to the Windows box and click OK.

Now, from Linux, you can use either `rdesktop` or `tsclient` (a graphical wrapper around `rdesktop`) to connect to the Windows system using Remote Desktop Protocol

(RDP). If those applications are not already installed, type the following from your Linux system:

```
# yum install rdesktop tsclient
```

Connecting to a Windows Desktop with tsclient

If you are used to using Windows' Remote Desktop Connection (formerly known as *Terminal Services Client*) to connect from one Windows box to another, you will probably find the tsclient tool a good way to connect to a Windows desktop from Linux. Running `tsclient` opens a Terminal Server Client window that mimics the Windows remote desktop client's user interface.

When the tsclient package is installed, launch `tsclient` by selecting Applications ➪ Internet ➪ Terminal Server Client from the GNOME desktop or by typing the following from the shell:

```
$ tsclient &
```

Figure 13-2 shows the Terminal Server Client window.

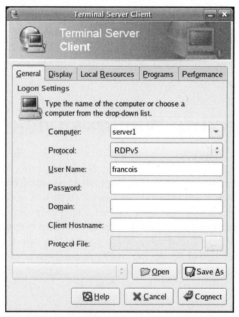

Figure 13-2: Terminal Server Client (tsclient) connects to Windows desktops.

Probably all you need to enter on this screen is the name or IP address of the Windows system. You will probably be prompted for user name and password, depending on how the Windows system is configured. Select different tabs to further refine your connection to the remote Windows desktop.

Note that `tsclient` can also be used as a client for VNC and XDMCP.

Connecting to a Windows Desktop with rdesktop

If you prefer not to use the `tclient` wrapper described above, you can **log in to a remote Windows desktop** using the `rdesktop` command. The `rdesktop` command requests a login to the Windows machine, then opens the Windows desktop for the user after you log in. Here are examples of the `rdesktop` command:

```
$ rdesktop 172.16.18.66          Login to desktop at IP address
$ rdesktop -u chris -p M6pyXX win1  Identify user/password for host win1
$ rdesktop -f win1                Run rdesktop in full-screen mode
$ rdesktop -0 -r sound:local win1  Direct sound from server to client
$ rdesktop -E win1                Disable client/server encryption
```

If you disable client/server encryption, the login packet is encrypted, but everything after that is not. Although this can improve performance greatly, anyone sniffing your LAN would be able to see your clear-text communications (including any interactive logins after the initial login packet). Other `rdesktop` options that can improve performance or your Windows desktop include -m (don't send mouse motion events), -D (hide window manager's decorations), and -K (don't override window manager key bindings).

Using Remote Linux Desktop and Applications

The X Window System (X) should not be run on typical production servers for security and performance reasons. But thanks to the client-server nature of X, you can run an X-enabled program on a remote machine with its graphical output directed to your desktop. In that relationship, the application running from the remote machine is referred to as the *X client*, and your desktop is the *X server*. When running remote X applications on untrusted networks or the Internet, use SSH forwarding as described earlier. On trusted LANs, do it without SSH, as described here.

By default, your X desktop will not allow remote X applications to connect (popup) on your desktop. You can **allow remote apps on your desktop** using the `xhost` command. On your local Linux display, use the `xhost` command to control which remote machines can connect to X and display applications on your desktop. Here are examples of `xhost`:

```
$ xhost                      List allowed hosts
access control enabled, only authorized clients can connect
$ xhost +                    Disable access control (dangerous)
access control disabled, clients can connect from any host
$ xhost -                    Re-enable access control
access control enabled, only authorized clients can connect
$ xhost remotemachine        Add an allowed host
remotemachine being added to access control list
```

Access control should be completely disabled only for troubleshooting purposes. However, with access enabled for a particular host machine (remotemachine in this case), you can do the following from a shell on the remote computer to have X applications from that machine appear on the local desktop (in this case called localmachine):

```
$ export DISPLAY=localmachine:0    Set the DISPLAY to localmachine:0
$ xterm &                          Open remote Terminal on local
$ xclock &                         Open remote clock on local
$ gtali &                          Open remote dice game on local
```

After setting the `DISPLAY` variable on remotemachine to point to localmachine, any application run from that shell on remotemachine should appear on Desktop 0 on localmachine. In this case, we started the Terminal window, clock, and game applications.

> **NOTE** *On recent versions of Fedora, the X server doesn't listen for TCP connections by default. To allow remote X connections, edit the* `/etc/gdm/custom.conf` *file on the X server as follows:*
>
> ```
> [security]
> DisallowTCP=false
> ```
>
> *Then restart X Window.*

Sharing X applications in this way between Linux and Unix hosts is pretty easy. However, it is not trivial to use across other computer platforms. If your desktop runs Windows, you have to run an X server. A free solution is Cygwin, which includes an X server. There are also feature-rich commercial X servers, but they can be very expensive. To share remote desktops across different operating system platforms, we suggest you use Virtual Network Computing (VNC).

Sharing Desktops Using VNC

Virtual Network Computing (VNC) consists of server and client software that enables you to assume remote control of a **full desktop display from one computer on another**. In Fedora, RHEL, and similar systems, you need the vnc package to access a remote desktop on your display (client) and vnc-server to share a desktop from your computer (server). To install those packages, type either (or both) of the following:

```
# yum install vnc
# yum install vnc-server
```

VNC clients and servers are available for, and interoperable with, many different operating systems. VNC servers are available on Linux, Windows (32-bit), Mac OS X, and Unix systems. VNC clients are offered on those, and many other types of systems (including OS/2, PalmOS, and even as a Java application running in a web browser).

Setting Up the VNC Server

From your Linux desktop, we'll assume you are using the default display (DISPLAY=:0) as your local desktop. So we'll set out to create independent displays accessible via VNC. To start, open the vncservers file on the Linux system acting as your VNC server (as root user) using any text editor:

```
# vi /etc/sysconfig/vncservers
```

In that file, create a display:user pair to identify a VNC desktop. These user accounts must be valid user names for your system. Here are two different examples:

```
VNCSERVERS="1:francois"
VNCSERVERS="1:francois 2:chris"
```

Then as each user, run the vncpasswd command to create the password each of those users will need to connect to their own desktops on the VNC server. In our example, we run the following as the user francois:

```
$ vncpasswd
Password: *******
Verify: *******
```

Finally, you can start the VNC service (vncserver) as you would any other service in Fedora and similar systems. Type the following as root user:

```
# chkconfig vncserver on
# service vncserver start
```

If you are using the iptables firewall built into your system, make sure you open the port(s) for VNC. Each display runs on its own port. Display number N is accessed on TCP port 5900+N. For example, display 1 is accessible on port 5901. Refer to Chapter 14 for more details on iptables.

Starting Up the VNC Client

With the VNC server running, you can connect to a desktop on that server from any of the client systems mentioned earlier (Windows, Linux, Mac OSX, UNIX, and so on). For example, assuming your VNC server is on a system named `myserver`, you could type the following command to **start that remote desktop** from another Linux system:

```
$ vncviewer myserver:1        Connect as francois on display 1
$ vncviewer myserver:2        Connect as chris on display 2
```

You can also use `tsclient` to connect; for this example, you would just specify `myserver:1` as the computer and VNC as the protocol. By default, once you connect via VNC, all you get is a very basic window manager (`twm`) and a terminal. **To get the full Fedora desktop** next time the user logs in, you should edit your VNC `xstartup` file on the VNC server. For example, log in as the user (in this example, francois or chris) and type the following:

```
$ vi ~/.vnc/xstartup
```

When editing that file, remove the comment characters from two lines so they appear as follows:

```
unset SESSION_MANAGER
exec /etc/X11/xinit/xinitrc
```

On older versions of the VNC software, the file may not exist. So create it and add the two lines above. After creating the file, set its permissions as follows:

```
# chmod 755 ~/.vnc/xstartup
```

Then, for the changes to take effect, you need to restart the VNC server. As root user, type:

```
# service vncserver restart
```

Using VNC on Untrusted Networks with SSH

VNC is a considered to be an insecure protocol. The password is sent using fairly weak encryption, and the rest of the session is not encrypted at all. For that reason, when using VNC over an untrusted network or Internet, we recommend you tunnel it over SSH.

For a general description of how the SSH service works, refer to the "Doing Remote Login and Tunneling with SSH" section earlier in this chapter. To forward VNC display 2 (port 5902) on the computer named `myserver`, to the same local port, type the following:

```
$ ssh -L 5902:localhost:5902 myserver
```

NOTE *If you start using VNC routinely, you may want to look at* tightvnc. *Although it's not included with Fedora,* tightvnc *is another open source implementation of the VNC protocol, under active development and with newer features and optimizations. These features include built-in ssh tunneling.*

Sharing a VNC Desktop with Vino

If you're running GNOME and would like to **share your existing GNOME desktop** (display :0), you can do so with Vino (vino package). From the GNOME Desktop panel, select System ➪ Preference ➪ Remote Desktop to display the Remote Desktop Preferences window (vino-preferences command) shown in Figure 13-3.

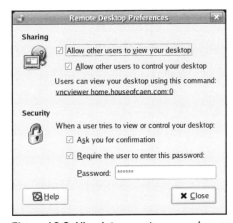

Figure 13-3: Vino lets remote users view, and possibly control, your desktop.

In the Remote Desktop Preferences window, selecting the Allow other users to view your desktop check box enables remote VNC viewers to view your desktop. Selecting the Allow other users to control your desktop check box enables others to manipulate your desktop with their mouse and keyboard.

If the Ask you for confirmation check box is selected, a remote request to view your desktop causes a pop-up window to okay the connection before the requestor can see your desktop. Selecting the Require the user to enter this password check box is a good idea, to prevent those without a password from viewing your desktop. (Be sure the password is at least eight characters.)

As the Remote Desktop Preferences window notes, you can use vncviewer from another Linux system (with the address and display number shown) to display the shared desktop to another system. However, VNC clients from many different operating systems should work as well.

Summary

If you ever find yourself in a position where you need to administer multiple Linux systems, you have a rich set of commands with Linux for doing remote system administration. The Secure Shell (SSH) facility offers encrypted communications between clients and servers for remote login, tunneling, and file transfer.

Virtual Network Computing (VNC) lets one Linux system share its desktop with a client system so that the remote desktop appears right on the client's desktop. With tools such as Vino, you can even share a desktop in such a way that the VNC server and client can both work from the same desktop at the same time.

14

Locking Down Security

Securing your Linux system means first restricting access to the user accounts and services on that system. After that, security means checking that no one has gotten around the defenses you have set up.

Fedora, Red Hat Enterprise Linux, CentOS, and other systems based on those Linux distributions are designed to be secure by default. That means that there are no user accounts with blank passwords, that the firewall is restrictive by default, and that most network services (Web, FTP, and so on) are off by default (even if their software is installed).

Although many of the commands covered in this book can be used to check and improve the security of your Linux system, some basic Linux features are particularly geared toward security. For example, secure user accounts with good password protection, a solid firewall, and consistent logging (and log monitoring) are critical to having a secure Linux system. Commands related to those features, plus some advanced features, such as SELinux and tripwire, are covered in this chapter.

Working with Users and Groups

During most Linux installation procedures, you are asked to assign a password to the root user (for system administration). Then you might be asked to create a user name of your choice and assign a password to that as well (for everyday computer use). We encourage you to always log in as a regular user and only su or sudo to the root account when necessary. When Linux is installed, you can use commands or graphical tools to add more users, modify user accounts, and assign and change passwords.

Managing Users the GUI Way

For a desktop system with X, you can manage users and groups with the User Manager window (System ➪ Administration ➪ Users and Groups). When managing user accounts for servers, one option is to use web-based GUIs. The most commonly used general-purpose tool is Webmin (www.webmin.com). Make sure you do not run Webmin on its default port (10000) for security reasons. You can also use special-purpose web interfaces. For example, there are many web-hosting automation GUIs, such as cPanel (www.cpanel.com), Plesk (www.swsoft.com/plesk), and Ensim (www.ensim.com).

Adding User Accounts

To **add new users**, you can use the useradd command. The only option that is required to add a new user is the user name you are adding. You can see some of the default settings for adding a new user by entering the -D option:

```
# useradd -D              Show useradd default values
GROUP=100                 Set group ID to 100 (users)
HOME=/home                Set base home directory to /home
INACTIVE=-1               Password expiration is disabled (-1)
EXPIRE=                   Don't set date to disable user account
SHELL=/bin/bash           Set the default shell to /bin/bash
SKEL=/etc/skel            Copy default config files from /etc/skel to $HOME
CREATE_MAIL_SPOOL=yes      Create a mail spool directory
```

Fedora and other Red Hat–sponsored systems override the default group (100) and create a new group for every user. By default, the user ID assigned to the first user created is 500 and the group ID is also 500. The group name is the same as the user name. The home directory is the user name appended to /home. So, for example, if you created the first regular user account on the system as follows:

```
# useradd willz
```

The result would be a new user account with a willz user name (UID 500), willz group name (GID 500), a home directory of /home/willz, and a set of configuration files (each beginning with a ".") copied to the home directory from /etc/skel. The account would remain active indefinitely (no expiration date). **Add a password** as follows, and in most cases that's all you need to do to have a working user account.

```
# passwd horatio
Changing password for user horatio.
New UNIX password: ********
Retype new UNIX password: ********
passwd: all authentication tokens updated successfully.
```

> **NOTE** Remember to use strong, non–dictionary-based passwords.

There are many options you can enter to **override the defaults** when you create a user. Combine the different options as you choose. Here are some examples:

```
# useradd -u 1001 -g 300 skolmes   Use specific UID and GID for user
# useradd -d /home/jj jones        Create /var/x/jj home directory
# useradd -G support,sales timd    Add user to support and sales groups
# useradd -c "Tom G. Lotto" tlot   Add user's full name to comment field
# useradd -s /bin/tcsh joeq        Assign a new default shell (tcsh)
# useradd -e 2008-04-01 jerry      Add account to expire April 01, 2008
# useradd -f 0 jdoe                Create a disabled account
# useradd -s /sbin/nologin billt   Keep user from shelling in
# useradd -M billyq                Prevent creation of home directory
```

The -e option example is useful for setting an expiration date for a user that you know to be temporary. Change the default shell to nologin when you want a user to be able to access the computer (via FTP, POP3, and so on), but you don't want to allow access to a regular Linux login shell. Likewise, the last example (-M) might allow a user to access a machine, but not have a home directory.

Before you can add a user to a group, that group must exist (see the groupadd command in the "Adding Groups" section later in this chapter). A user must belong to one initial group that can be defined with -g and can also belong to supplementary groups, defined with -G.

To **list the group(s) that a user belongs to,** use the groups command:

```
$ groups francois                  List the groups that a user belongs to
francois ftpusers
```

Changing useradd Defaults

The default values you get when you create a new user account with useradd (default shell, GID, expire dates, and so on) are set by values in the /etc/login.defs and /etc/default/useradd files. You can edit those files to change defaults or run the useradd command with the -D option to list or selectively change values:

```
# useradd -D                       List default settings for useradd
# useradd -D -b /home2 -s /bin/csh Set default base dir and shell
# useradd -D -e 2009-01-01         Set all new users to expire in 2009
```

As noted earlier, files and directories from the /etc/skel directory are copied to the new user's home directory when the account is created. Those files include some bash shell files and configuration files in the .kde directory. You can add other files and directories to /etc/skel so that each new user gets them. For example, if you are configuring a web server, you might create public_html and public_ftp directories for users to add web pages and files they want to share.

Modifying User Accounts

After a user account is created, you can change values for that account with the usermod command. Most options are the same ones you would use with `useradd`. For example:

```
# usermod -c "Thomas Lotto" tlot   Change user's name in comment field
# usermod -s /bin/sh joeq          Change default shell to sh
# usermod -L swanson               Lock the user account named swanson
# usermod -U travis                Unlock user account named travis
```

Note that the last two examples lock and unlock a user account, respectively. Locking a user account does not remove the user's account from the system or delete any of the user's files and directories. However, it does keep the user from logging in. Locking an account can be useful if an employee is leaving the company, but the work in that employee's files needs to be passed to another person. Under those circumstances, locking the user instead of deleting it prevents the files owned by that user from appearing as belonging to an unassigned UID.

Because a regular user can't use the `useradd` or `usermod` command, there are special commands for changing personal account information. Here are examples:

```
$ chsh -s /bin/sh            Change current user's shell to /bin/sh
# chsh -s /bin/sh francois    Change a user's shell to /bin/sh
$ chfn -f "Francois Caen" \   Change full name
     -o "B-205"          \   Change office number
     -h 212-555-1212     \   Change home phone number
     -p 212-555-1957         Change office phone number
$ finger francois
Login: francois                      Name: Francois Caen
Directory: /home/francois            Shell: /bin/bash
Office: B-205, 212-555-1212    Home Phone: 212-555-1957
On since Sat Aug  4 13:39 (CDT) on tty1    4 seconds idle
No mail.
No Plan.
```

The information changed above with the chfn command and displayed with finger are stored in the fifth field of the /etc/password file for the selected user. (The /etc/passwd file can only be edited directly by the root user, and should only be edited using the vipw command and extreme caution.)

Deleting User Accounts

With the userdel command, you can remove user accounts from the system, as well as other files (home directories, mail spool files, and so on) if you choose. Here are examples:

```
# userdel jimbo           Delete user, not user's home directory
# userdel -r lily         Delete user, home directory, and mail spool
```

Managing Passwords

Adding or changing a password is usually done quite simply with the `passwd` command. However, there are additional options available with `passwd` that let an administrator manage such things as user account locking, password expiration, and warnings to change passwords. Besides `passwd`, there are commands such as `chage`, `chfn`, and `vipw`, for working with user passwords.

Regular users can **change only their own passwords**, whereas the root user can change the password for any user. For example:

```
$ passwd                        Change a regular user's own password
Changing password for user chris.
Changing password for chris.
(current) UNIX password: ********
New UNIX password: *
BAD PASSWORD: it's WAY too short
New UNIX password: *********
Retype new UNIX password: *********
passwd: all authentication tokens updated successfully.
# passwd joseph                 Root can change any user's password
Changing password for user joseph.
New UNIX password: *
BAD PASSWORD: it's WAY too short
Retype new UNIX password: *
passwd: all authentication tokens updated successfully.
```

In the first example, a regular user (chris) changes his own password. Even while logged in, the user must type the current password before entering a new one. Also, `passwd` keeps a regular user from setting a password that is too short, based on a dictionary word, doesn't have enough different characters, or is otherwise easy to guess. The root user, in the second example, can change any user password without the old password. Likewise, the root user is warned about a password that's considered insecure. However, the root user can assign a short or easy-to-guess password, despite those warnings.

Passwords should be at least eight characters, be a combination of letters and other characters (numbers, punctuation, and so on), and not include real words. Make passwords easy to remember but hard to guess.

A system administrator can use `passwd` to **lock and unlock user accounts**. For example:

```
# passwd -l carl               Lock the user account (carl)
Locking password for user carl.
passwd: Success
# passwd -u carl               Unlock a locked user account (carl)
Unlocking password for user carl.
passwd: Success
```

```
# passwd -u jordan          Fails to unlock account with blank password
Unlocking password for user jordan.
passwd: Warning: unlocked password would be empty.
passwd: Unsafe operation (use -f to force)
# passwd -u -f jordan       Able to unlock user with blank password
Unlocking password for user jordan.
passwd: Success
```

Locking a user account with `passwd` causes two exclamation marks (`!!`) to be placed at the front of the password field in the `/etc/shadow` file (where user passwords are stored). When a user account is unlocked, the exclamation marks are removed and the user's previous password is restored.

An administrator can use the `passwd` command to **require users to change passwords regularly**, as well as **warn users when passwords are about to expire**. To use the password expiration feature, the user account needs to have had password expiration enabled. The following examples use `passwd` to modify password expiration:

```
# passwd -n 2 vern          Set minimum password life to 2 days
# passwd -x 300 vern        Set maximum password life to 300 days
# passwd -w 10 vern         Warn of password expiration 10 days in advance
# passwd -i 14 vern         Days after expiration account is disabled
```

In the first example, the user must wait at least two days (`-n 2`) before changing to a new password. In the second, the user must change the password within 300 days (`-x 300`). In the next example, the user is warned 10 days before the password expires (`-w 10`). In the last example, the user account is disabled 14 days after the password expires (`-i 14`).

To **view password expiration**, you can use the `chage` command as follows:

```
# chage -l vern             View password expiration information
Last password change                             : Aug 04, 2007
Password expires                                 : May 31, 2008
Password inactive                                : Jun 14, 2008
Account expires                                  : never
Minimum number of days between password change   : 2
Maximum number of days between password change   : 300
Number of days of warning before password expires : 10
```

As system administrator, you can also use the `chage` command to manage password expiration. Besides being able to set minimum (`-m`), maximum (`-M`), and warning (`-W`) days for password expiration, `chage` can also set the day when a user must set a new password or a particular date the account becomes inactive:

```
# chage -I 40 frank         Make account inactive in 40 days
# chage -d 5 perry          Force user's password to expire in 5 days
```

Instead of five days (-d 5), you could set that option to 0 and cause the user to have to set a new password the next time he or she logs in. For example, the next time the user perry logs in, if -d 0 is set, perry will be prompted for a new password as follows:

```
login: perry
Password: ********
You are required to change your password immediately (root enforced)
Changing password for perry.
(current) UNIX password:
New UNIX password: *********
Retype new UNIX password: *********
```

Adding Groups

Each new user is assigned to one or more groups. You can create groups at any time and add users to those groups. The permissions that each group has to use files and directories in Linux depend on how the group permission bits are set on each item. Assigning users to a group enables you to attach ownership to files, directories, and applications so that those users can work together on a project or have common access to resources.

Commands similar to those for working with users are available for managing your groups. You can add groups (groupadd), change group settings (groupmod), delete groups (groupdel), and add and delete members from those groups (groupmems). Here are some examples for **adding new groups** with the groupadd command:

```
# groupadd marketing        Create new group with next available GID
# groupadd -g 701 sales      Create new group with GID of 701
# groupadd -r myadmin        Create group with admin GID (under 499)
# groupadd -o -g 74 mysshd   Create group with existing GID
```

With the groupmod command, you can **change the name or group ID** of an existing group. Here are examples:

```
# groupmod -g 491 myadmin    Modify myadmin to use GID 491
# groupmod -n myad myadmin   Change name of myadmin group to myad
```

To remove an existing group, use the groupdel command. Here is an example:

```
# groupdel myad              Remove existing myad group
```

Keep in mind that removing a group or user doesn't remove the files, directories, devices, or other items owned by that group or user. If you do a long listing (ls -l) of a file or directory assigned to a user or group that was deleted, the UID or GID of the deleted user or group is displayed.

Checking on Users

After you have created user accounts, and let those users loose on your computer, you can use several commands to keep track of how they are using your computer. Commands for checking on user activity on your Linux system that are covered in other chapters include the following:

❑ The find command to search the system for files anywhere on the system that are owned by selected users (see Chapter 4)

❑ The du command to see how much disk space has been used in selected users' home directories (see Chapter 7)

❑ Commands such as fuser, ps, and top to find out which processes users are running (see Chapter 9)

Aside from the commands just mentioned, there are commands for checking such things as who is logged into your system and getting general information about the users with accounts on your system. Here are examples of commands for getting information about people logging into your system:

```
$ last          List the most recent successful logins
greek    tty3                 Sun Aug  5 18:05   still logged in
chris    tty1                 Sun Aug  4 13:39   still logged in
root     pts/4    thompson    Sun Aug  5 14:02   still logged in
chris    pts/1    :0.0        Sat Aug  4 15:47   still logged in
jim      pts/0    10.0.0.50   Fri Aug  3 13:46 - 15:40  (01:53)
francois pts/2                Thu Aug  2 11:14 - 13:38 (2+02:24)
$ last -a       Makes it easier to read the remote client hostname
# lastb         List the most recent unsuccessful logins
julian   ssh:notty   ritchie       Mon Aug  6 12:28 - 12:28  (00:00)
morris   ssh:notty   thompson      Tue Jul 31 13:08 - 13:08  (00:00)
baboon   ssh:notty   10.0.0.50     Sun Jul  8 09:40 - 09:40  (00:00)
francois ssh:notty   000db9034dce.cli Fri Jun 22 17:23 - 17:23  (00:00)
$ who -u        List who is currently logged in (long form)
greek    tty3    2007-08-05 18:05 17:24    18121
jim      pts/0   2007-08-06 12:29  .       20959 (server1.example.com)
root     pts/3   2007-08-04 18:18 13:46    17982 (server2.example.com)
francois pts/2   2007-07-31 23:05 old      4700  (0a0d9b34x.example.com)
chris    pts/1   2007-08-04 15:47 old      17502 (:0.0)
$ users         List who is currently logged in (short form)
chris francois greek jim root
```

With the last command, you can see when each user logged in (or opened a new shell) and either how long they were logged in or a note that they are "still logged in." The tty1 and tty3 terminal lines show users working from virtual terminals on the console. The pts lines indicate a person opening a shell from a remote computer (thompson) or local X display (:0.0). We recommend you use the -a option for improved readability. The lastb command shows failed login attempts and where they are from. The who -u and users commands show information on currently logged-in users.

Here are some commands for finding out more about individual users on your system:

```
$ id                    Your identity (UID, GID and group for current shell)
uid=501(chris) gid=501(chris) groups=501(chris)
$ who am i              Your identity (user, tty, login date, location)
chris    pts/0     Aug 3 2140 (:0.0)
$ finger -s chris    User information (short)
Login    Name         Tty    Idle   Login Time     Office   Office Phone
chris    Chris Negus  tty1    1d    Aug  4 13:39   A-111     555-1212
$ finger -l chris    User information (long)
Login: chris                        Name: Chris Negus
Directory: /home/chris              Shell: /bin/bash
Office: A-111, 555-1212             Home Phone: 555-2323
On since Sat Aug  4 13:39 (CDT) on tty1     2 days idle
New mail received Mon Aug  6 13:46 2007 (CDT)
    Unread since Sat Aug  4 09:32 2007 (CDT)
No Plan.
```

Besides displaying basic information about the user (login, name, home directory, shell, and so on), the `finger` command will also display any information stored in special files in the user's home directory. For example, the contents of the user's `~/.plan` and `~/.project` files, if those files exist, are displayed at the end of the `finger` output. With a one-line `.project` file and multi-line `.plan` file, output could appear as follows:

```
$ finger -l chris    User information (long, .project and .plan files)
     . . .
Project:
My project is to take over the world.
Plan:
My grand plan is
to take over the world
by installing Linux on every computer
```

Configuring the Built-In Firewall

A firewall is a critical tool for keeping your computer safe from intruders over the Internet or other network. It can protect your computer by checking every packet of data that comes to your computer's network interfaces, then making a decision about what to do with that packet based on the parameters you set. The firewall facility built into the current Linux kernel is called iptables. (You may also hear of ipchains, which was iptables' predecessor in kernel 2.2 and below.)

The iptables facility (www.netfilter.org) is extraordinarily powerful, yet complex to use from the command line. For that reason, many people set up their basic firewall rules using a graphical interface. Fedora comes with the Security Level and Configuration window (select System ➪ Administration ➪ Firewall and SELinux) for configuring basic firewalls. It also offers add-on packages such as Firestarter (firestarter package), FWBuilder (fwbuilder package) and Shorewall (shorewall package) for graphically configuring firewalls.

When you install Fedora, you have the option to enable the firewall on your system. This generates an iptables configuration that is a good starting point for simple server firewalling, which consists of opening just a few ports for running daemons and blocking the rest. You can customize this default configuration by editing /etc/sysconfig/iptables and using simple copy-and-paste to add or remove ports. To make your changes take effect, use the following command:

```
# service iptable restart
```

For more complex needs, as when iptables is used as the firewall in front of multiple machines, we recommend using one of the graphical tools mentioned above. However, there are times when either you don't have a GUI available or you need a firewall rule that isn't available through a GUI. In those cases, it's useful to know the syntax of the iptables command to list current rules and add a new rule yourself.

Before you start messing around with your firewall in Fedora, RHEL, or CentOS, you should check how the firewall is set on your system. Here is how to **list the current rules set** on your Linux system's firewall:

```
# iptables -L                    Display current iptables filter table
Chain INPUT (policy ACCEPT)
target    prot opt source        destination
   ...
ACCEPT    udp  --  anywhere    anywhere    udp dpt:ipp
ACCEPT    tcp  --  anywhere    anywhere    tcp dpt:ipp
ACCEPT    0    --  anywhere    anywhere    state RELATED,ESTABLISHED
ACCEPT    tcp  --  anywhere    anywhere    state NEW tcp dpt:ftp
ACCEPT    tcp  --  anywhere    anywhere    state NEW tcp dpt:ssh
ACCEPT    tcp  --  anywhere    anywhere    state NEW tcp dpt:http
REJECT    0    --  anywhere    anywhere    reject-with icmp-host-prohibited


Chain FORWARD (policy ACCEPT)
target    prot opt source        destination
REJECT    0    --  anywhere    anywhere    reject-with icmp-host-prohibited


Chain OUTPUT (policy ACCEPT)
target       prot opt source                  destination
```

The example illustrates the default *filter* iptables firewall table. It shows that for packets coming into the computer's network interfaces, packets for Internet Printing Protocol (ipp) on udp and tcp protocols are allowed. Likewise, tcp packets matching the FTP (ftp), Secure Shell (ssh), and web (http) destination ports are accepted. Packets are also accepted if they are associated with an established connection. Next you can **look at the nat table**:

```
# iptables -t nat -L           Display current iptables nat table
Chain PREROUTING (policy ACCEPT)
target    prot opt source        destination
DNAT      tcp  --  0.0.0.0/0    11.22.33.44  tcp dpt:8785 to:10.0.0.155:22
DROP      tcp  --  0.0.0.0/0    0.0.0.0/0    tcp dpt:135
DROP      udp  --  0.0.0.0/0    0.0.0.0/0    udp dpt:135
```

```
Chain POSTROUTING (policy ACCEPT)
target     prot opt source              destination
MASQUERADE  all  --  0.0.0.0/0           0.0.0.0/0

Chain OUTPUT (policy ACCEPT)
target     prot opt source              destination
```

The nat table just shown applies to a feature called *Network Address Translation* (NAT). NAT enables you to do such things as use private addresses behind your firewall. As the packets from internal LAN machines exit the firewall, the source private address is rewritten with the IP address of the firewall's external interface. The firewall keeps track of these sessions in order to allow the return traffic through to the LAN machines. All this is configured with the MASQUERADE line on the POSTROUTING chain.

In the example above, the DNAT line in the PREROUTING chain causes any requests to port 8785, at IP address 11.22.33.44, to be forwarded to the internal LAN IP address 10.0.0.155 on port 22 (a trick to let someone ssh into a computer behind the firewall through a non-standard port).

Here are other examples for **listing information about your firewall**, The iptstate command is part of the iptstate package.

```
# iptables -n -L              Filter rules, IP numbers (no DNS lookup)
# iptables -v -L              Verbose output (with packet/byte counts)
# iptables -L --line-numbers  Show line number in chain for each rule
# iptables -nvL --line-numbers Our Tech Editor's favorite combination
# iptstate                    Show top-like listing of iptables entries
# iptstate -tl                Same thing with DNS names and totals
```

In Fedora systems, if iptables is not started you can **start iptables manually** by typing the following:

```
# service iptables start    To start iptables now
# chkconfig iptables on      To set iptables to start at boot time
```

Here is how you can **stop or flush all iptables rules** on a Fedora system:

```
# iptables -F               Flush all iptables rules
# service iptables stop     To turn off iptables service now
# chkconfig iptables off    To set iptables to not start at boot time
```

The iptables rules that are reinstated on your next reboot are stored permanently in the /etc/sysconfig/iptables file. Firewall changes you make with the iptables command will be lost on your next reboot if they are not added to this file. To **save the currently active firewall rules** to the permanent /etc/sysconfig/iptables file, type either of the following commands:

```
# service iptables save                      Permanently save settings
# iptables-save > /etc/sysconfig/iptables  Same as above
```

Now that you know how to start, stop, list settings, and save settings related to your system's iptables facility, you might want to see some examples of how the `iptables` command can be used to **change rules on an active firewall:**

```
# iptables -A INPUT -p TCP \    Add filter input rule for TCP packets
    -i eth0                \    on the first Ethernet interface
    --destination-port 25  \    destined for mail service port (25)
    -j ACCEPT                   to accept those packets when encountered

# iptables -t nat          \    Add nat rule
    -A POSTROUTING         \    POSTROUTING chain
    -o eth1                \    for packets received on eth1 interface
    -j SNAT                \    jump to network address translation
    --to-source 11.22.33.1      using outgoing address 11.22.33.1
```

Of the two examples shown, the first example creates a rule that allows new incoming requests to your system on port 25. This is presumably because you have configured your computer as a mail server (with sendmail, postfix, or other SMTP service). The second example creates a NAT table rule to allow the firewall to do Source Network Address Translation (SNAT). The SNAT feature lets you have private IP addresses behind your firewall that can communicate to the public Internet using the firewall's external IP address.

To use SNAT or any other form of NAT, you must **also enable IP forwarding** on the machine. This can be done temporarily with the `echo` command:

```
# echo 1 > /proc/sys/net/ipv4/ip_forward   Allow port forwarding
```

To make the change permanent across reboots, edit the `/etc/sysctl.conf` file and change the following variable:

```
net.ipv4.ip_forward = 1
```

In cases where you have an Internet-facing service offered on a machine behind your firewall, you can instruct the firewall to **forward requests for that service** to that machine. The following example uses a feature called *port forwarding* to pass requests for a service through the firewall to the destination machine behind the firewall:

```
# iptables -t nat -A PREROUTING \   Add nat PREROUTING rule
    -p tcp -d 11.22.33.1        \   accepts tcp requests on 11.22.33.1
    --dport 80                  \   for port 80 (Web service)
    -j DNAT                     \   jump to the DNAT target
    --to-destination 10.0.0.2       forward those packets to 10.0.0.2
```

You can create many other types of rules to change how your firewall behaves. Refer to the iptables man page or the Netfilter web site (`www.netfilter.org`) for further information on using the iptables facility.

Working with System Logs

Most Linux systems are configured to log many of the activities that occur on those systems. Those activities are then written to log files located in the /var/log directory or its subdirectories. This logging is done by the Syslog facility.

Fedora, RHEL, and CentOS use the syslogd (system log daemon) and klogd (kernel log daemon) from the sysklogd package to manage system logging. Those daemons are started automatically from the syslog init script (/etc/init.d/syslog). Information about system activities is then directed to files in the /var/log directory such as messages, secure, cron, and boot.log, based on settings in the /etc/syslog .conf file.

Automatic log rotation is handled by logrotate, based on settings in the /etc/ logrotate.conf file and /etc/logrotate.d directory. The /etc/cron.daily/ logrotate cronjob causes this daily log rotating to take place.

You can check any of the log files manually (using vi or another favorite text editor). However, if the logwatch package is installed (which it should be by default), highlights of your log files will automatically be mailed to your root user's mailbox every day. You can change both the recipient and the sender address of that mail by editing the /etc/cron.daily/0logwatch file. To prevent e-mail loops, you should change the sender address to a real e-mail address when the recipient is not on the local machine. Another way to change the recipient is to forward root's e-mail to another address by editing /etc/aliases and running newaliases to enact the changes. Otherwise, just log in as root and type the following to read your logwatch e-mail messages:

```
# mail
>U  1 logwatch@joe Sat Jun 16 0432 88/2536 "Logwatch for joe (Linux)"
& 1
```

Type 1 to page through the logwatch message. You will see information about SELinux audits, system startup, SSHD daemon, disk space in each partition, login problems caught by PAM, and new packages installed by yum.

You can **send your own messages to the syslogd logging facility** using the logger command. Here are a couple of examples:

```
# logger Added new video card          Message added to messages file
# logger -p info -t CARD -f /tmp/my.txt   Priority, tag, message file
```

In the first example the words "Added new video card" are sent to the messages file. In the second example, the priority of the message is set to info, and a tag of CARD is added to each line in the message. The message text is taken from the /tmp/my.txt file. To see these log entries in real time, use tail -f or less as described in Chapter 5.

Using Advanced Security Features

A dozen or so pages covering security-related commands are not nearly enough to address the depth of security tools available to you as a Linux system administrator. Beyond the commands covered in this chapter, here are descriptions of some features you may want to look into to further secure your Linux system:

❑ **Security Enhanced Linux (SELinux):** The SELinux feature provides a means of securing the files, directories, and applications in your Linux system in such a way that exploitation of one of those areas of your system cannot be used to breach other areas. For example, if intruders were to compromise your web daemon, they wouldn't necessarily be able to compromise the rest of the system. SELinux was developed by the U.S. National Security Agency (NSA), who hosts a related FAQ at www.nsa.gov/selinux/info/faq.cfm.

SELinux can be enabled when you install Fedora, RHEL, or CentOS. To protect selected services with SELinux, you can use the Security Level Configuration window. Simply enable SELinux, and then check the services you want enabled on the SELinux tab of that window. SELinux can also be configured from the CLI.

❑ **Central logging:** If you're managing more than a couple of Linux servers, it becomes preferable to have all your systems log to a central syslog server. When you implement your syslog server, you may want to explore using syslog-ng. Also, if you outgrow logwatch, you should consider using a log parser such as Splunk.

❑ **Tripwire:** Using the tripwire package, you can take a snapshot of all the files on your system, then later use that snapshot to find if any of those files have been changed. This is particularly useful to find out if any applications have been modified that should not have been. First, you take a baseline of your system file. Then at regular intervals, you run a tripwire integrity check to see if any of your applications or configuration files have been modified.

❑ **RPM database:** Another way to check if any of your applications have been modified is by using the rpm command to validate the applications and configuration files you have installed on your system. Using rpm -V, you can verify the size, MD5sum, permissions, type, and ownership of every item in an RPM package. See Chapter 2 for information on using rpm to verify the contents of installed RPM packages.

❑ **chkrootkit:** If you suspect your system has been compromised, download and build chkrootkit from www.chkrootkit.org. This will help you detect rootkits that may have been used to take over your machine. We recommend you run chkrootkit from a LiveCD or after mounting the suspected drive on a clean system.

Summary

Although there are many tools available for securing your Linux system, the first line of security starts with securing the user accounts on your system and the services that run on your system. Commands such as `useradd, groupadd,` and `password` are standard tools for setting up user and group accounts.

Because most serious security breaches outside your organization can come from intruders accessing your systems on public networks, setting up secure firewalls is important for any system connected to the Internet. The iptables facility provides the firewall features that are built into the Linux kernel.

To keep track of activities on your system, the Syslog facility logs information about nearly every aspect of the actions that take place on your system. Packages that are installed by default, such as logrotate and logwatch, make it easy to manage and do daily checks on your system logs.

A

Using vi or Vim Editors

Although easy-to-use graphical text editors (such as `gedit` and `kedit`) are readily available with Linux, most power users still use vi or Emacs to edit text files. Besides the fact that vi and Emacs will work from any shell (no GUI required), they offer other advantages such as your hands never having to leave the keyboard and integration with useful utilities. And unlike GUI editors, text-based editors are usable over slow Internet connections such as dial-up or satellite.

IN THIS APPENDIX

Using the vi editor

Starting/quitting the vi editor

Moving around in vi

Changing and deleting text

Using Ex commands

Using visual mode

This appendix focuses on features of the vi editor that can not only help you with basic editing, but also help you do some advanced text manipulation. We chose to cover vi rather than Emacs because vi is more universal and leaner, and also because vi keyboard shortcuts only require two arms. Because many Linux systems use the Vim (Vi IMproved) editor in place of the older vi editor, the descriptions in this appendix are extended to cover Vim as well. Some features in Vim that are not in vi include multiple undo levels, syntax highlighting, and online help.

> **NOTE** *If you have never used vi or Vim before, try out the tutor that comes with the* vim-enhanced *package. Run the* vimtutor *command and follow the instructions to step through many of the key features of vi and Vim.*

Starting and Quitting the vi Editor

If you want to experiment with using vi, you should copy a text file to practice on. For example, type:

```
$ cp /etc/inittab /tmp
```

Then open that file using the `vi` command as follows:

```
$ vi /tmp/inittab
```

To benefit from all the improvements of Vim, make sure you have the vim-enhanced RPM installed. On many systems, vi is aliased to the vim command. You may want to double-check that using the alias command. If you specifically want to use the older-style vi command, use the full path to the vi command instead:

```
/bin/vi /tmp/text.txt
```

Here are a few other ways you can **start vi**:

```
$ vi +25 /tmp/inittab      Begin on line 25
$ vi + /tmp/inittab        Begin editing file on the last line
$ vi +/tty /tmp/inittab    Begin on first line with word "tty"
$ vi -r /tmp/inittab       Recover file from crashed edit session
$ view /tmp/inittab        Edit file in read-only mode
```

When you are done with your vi session, there are several different ways to save and quit. To **save the file before you are ready to quit,** type **:w**. To **quit and save changes,** type either **ZZ** or **:wq**. To **quit without saving changes,** type **:q!**. If you find that you can't write to the file you are editing, it may be opened in read-only mode. If that's the case, you can try forcing a write by typing **:w!** or you can **save the contents of the file to a different name.** For example, type the following to save the contents of the current file to a file named myfile.txt:

```
:w /tmp/myfile.txt
```

The vi editor also enables you to **line up several files at a time to edit.** For example, type:

```
$ cd /tmp
$ touch a.txt b.txt c.txt
$ vi a.txt b.txt c.txt
```

In this example, vi will open the a.txt file first. You can **move to the next file** by typing **:n**. You may want to **save changes before moving to the next file (:w)** or **save changes as you move to the next file (:wn)**. To **abandon changes while moving to the next file,** type **:n!**.

You will probably find it easier to open multiple files by splitting your vi screen. When you're in vi and have a file open, you can **split your screen multiple times** either horizontally or vertically:

```
:split /etc/httpd/conf/httpd.conf
:vsplit /etc/init.d/httpd
```

Use <Tab> to complete the path to the files, just like you would in a bash shell. To **navigate between split windows,** press Ctrl+w, followed by the w key. To close the current window, use the usual vi exit command (:q).

Moving Around in vi

The first thing to get used to with vi is that you can't just start typing. Vi has multiple modes that enable you to perform a different set of tasks. You start a vi session in Normal mode, where vi is waiting for you to type a command to get started. While you are in Normal mode, you can move around the file, to position where you want to be in the file. To enter or modify text, you need to go into Insert or Replace modes.

Assuming vi is open with a file that contains several pages of text, Table A-1 shows some keys and combinations you can type to **move around the file while in normal mode.**

Table A-1: Keystroke Commands for Moving Around

Key	Result	Key	Result
PageDown or Ctrl+f	Move down one page	PageUp or Ctrl+b	Move up one page
Ctrl+d	Move down half page	Ctrl+u	Move up half page
Shift+g	Go to last line of file	:1	Go to first line of file (use any number to go to that line)
Shift+h	Move cursor to screen top	Shift+l	Move cursor to screen bottom
Shift+m	Move cursor to middle of screen	Ctrl+l	Redraw screen (if garbled)
Enter	Move cursor to beginning of the next line	-	Move cursor to beginning of the previous line
Home or $	Move cursor to end of line	End or ^ or 0	Move cursor to line beginning
(	Move cursor to beginning of previous sentence	)	Move cursor to beginning of next sentence
{	Move cursor to beginning of previous paragraph	}	Move cursor to beginning of next paragraph
w	Move cursor to next word (space, new line, or punctuation)	Shift+w	Move cursor to next word (space or new line)

Continued

Table A-1: Keystroke Commands for Moving Around (*continued*)

Key	Result	Key	Result
b	Move cursor to previous word (space, new line, or punctuation)	Shift+b	Move cursor to previous word (space or new line)
e	Move cursor to end of next word (space, new line, or punctuation)	Shift+e	Move cursor to end of next word (space or new line)
Left arrow or Backspace	Move cursor left one letter	Right arrow or l	Move cursor right one letter
k or up arrow	Move cursor up one line	j or down arrow	Move cursor down one line
/*string*	Find next occurrence of *string*	?*string*	Find previous occurrence of *string*
n	Find same string again (forward)	Shift+n	Find same string again (backwards)

Changing and Deleting Text in vi

To begin changing or adding to text with vi, you can enter Insert or Replace modes, as shown in Table A-2. When you enter Insert or Replace mode, the characters you type will appear in the text document (as opposed to being interpreted as commands).

Press the Esc key to exit to normal mode after you are done inserting or replacing text.

Table A-2: Commands for Changing Text

Key	Result	Key	Result
i	Typed text appears before current character	Shift+i	Typed text appears at the beginning of current line
a	Typed text appears after current character	Shift+a	Typed text appears at the end of current line

Table A-2: Commands for Changing Text (*continued*)

Key	Result	Key	Result
o	Open a new line below current line to begin typing	Shift+o	Open a new line above current line to begin typing
s	Erase current character and replace with new text	Shift+s	Erase current line and enter new text
c?	Replace ? with l, w, $, or c to change the current letter, word, end of line, or line	Shift+c	Erase from cursor to end of line and enter new text
r	Replace current character with the next one you type	Shift+r	Overwrite as you type from current character going forward

Table A-3 contains keys you type to delete or paste text.

Table A-3: Commands for Deleting and Pasting Text

Key	Result	Key	Result
x	Delete text under cursor	Shift+x	Delete text to left of cursor
d?	Replace ? with l, w, $, or d to cut the current letter, word, end of line from cursor, or entire line	Shift+d	Cut from cursor to end of line
y?	Replace ? with l, w, or $ to copy (yank) the current letter, word, or end of line from cursor	Shift+y	Yank current line
p	Pastes cut or yanked text after cursor	Shift+p	Pastes cut or yanked text before cursor

Using Miscellaneous Commands

Table A-4 shows a few miscellaneous, but important, commands you should know.

Table A-4: Miscellaneous Commands

Key	Result
u	Type **u** to undo the previous change. Multiple u commands will step back to undo multiple changes.
.	Typing a period (.) will repeat the previous command. So, if you deleted a line, replaced a word, changed four letters, and so on, the same command will be done wherever the cursor is currently located. (Entering input mode again resets it.)
Shift+j	Join the current line with the next line.
Esc	If you didn't catch this earlier, the Esc key returns you from an input mode back to command mode. This is one of the keys you will use most often.

Modifying Commands with Numbers

Nearly every command described so far can be modified with a number. In other words, instead of deleting a word, replacing a letter, or changing a line, you can delete six words, replace 12 letters, and change nine lines. Table A-5 shows some examples.

Table A-5: Modifying Commands with Numbers

Command	Result
7cw	Erase the next seven words and replace them with text you type
5, Shift+d	Cut the next five lines (including the current line)
3p	Paste the previously deleted text three times after the current cursor
9db	Cut the nine words before the current cursor
10j	Move the cursor down ten lines
y2)	Copy (yank) text from cursor to end of next two sentences
5, Ctrl+f	Move forward five pages
6, Shift+j	Join the next six lines

From these examples, you can see that most vi keystrokes for changing text, deleting text, or moving around in the file can be modified using numbers.

Using Ex Commands

The vi editor was originally built on an editor called Ex. Some of the vi commands you've seen so far start with a semicolon and are known as *Ex* commands. To enter Ex commands, start from normal mode and type a colon (:). This switches you to command line mode. In this mode, you can use the Tab key to complete your command or file name, and the arrow keys to navigate your command history, as you would in a bash shell. When you press Enter at the end of your command, you are returned to normal mode.

Table A-6 shows some examples of Ex commands.

Table A-6: Ex Command Examples

Command	Result
:!bash	Escape to a bash shell. When you are done, type exit to return to vi.
:!date	Run date (or any command you choose). Press Enter to return.
:!!	Rerun the command previously run.
:20	Go to line 20 in the file.
:5,10w abc.txt	Write lines 5 through 10 to the file abc.txt.
:e abc.txt	Leave the current file and begin editing the file abc.txt.
:.r def.txt	Read the contents of def.txt into the file below the current line.
:s/RH/RedHat	Substitute Red Hat for the first occurrence of RH on the current line.
:s/RH/Red Hat/g	Substitute Red Hat for all occurrences of RH on the current line.
:%s/RH/Red Hat/g	Substitute Red Hat for the all occurrences of RH in the entire file.
:g/Red Hat/p	List every line in the file that contains the string "Red Hat".
:g/gaim/s//pidgin/gp	Find every instance of gaim and change it to pidgin.

From the ex prompt you can also see and change settings related to your vi session using the set command. Table A-7 shows some examples.

Table A-7: set Commands in ex Mode

Command	Result
`:set all`	List all settings.
`:set`	List only those settings that have changed from the default.
`:set number`	Have line numbers appear left of each line. (Use set nonu to unset.)
`:set ai`	Sets autoindent, so opening a new line follows the previous indent.
`:set ic`	Sets ignore case, so text searches will match regardless of case.
`:set list`	Show $ for end of lines and ^I for tabs.
`:set wm`	Causes vi to add line breaks between words near the end of a line.

Working in Visual Mode

The Vim editor provides a more intuitive means of selecting text called *visual mode*. To begin visual mode, move the cursor to the first character of the text you want to select and press the v key. You will see that you are in visual mode because the following text appears at the bottom of the screen:

```
-- VISUAL --
```

At this point, you can use any of your cursor movement keys (arrow keys, Page Down, End, and so on) to move the cursor to the end of the text you want to select. As the page and cursor move, you will see text being highlighted. When all the text you want to select is highlighted, you can press keys to act on that text. For example, d deletes the text, c lets you change the selected text, :w /tmp/test.txt saves selected text to a file, and so on.

B

Shell Special Characters and Variables

Fedora provides bash as the default shell. Chapter 3 helps you become comfortable working in the shell. This appendix provides a reference of the numerous characters and variables that have special meaning to the bash shell. Many of those elements are referenced in Table B-1 (Shell Special Characters) and Table B-2 (Shell Variables).

IN THIS APPENDIX

Using special shell characters

Using shell variables

Using Special Shell Characters

You can use special characters from the shell to match multiple files, save some keystrokes, or perform special operations. Table B-1 shows some shell special characters you may find useful.

Table B-1: Shell Special Characters

Character	Description
*	Match any string of characters.
?	Match any one character.
[...]	Match any character enclosed in the braces.
' ... '	Remove special meaning of characters between quotes. Variables are not expanded.
" ... "	Same as simple quotes except for the escape characters ($ ` and \ ) that preserve their special meaning.
\	Escape character to remove the special meaning of the character that follows.

Continued

Table B-1: Shell Special Characters (*continued*)

Character	Description
~	Refers to the $HOME directory.
~+	Value of the shell variable PWD (working directory).
~-	Refers to the previous working directory.
.	Refers to the current working directory.
..	Refers to the directory above the current directory. Can be used repeatedly to reference several directories up.
$param	Used to expand a shell variable parameter.
cmd1 `cmd2` or cmd1 $(cmd2)	cmd2 is executed first. Then the call to cmd2 is substituted with the output of cmd2, and cmd1 is executed.
cmd1 >	Redirects standard output from command.
cmd1 <	Redirects standard input to command.
cmd1 >>	Appends standard output to file from command, without erasing its current contents.
cmd1 | cmd2	Pipes the output of one command to the input of the next.
cmd &	Runs the command in the background.
cmd1 && cmd2	Runs first command, then if it returns a zero exit status, runs the second command.
cmd1 || cmd2	Runs first command, then if it returns a non-zero exit status, runs the second command.
cmd1 ; cmd2	Runs the first command and when it completes, runs the second command.

Using Shell Variables

You identify a string of characters as a parameter (variable) by placing a $ in front of it (as in $HOME). Shell environment variables can hold information that is used by the shell itself, as well as by commands you run from the shell. Not all environment variables will be populated by default. Some of these variables you can change (such as the default printer in $PRINTER or your command prompt in $PS1). Others are managed by the shell (such as $OLDPWD). Table B-2 contains a list of many useful shell variables.

Table B-2: Shell Variables

Shell Variable	Description
BASH	Shows path name of the bash command (/bin/bash).
BASH_COMMAND	The command that is being executed at the moment.
BASH_VERSION	The version number of the bash command.
COLORS	Path to the configuration file for ls colors.
COLUMNS	The width of the terminal line (in characters).
DISPLAY	Identifies the X display where commands launched from the current shell will be displayed (such as :0.0).
EUID	Effective user ID number of the current user. It is based on the user entry in /etc/passwd for the user that is logged in.
FCEDIT	Determines the text editor used by the fc command to edit history commands. The vi command is used by default.
GROUPS	Lists groups of which the current user is a member.
HISTCMD	Shows the current command's history number.
HISTFILE	Shows the location of your history file (usually located at $HOME/.bash_history).
HISTFILESIZE	Total number of history entries that will be stored (default, 1000). Older commands are discarded after this number is reached.
HISTCMD	The number of the current command in the history list.
HOME	Location of the current user's home directory. Typing the cd command with no options returns the shell to the home directory.
HOSTNAME	The current machine's host name.
HOSTTYPE	Contains the computer architecture on which the Linux system is running (i386, i486, i586, i686, x86_64, ppc, or ppc64).
LESSOPEN	Set to a command that converts content other than plain text (images, RPMs, zip files, and so on) so it can be piped through the less command.
LINES	Sets the number of lines in the current terminal

Continued

Table B-2: Shell Variables (*continued*)

Shell Variable	Description
LOGNAME	Holds the name of the current user.
LS_COLORS	Maps colors to file extensions to indicate the colors the ls command displays when encountering those file types.
MACHTYPE	Displays information about the machine architecture, company, and operating system (such as i686-redhat-linux-gnu)
MAIL	Indicates the location of your mailbox file (typically the user name in the /var/spool/mail directory).
MAILCHECK	Checks for mail in the number of seconds specified (default is 60).
OLDPWD	Directory that was the working directory before changing to the current working directory.
OSTYPE	Name identifying the current operating system (such as linux or linux-gnu)
PATH	Colon-separated list of directories used to locate commands that you type (/bin, /usr/bin, and $HOME/bin are usually in the PATH).
PPID	Process ID of the command that started the current shell.
PRINTER	Sets the default printer, which is used by printing commands such as lpr and lpq.
PROMPT_COMMAND	Set to a command name to run that command each time before your shell prompt is displayed. (For example, PROMPT_COMMAND=ls lists commands in the current directory before showing the prompt).
PS1	Sets the shell prompt. Items in the prompt can include date, time, user name, hostname, and others. Additional prompts can be set with PS2, PS3, and so on.
PWD	The directory assigned as your current directory.
RANDOM	Accessing this variable generates a random number between 0 and 32767.
SECONDS	The number of seconds since the shell was started.
SHELL	Contains the full path to the current shell.
SHELLOPTS	Lists enabled shell options (those set to on)

C

Getting Information from /proc

Originally intended to be a location for storing information used by running processes, the /proc file system eventually became the primary location for storing all kinds of information used by the Linux kernel. Despite the emergence of /sys to provide a more orderly framework for kernel information, many Linux utilities still gather and present data about your running system from /proc.

IN THIS APPENDIX

Viewing /proc information

Changing /proc information variables

If you are someone who prefers to cut out the middleman, you can bypass utilities that read /proc files and read (and sometimes even write to) /proc files directly. By checking /proc, you can find out the state of processes, hardware devices, kernel subsystems, and other attributes of Linux.

Viewing /proc information

Checking out information in files from the /proc directory can be done by using a simple cat command. In /proc, there is a separate directory for each running process (named by its process ID) that contains information about the process. There are also /proc files that contain data for all kinds of other things, such as your computer's CPU, memory usage, software versions, disk partitions, and so on.

The following examples describe some of the information you can get from your Linux system's /proc directory:

```
$ cat /proc/cmdline        Shows options passed to the boot prompt
ro root=LABEL=/123 rhgb quiet
$ cat /proc/cpuinfo        Shows information about your processor
Processor     : 0
vendor_id     : GenuineIntel
cpu family    : 6
model         : 8
model name    : Pentium III (Coppermine)
```

```
stepping : 3
cpu MHz        : 648.045
cache size     : 256 KB
   ...
```

In the example above, the MHz speed may be well below your actual system speed if a CPU governor such as cpuspeed is running.

```
$ cat /proc/devices        Shows existing character and block devices
Character devices:
  1 mem
  4 /dev/vc/0
  4 tty
  4 ttys
  5 /dev/tty
   ...
Block devices:
  1 ramdisk
  7 loop
  8 sd
  9 md
$ cat /proc/diskstats      Display disks, partitions, and statistics
    1    0 ram0 0 0 0 0 0 0 0 0 0 0 0
    1    1 ram1 0 0 0 0 0 0 0 0 0 0 0
   ...
    8    0 sda 2228445 1032474 68692149 21672710 1098740 4003143
47790770 101074392 0 15385988 122799055
    8    1 sda1 330077 13060510 188002 8443280
    8    1 sda2 1491 1759 50 162
   ...
    7    0 loop0 0 0 0 0 0 0 0 0 0 0 0
```

In the diskstats output just shown, you can see ramdisk (ram0, ram1, and so on) and loopback devices (loop0, loop1, and so on). For hard disk partitions, the example shows statistics for the whole hard disk (sda) and each partition (sda1, sda2, and so on).

The 11 fields for the entire hard disk show (from left to right): total number of reads, number of reads merged, number of sectors read, number of milliseconds spent by all reads, number of writes completed, number of writes merged, number of sectors written, number of milliseconds spent writing, number of input/output requests currently in progress, number of milliseconds spent doing input/output, and weighted number of milliseconds spend doing input/output. Fields for a particular partition show (from left to right): number of reads issued, number of sectors read, number of writes issued, and number of sectors written.

```
$ cat /proc/filesystems    List filesystem types supported by current kernel
nodev   sysfs              nodev means type is not currently used by any device
nodev   rootfs
   ...
        ext3               ext3 is used on a mounted block device
        iso9660            iso9660 is used on a mounted block device
```

```
$ cat /proc/interrupts        View IRQ channel assignments
          CPU0
   0:  198380901   XT-PIC-XT       timer
   1:      28189   XT-PIC-XT       i8042
   2:          0   XT-PIC-XT       cascade
   6:    3770197   XT-PIC-XT       Ensoniq AudioPCI
   7:        660   XT-PIC-XT       parport0
       ...
$ cat /proc/iomem             Show physical memory addresses
00000000-0009fbff : System RAM
  00000000-00000000 : Crash kernel
0009fc00-0009ffff : reserved
000a0000-000bffff : Video RAM area
000c0000-000c7fff : Video ROM
000c8000-000c8fff : Adapter ROM
000f0000-000fffff : System ROM
00100000-0febffff : System RAM
       ...
$ cat /proc/ioports           Show virtual memory addresses
0000-001f : dma1
0020-0021 : pic1
0040-0043 : timer0
0050-0053 : timer1
0060-006f : keyboard
0070-0077 : rtc
0080-008f : dma page reg
00a0-00a1 : pic2
00c0-00df : dma2
00f0-00ff : fpu
       ...
$ cat /proc/keys         Displays a list of keys being kept by kernel
00000001 I — — -   1 perm 1f3f0000   0   0 keyring   _uid_ses.0: 1/4
00000002 I — — -   7 perm 1f3f0000   0   0 keyring   _uid.0: empty
0442d29e I — Q —   2 perm 1f3f0000   0   0 keyring   _ses.20729: 1/4
       ...
$ cat /proc/loadavg          Shows 1, 5, and 15 minute load averages,
1.77 0.56 0.19 2/247 1869      running processes/total and highest PID
$ cat /proc/meminfo          Shows available RAM and swap
MemTotal:       482992 kB
MemFree:         25616 kB
Buffers:         12204 kB
Cached:          64132 kB
SwapCached:     117472 kB
Active:         321344 kB
Inactive:        93168 kB
HighTotal:           0 kB
HighFree:            0 kB
LowTotal:       482992 kB
       ...
$ cat /proc/misc           Shows name/minor number of devices
229 fuse                     registered with misc major device (10)
 63 device-mapper
175 agpgart
```

```
144 nvram
      . . .
$ cat /proc/modules               Shows loaded modules, memory size,
nls_utf8 6209 1 - Live 0xd0c59000     instances loaded, dependencies
cifs 213301 0 - Live 0xd0e3b000       load state, and kernel memory
nfs 226861 0 - Live 0xd0e02000
nfsd 208689 17 - Live 0xd0d8a000
exportfs 9537 1 nfsd, Live 0xd0cfb000
lockd 62409 3 nfs,nfsd, Live 0xd0d45000
nfs_acl 7617 2 nfs,nfsd, Live 0xd0c56000
fuse 45909 2 - Live 0xd0d24000
vfat 16193 0 - Live 0xd0cf6000
      . . .
$ cat /proc/mounts        Show mounted local/remote file system info
rootfs / rootfs rw 0 0
/dev/root / ext3 rw,data=ordered 0 0
/dev /dev tmpfs rw 0 0
/proc /proc proc rw 0 0
/sys /sys sysfs rw 0 0
$ cat /proc/partitions    Show mounted local disk partitions
major minor  #blocks  name

   8     0   40031712 sda
   8     1     200781 sda1
   8     2   10241437 sda2
   8     3    6160927 sda3
   . . .
   7     0     682998 loop0


$ cat /proc/mdstat        If using software RAID, show RAID status
Personalities : [raid1]
read_ahead 1024 sectors
Event: 1
md0 : active raid1 sdb1[1] sda2[0]
      69738048 blocks [2/2] [UU]

unused devices: <none>
```

The /proc/mdstat file contains detailed status information on your software RAID devices. In this example, md0 is a RAID1 (mirror) composed of the /dev/sdb1 and /dev/sda1 partitions. On the following line, there is one U for each healthy RAID member. If you lose a drive, the output would appear as [U_].

```
$ cat /proc/stat               Shows kernel stats since system boot
cpu  1559592 1488475 710279 218584583 1446866 5486 16708
cpu0 1559592 1488475 710279 218584583 1446866 5486 16708
intr 215956694 200097282 28242 0 1 3 0 3770197 660 1 1 0 3753340  ...
ctxt 281917622
btime 1181950070
processes 519308
procs_running 1
procs_blocked 0
```

The /proc/stat file contains statistics related to CPU and process activities. The cpu line shows totals for all CPUs, while separate lines for each processor (cpu0, cpu1, and so on) show stats for each CPU on the computer. There are seven fields (from left to right) of CPU information: number of normal processes executed in user mode, niced processes executed in user mode, kernel mode processes, idle processes, iowait processes (waiting for input/output to finish), servicing interrupts (IRQ), and servicing soft IRQs.

```
$ cat /proc/swaps              List information about swap space
Filename       Type      Size    Used   Priority
/dev/sda2      partition 1020088 201124 -1
$ cat /proc/uptime             Seconds since system booted/total seconds idle
2300251.03 2261855.31
$ cat /proc/version            List kernel version and related compiler
Linux version 2.6.21-1.3194.fc7
(kojibuilder@xenbuilder4.fedora.phx.redhat.com)
(gcc version 4.1.2 20070502 (Red Hat 4.1.2-12))
#1 SMP Wed May 23 22:35:01 EDT 2007
```

Changing /proc information

Some values in the /proc/sys directory can actually be changed on the fly. For /proc/sys files that accept binary values (0 disabled or 1 enabled) people would often simply echo a value to any files they wanted to change. For example, to allow forwarding of IPv4 packets, such as to allow a system to do Network Address Translation (NAT) or IP Masquerading, you could type:

```
# echo 1 > /proc/sys/net/ipv4/ip_forward
```

Although you could still use this technique to make temporary changes to your system, the preferred method of changing /proc/sys information on the fly is using the sysctl command. To change those settings on a more permanent basis, you should add entries to the /etc/sysctl.conf file. Here are some examples of the sysctl command:

```
# sysctl -A | less              Display all kernel runtime parameters
# sysctl -w net.ipv4.ip_forward=1   Turn on IPV4 packet forwarding
```

See Chapter 10 as well as the sysctl and sysctl.conf man pages for further information.

Index

A

D

G

L

U

V

Take a look inside the Linux® toolbox.

Check out other books available in the series.

Available now at www.wiley.com